Pro Apache Geronimo

Kishore Kumar

Apress®

Pro Apache Geronimo

Copyright © 2006 by Kishore Kumar

ISBN-13 (pbk): 978-1-59059-642-5

ISBN-10 (pbk): 1-59059-642-0

Printed and bound in the United States of America 9 8 7 6 5 4 3 2 1

Lead Editor: Steve Anglin
Technical Reviewer: Harshad Oak, Dilip Thomas
Editorial Board: Steve Anglin, Dan Appleman, Ewan Buckingham, Gary Cornell, Jason Gilmore,
    Jonathan Hassell, James Huddleston, Chris Mills, Matthew Moodie, Dominic Shakeshaft, Jim Sumser,
    Matt Wade
Project Manager: Beth Christmas
Copy Edit Manager: Nicole LeClerc
Copy Editor: Elizabeth Cate
Assistant Production Director: Kari Brooks-Copony
Production Editor: Kelly Gunther
Compositor: Linda Weidemann, Wolf Creek Press
Proofreader: Elizabeth Berry
Indexer: Rebecca Plunkett
Artist: Kinetic Publishing Services, LLC
Cover Designer: Kurt Krames
Manufacturing Director: Tom Debolski

Distributed to the book trade worldwide by Springer-Verlag New York, Inc., 233 Spring Street, 6th Floor, New York, NY 10013. Phone 1-800-SPRINGER, fax 201-348-4505, e-mail orders-ny@springer-sbm.com, or visit http://www.springeronline.com.

For information on translations, please contact Apress directly at 2560 Ninth Street, Suite 219, Berkeley, CA 94710. Phone 510-549-5930, fax 510-549-5939, e-mail info@apress.com, or visit http://www.apress.com.

The source code for this book is available to readers at http://www.apress.com in the Source Code section.

Contents at a Glance

Contents

About the Author

 **KISHORE KUMAR** is a J2EE solutions architect and a senior technology evangelist at US Technology (http://www.ustri.com). Apart from his project roles, he leads the Java Center of Excellence (JCOE), the primary community for competency development and efficiency improvement within his company. At US Technology, he works with the latest Java and J2EE technologies. As leader of JCOE, Kishore works on many projects, such as framework developments, Eclipse plug-in developments, and concept proof for the latest technologies.

About the Technical Reviewer

HARSHAD OAK is the founder of Rightrix Solutions and the editor-in-chief of the sites IndicThreads.com, QThreads.com, and PythonThreads.com. He is the author of the books *Pro Jakarta Commons* (Apress, 2004) and *Oracle JDeveloper 10g: Empowering J2EE Development* (Apress, 2004) and coauthor of *Java 2 Enterprise Edition 1.4 Bible* (John Wiley & Sons, 2003). He is also currently a regional director for Oracle Fusion Middleware. He can be reached at harshad@rightrix.com.

Acknowledgments

My life changed considerably after I joined US Technology and met its founder and ex-chairman, the late Mr. G. A. Menon. Every time I talked with him, the experience was nothing short of enlightening. He taught me to have big dreams because only then I could have my dreams come true. The publication of my first book is one of those dreams come true. I am dedicating this book to Mr. Menon, his family, and to his greatest dream, US Technology.

The past few months had been extremely tough with all the hard work I had to do to bring this book out on time. I would like to thank my wife, Nithya, and all my family members for their kind understanding and support, without which this book would have never been a reality.

Next, I would like to mention my special regard for my mentor and guide, Shankar Rajamoney, for all his help all throughout, and for Arun Narayanan, for always encouraging me to perform my best.

My special thanks to Beth Christmas at Apress for keeping track of this book's progress, coordinating reviews, and reminding me of the schedule whenever I lost track. I am grateful to Steve Anglin for generously accepting my proposal for this book and guiding me throughout the process. My sincere thanks go to Dilip Thomas and Harshad Oak for their sharp technical reviews and comments. Elizabeth Cate has helped me a lot with her copy editing reviews and correcting all my mistakes; I am extremely thankful for her patience and support. And last but not least, I would like to thank Kelly Gunther and everyone else on the Apress production team who worked directly or indirectly to publish this book.

Thanks and regards,
Kishore Kumar

Introduction

Pro *Apache Geronimo* is a hands-on guide to enterprise Java programming using the Apache Geronimo open source application server. Apart from discussing the Geronimo architecture in great detail, this book uses simple examples to explain Java enterprise concepts such as web applications, Enterprise JavaBeans (EJB), message-driven beans, and connectors. All code samples from this book are available for download from http://www.apress.com.

This book also details how to package application components as an enterprise application and the process for developing, packaging, and running client applications using the client container. Additionally, I have included some discussion on advanced concepts, such as how Geronimo supports security.

If you have any questions or comments regarding this book, please feel free to contact me at kishore.kumar@ustri.com or kishorekollam@gmail.com.

CHAPTER 1

■ ■ ■

Getting Started

Apache Geronimo is an open source Java 2 Platform, Enterprise Edition (J2EE) application server from the Apache Software Foundation. It is a framework that integrates a large base of open source projects to provide a J2EE 1.4–compliant, production-quality container for J2EE applications. With Geronimo, you can deploy and run your web, Enterprise JavaBeans (EJB), and enterprise applications. You can create your enterprise applications by using servlets, JavaServer Pages (JSPs), and EJBs; access your database by using Java Database Connectivity (JDBC) connectors; access the directory services through Java Naming and Directory Interface (JNDI); and so on.

At its core, Geronimo is more than a J2EE server; it provides an Inversion of Control (IOC) platform. Many other applications can also make use of this platform to build their services and servers. As a platform, Geronimo provides a modular infrastructure for building any system by implementing the common basic facilities, including service life cycle and service modules (configurations).

Although many open source J2EE servers already exist, Geronimo is unique because of its Apache license. The Apache license is the most liberal of all the open source licenses. You can use Geronimo as it is or even modify and use it in your commercial and noncommercial applications. The only requirement from the user is an acknowledgement of the source.

In Chapter 1, I'll summarize Geronimo's history and present an overview of its features. I'll then explain how to install Geronimo. Last, I'll demonstrate how to start and stop the server.

History

Geronimo started as an Apache Incubator project in the summer of 2003, and by May 2004, it had become a top-level Apache project. In June 2004, the Geronimo Milestone 4 release passed the automated J2EE Technology Compatibility Kit (TCK) 1.4.1a test suite. The Milestone 4 release had many significant advantages over the Milestone 3 release, including full support for EJB, Java Specification Request (JSR) 77, and web services.

In October 2005, Apache released Milestone 5, which is a fully certified J2EE 1.4 application server. This milestone contains a number of enhancements, including a complete Tomcat integration, a more flexible and dynamic service configuration, and a developer preview of a portlets-based management console. In January 2006, Apache announced the Geronimo 1.0 release.

A good number of Geronimo committers were from a company called Gluecode, which built a Geronimo-based portal product, JOE. Recently, IBM took over this company and has since been a significant contributor to the Apache Geronimo project. IBM has also released WebSphere Application Server Community Edition, which is based on the core Geronimo technology.

Features

The goal in creating Geronimo was to provide the best open source, fully certified application server, a J2EE platform for high-end production use, and a high-performance J2EE server. To meet this goal, Geronimo's designers focused on the following aspects:

- Manageability of all services and components

- Flexible configuration capabilities

- Full support for J2EE specifications through integration of open source components

- Custom-developed components that meet Geronimo's stringent performance goals

Geronimo's features match those of any other commercial application server on the market. The sections that follow describe Geronimo's key features.

IOC Container As the Core Geronimo Platform

Geronimo is based on an IOC framework for service components called GBeans. In addition, Geronimo integrates with other popular IOC containers, like Spring.

GBean-Based Modular Services

One or more GBeans implement a specific service, like a web container, an EJB container, or the security infrastructure. Most GBean-based services are either wrappers over an open source component or custom implementations. For instance, the GBeans that provide the web container functionality are wrappers over a Jetty or a Tomcat Hypertext Transfer Protocol (HTTP) server. In short, the Geronimo J2EE server is a set of GBeans deployed and run in the Geronimo platform that implement and provide the J2EE services as required by the J2EE specification. Even J2EE applications are also deployed and run as GBeans.

JSR 77 Support

Geronimo implements JSR 77, which is the J2EE management specification. JSR 77 is based on the Java Management Extension (JMX) specification and defines a standard model for J2EE-managed objects. It abstracts the manageable parts of a J2EE server (including deployed J2EE applications) and defines a standard interface for clients and management consoles to access management information. Geronimo implements the JSR 77 management EJB and exposes all its deployed GBean services to JSR 77 clients. Geronimo's JMX implementation utilizes the open source MX4J product.

JSR 88 Support

Geronimo also supports JSR 88, a standard application programming interface (API) that enables tools to interact with any application server to configure and deploy J2EE applications. Application configuration involves creating the required deployment descriptors, including standard and application server–specific deployment descriptors for J2EE components. Many tools use a graphical user interface (GUI) to collect relevant information from the user, generate required deployment descriptors, and package the component ready for deployment. Application deployment involves application server interactions to deploy, undeploy, start, and stop applications.

J2EE Application Containers

Geronimo implements containers for all the J2EE application module types: web applications, EJB applications, J2EE Application Clients, and Connectors.

Web Applications

Geronimo 1.0 offers one of two open source web containers—Jetty or Apache Tomcat—that can host and run web applications packaged as Web Archive (WAR) files. The web container supports Servlets 2.4 and the JSP 2.0 specification. The Geronimo Milestone 5 release includes both web containers. Jetty is the default web container, but you can manually reconfigure Milestone 5 to use Tomcat.

EJB and Enterprise Applications

Geronimo uses the OpenEJB container to host and run EJB applications. It supports session, entity, and message-driven beans. It also supports advanced J2EE features like timers and web services. Currently, it implements the EJB 2.1 specification.

You can deploy EJBs as a standard EJB Java Archive (JAR) file. You can also package your enterprise application consisting of one or more web applications (packaged as WAR files), one or more EJB applications (packaged as EJB JAR files), and one or more connectors (packaged as Resource Archive [RAR] files) into Enterprise Archive (EAR) files and deploy these elements as a single unit.

J2EE Client Applications

Geronimo has a client container for J2EE application clients. Geronimo uses custom code to implement and provide the client container. Client applications can access and use all server resources available through JNDI.

J2EE Connectors

Geronimo has a J2EE Connector Architecture (J2CA) container that can host and run J2EE connectors. Connectors are J2EE application components that run within the application server environment and provide Enterprise Information System (EIS) connectivity to other J2EE application components, like EJB. Geronimo uses custom code to implement the Java Connector Architecture (JCA) container and supports both inbound and outbound connectors. Inbound connectors pass information from the EIS to the application server, and outbound connectors pass information from the application server to the EIS.

Web Services

Geronimo uses Apache Axis and custom code to support web services. It implements the enterprise web services specification (JSR 109) and can export Plain Old Java Object (POJO)–based and EJB-based service endpoints as web services.

Java Message Service (JMS) and Messaging Services

Geronimo uses the ActiveMQ JMS provider to enable JMS applications. You can deploy JMS destinations (queues and topics) as part of a server configuration or as part of an application configuration. Serverwide JMS destinations are available to all applications on the server, and application-wide JMS destinations are available to a specific application only.

ActiveMQ is an open source messaging server, released under the Apache license, that implements the JMS 1.1, J2EE 1.4, JCA 1.5, and XA standards. It supports many different transport mechanisms, including HTTP, Transmission Control Protocol (TCP), and User Datagram Protocol (UDP).

J2EE Security

The Geronimo security infrastructure is based on the Java Authentication and Authorization Service (JAAS) framework and the Java Authorization Contract for Containers (JACC) specification. JAAS defines a mechanism for supporting pluggable login modules for authentication and a standard mechanism for authorization. The JACC specification defines a standard contract between the security policy provider implementations and the J2EE containers. Geronimo comes with a generic security realm implementation and a variety of login modules, including file-based and database-based implementations.

Transactions

Geronimo uses ObjectWeb's Java Open Transaction Manager (JOTM) for providing its transaction support. JOTM is a transaction manager that allows resource managers to participate in global distributed transactions by coordinating the transactions and implementing the two-phase commit protocol. Geronimo uses High-Speed ObjectWeb Logger (HOWL) for transaction logging and transaction recovery.

JDBC Connection Pools

You can configure a JDBC connection pool by deploying a connector that provides database connectivity and connection pools. Geronimo provides TranQL, the open source product that has a J2EE connector that allows you to configure and deploy a connection pool.

JavaMail

Geronimo provides JavaMail 1.3.3 capability, allowing applications to send and receive e-mails. Geronimo provides GBeans that you can use to configure a JavaMail session and Simple Mail Transport Protocol (SMTP) transport.

Apache Active Directory Support

Geronimo includes Apache Directory, which allows applications to use active directory services. This enables applications to implement a unified security layer for applications.

Specification Support

Geronimo offers all the features of a typical J2EE 1.4 application server, including support for all specifications that J2EE 1.4 requires. These specifications are as follows:

- Servlet 2.4

- JSP 2.0

- EJB 2.1

- JMS 1.1

- JTA 1.0.1B (Java Transaction API)

- JTS 1.0 (Java Transaction Service)

- JMX 1.2

- J2EE Management API 1.0

- J2EE Deployment API 1.1

- JCA 1.5

- JAXR 1.0 (Java API for XML Registries)

- JAX-RPC 1.1 (Java API for XML RPC)

- SAAJ 1.2 (SOAP with Attachment API for Java)

- JACC 1.0

- JavaMail 1.2

Figure 1-1 depicts Geronimo and the components that provide a J2EE 1.4–certified application server.

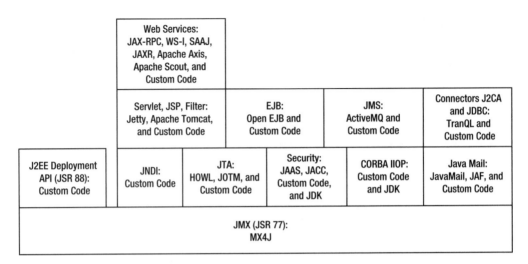

Figure 1-1. *Geronimo application server components*

Web-Based Administration Console

Geronimo has a web-based administration console application that you can use to administer the Geronimo server. You can also use this application to deploy, undeploy, and manage your own applications.

Other Features

Other useful Geronimo features include integration with the open source ServiceMix Enterprise Service Bus (ESB) and Eclipse tools and plug-ins for integrated development environment (IDE) integration. Geronimo supports the Java Business Integration (JBI) specification by using the ServiceMix ESB provider, and its deployer can deploy service components defined in the META-INF/jbi.xml file of any JAR file.

New Features in Geronimo 1.0

Some of the key features in Geronimo's 1.0 release are as follows:

- Hot deploy and undeploy of applications and services.

- A dynamic deploy directory for applications and services. You can deploy applications by copying their deployment artifacts to the Geronimo root/deploy directory.

- Remote deployment and management capabilities.

- Clustering support with Tomcat.

- Improved web-based administration console.

- Many configuration parameters that can be updated in the var/config/config.xml file.

- Improved documentation with samples.

> ### GERONIMO'S TO-DO LIST
>
> Here are some key features that Geronimo should offer in the next version:
>
> - Provide tooling support for all popular Java IDEs
>
> - Provide full clustering support
>
> - Completely implement the JSR 88 specification
>
> - Include a J2EE application client container that can work from a machine other than the server

Installing Geronimo

Geronimo is a pure Java application server; hence, it can run on any Java Development Kit (JDK) 1.4 platform. However, for all features to run with the 1.0 release, Geronimo requires Sun Java Virtual Machine (JVM) 1.4.2 or higher. This is primarily because Geronimo uses Sun's Common Object Request Broker Architecture (CORBA) implementation classes for its CORBA support—this limitation will likely be rectified with a later release, when Geronimo uses a bundled CORBA implementation.

Obtaining Geronimo

You can download Geronimo from http://geronimo.apache.org/downloads.html. There are three types of downloads available for each release: binary, installer, and source code. The binary release is a ZIP file or a TAR.GZ file, and the installer is a JAR file. You can use Subversion to check out Geronimo source code, as shown here:

```
svn co https://svn.apache.org/repos/asf/geronimo/trunk geronimo
```

This will create a directory called geronimo that contains the source code. You need Apache Maven to execute various Maven build commands to download dependencies and build Geronimo. This process is documented in the Geronimo wiki (http://wiki.apache.org/geronimo/Building).

Installing Geronimo Quickly

You can use the binary package for a quick installation. As mentioned, the binary package is a ZIP file (or a TAR.GZ file), and you simply unpack the ZIP file into a directory to complete the installation. (There are separate packages available for Tomcat and Jetty web containers, and you can select either one.) With this type of installation, you get Geronimo preconfigured with default settings. If you need to customize the various settings, including ports for services, you need to use the installer-based installation.

Installing Using the Installer

As of this writing, the Geronimo 1.0 final release does not have an installer download, and hence we will use the Geronimo 1.0 Milestone 4 release installer to explore the installation process. With future releases, the installer options are expected to change; however, the core installation process will remain the same.

The installer application is a JAR file. It guides you through an installation wizard that collects server configuration information and then installs and configures Geronimo for immediate use. To run the installer, use the following command:

```
java -jar geronimo-1.0-M4-installer.jar
```

A welcome screen appears, as shown in Figure 1-2.

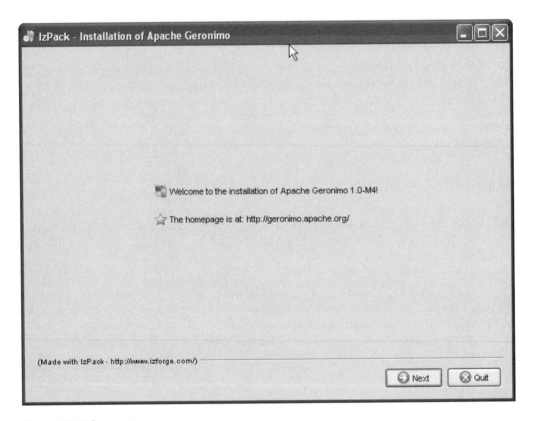

Figure 1-2. *Welcome screen*

Click the Next button. You will see the license screen, shown in Figure 1-3.

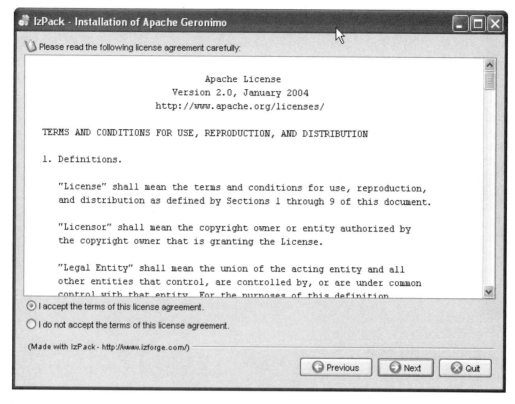

Figure 1-3. *License screen*

Accept the license, and click Next. In the next screen, choose an installation folder in which to install Geronimo, as shown in Figure 1-4. This folder will be the Geronimo root folder.

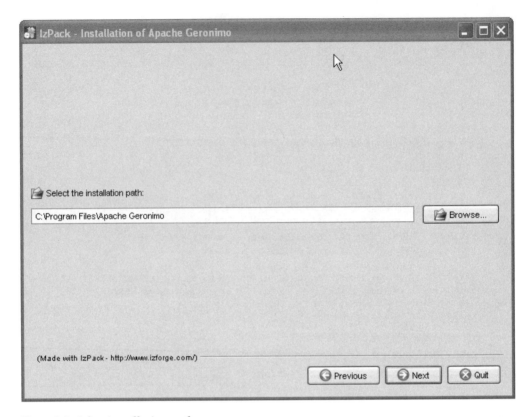

Figure 1-4. *Select installation path screen*

If the target directory does not exist, the installer indicates that it will create the directory. Click Next, and the installer displays the feature list, shown in Figure 1-5, from which you can select the optional features that you want to include in the installation. The core server, the J2EE features, and the web container are mandatory features. This feature list is expected to change in future releases.

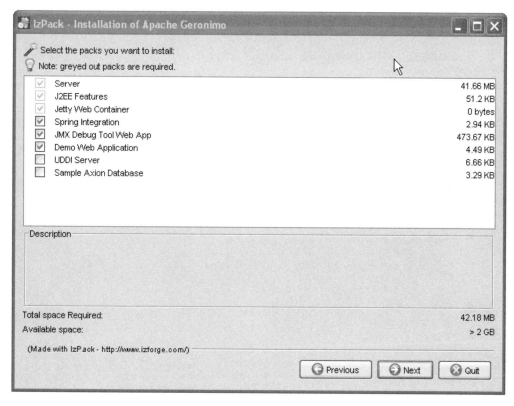

Figure 1-5. *Feature selection screen*

Click Next, and you will be prompted to enter a system user name and a password,
as shown in Figure 1-6. You need this user name and password to use the deployer and the
Geronimo administration web tool. You will also be prompted to enter port numbers for various services, like HTTP and JNDI. The web container will use the HTTP port number you
specify here to create a listener (connector) for handling HTTP requests, and it will use the
HTTPS port number to create another listener for handling secure HTTP (HTTPS) connections. You can choose to use the default values if you do not want to override these values.

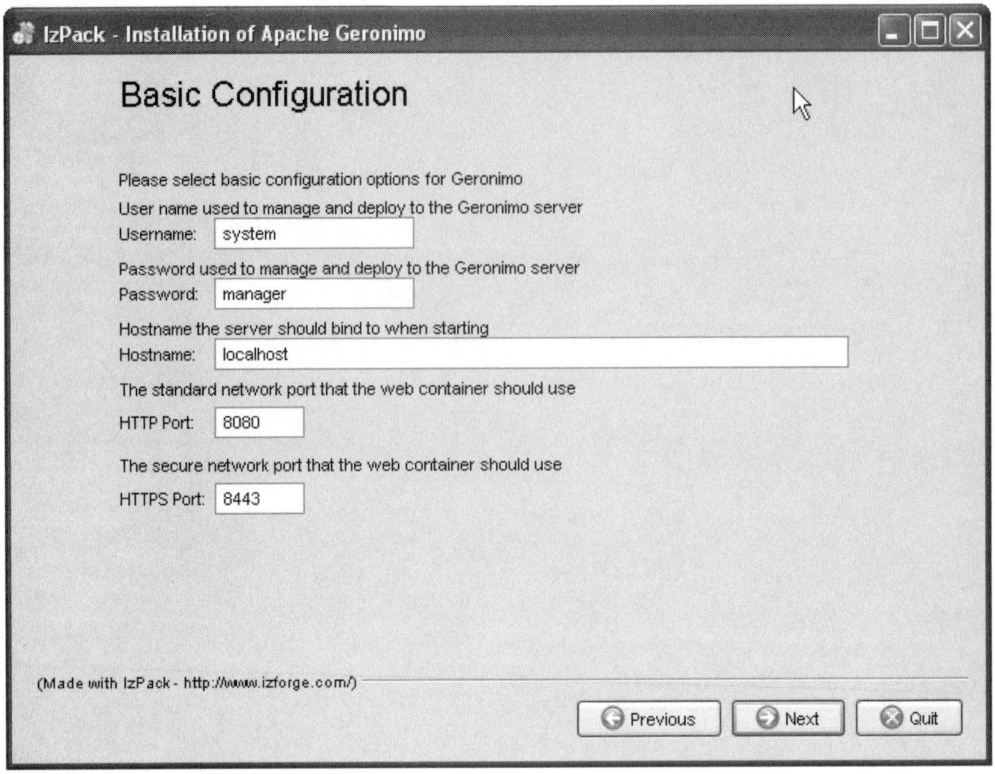

Figure 1-6. *Basic configuration screen*

Click Next to go to the advanced configuration screen, shown in Figure 1-7. Here, you need to enter configuration information for the following items:

- A naming port that Geronimo naming service should use to listen for JNDI connections

- A network port that the EJB container should use

- A list of client Internet Protocol (IP) addresses from which the EJB container should accept EJB client connections

- A network port for Remote Method Invocation over Internet Inter-Orb Protocol (RMI/IIOP) connections

- A network port that the IIOP Object Request Broker (ORB) should use

- A network port that the CORBA naming service should use

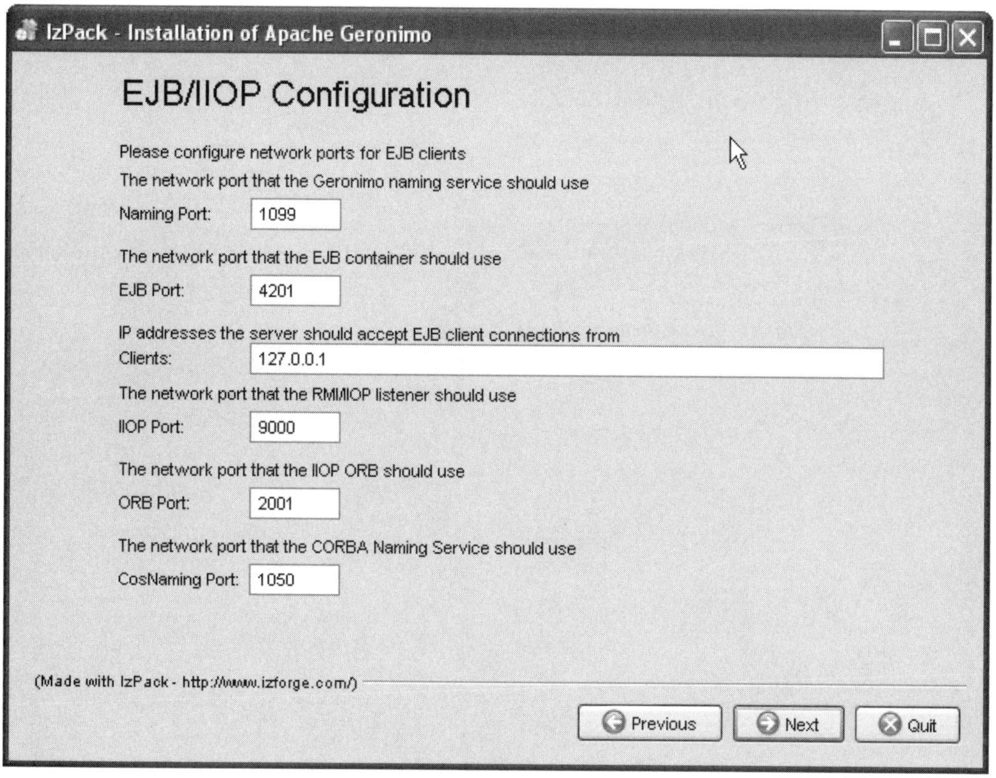

Figure 1-7. *Advanced configuration screen*

Click Next to advance to the final configuration screen, shown in Figure 1-8. Here, you need to provide configuration information for additional services, like JMS and Derby database.

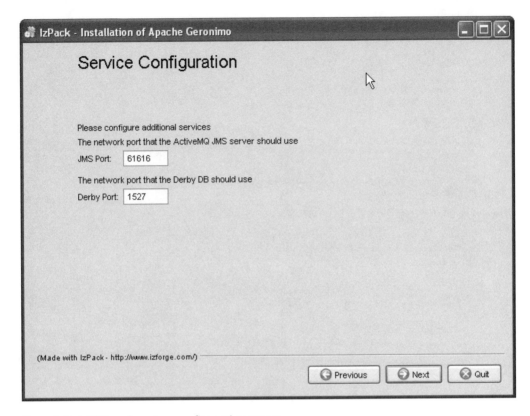

Figure 1-8. *Additional services configuration screen*

To start the installation, click Next. An installation progress screen, shown in Figure 1-9, appears.

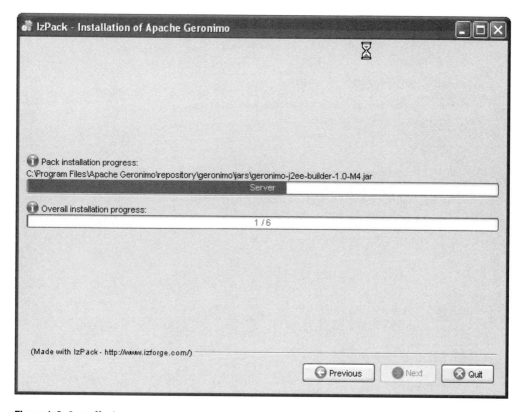

Figure 1-9. *Installation progress screen*

After installation, the installer displays the installation summary, as shown in Figure 1-10.

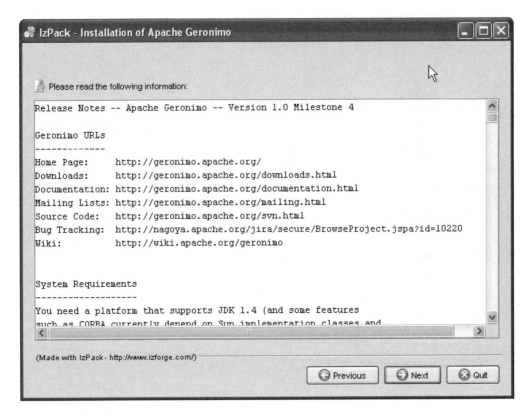

Figure 1-10. *Installation summary screen*

Finally, the installer displays the installation success screen, shown in Figure 1-11. If you require an installation script, you can create it and save it as an Extensible Markup Language (XML) file by selecting Generate an automatic installation script.

You can use the following installation script:

```
java -jar geronimo-1.0-M4-installer.jar install-file.xml
```

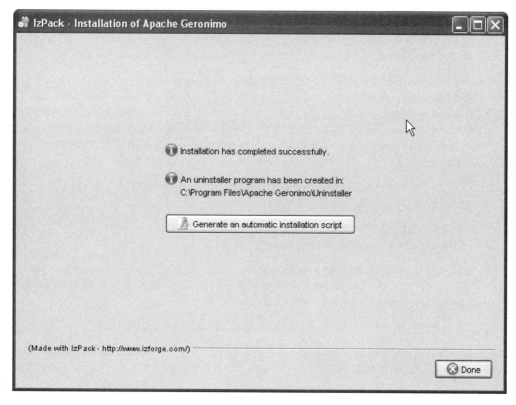

Figure 1-11. *Installation success screen*

Browsing the Geronimo Installation

During installation, the Geronimo installer creates the directory structure shown in Figure 1-12.

Figure 1-12. *Geronimo directory structure*

The following list describes the directories:

- *bin directory.* Contains JAR files (and scripts) that you can use to start the server and deploy applications to the server in both online and offline modes.

- *config-store directory.* Contains configuration modules in numbered subdirectories. A configuration module can be a user-deployed application or a system service. You can configure the server to start one or more configurations, as required. The default server configuration starts some of these modules. The file index.properties contains a mapping of configuration module names to subdirectory numbers. The Geronimo deploy tool maintains the contents of this directory automatically.

- *deploy directory.* Provides a hot-deployment directory into which you can copy your application artifacts for hot deployment.

- *lib directory.* Holds kernel libraries that are needed to start the bare server, which in turn loads all the required configuration modules.

- *repository directory.* Provides a store for all shared libraries. These libraries are loaded on a need basis. You can add database drivers and other libraries that need to be available to all application modules in this directory.

- *schema directory.* Holds a reference copy of all XML schema definitions.

- *var directory.* Holds server runtime contents like the log files, configuration information, and the security configuration files.

Starting the Server

To start Geronimo, run the following command from the home directory:

```
java -jar bin/server.jar
```

This command first starts the kernel and then loads the required configuration modules, which in turn load the following modules (also shown in Figure 1-13):

- A web container (Tomcat or Jetty on ports 8080 and 8443)

- An EJB container (OpenEJB with naming services on port 1099)

- A JMS broker (ActiveMQ on port 61616)

- An embedded database (Derby on port 1527)

- A log service that writes to var/log/geronimo.log

- A transaction manager

- A security realm based on security configurations in var/security/

- A JMX connector for outside JMX clients to manage and monitor server components

```
C:\geronimo-tomcat-j2ee-1.0\geronimo-1.0\bin>java -jar server.jar
Booting Geronimo Kernel (in Java 1.4.2_05)...
Starting Geronimo Application Server
[*********>              ] 40%  43s Starting geronimo/tomcat/1.0/car  12:54:03,6
71 INFO  [Http11Protocol] Initializing Coyote HTTP/1.1 on http-0.0.0.0-8443
[*********>              ] 40%  43s Starting geronimo/tomcat/1.0/car  12:54:03,7
11 INFO  [Http11Protocol] Starting Coyote HTTP/1.1 on http-0.0.0.0-8443
12:54:03,792 INFO  [Http11Protocol] Initializing Coyote HTTP/1.1 on http-0.0.0.0
-8080
12:54:04,052 INFO  [Http11Protocol] Starting Coyote HTTP/1.1 on http-0.0.0.0-808
0
[************************] 100%  75s Startup complete
  Listening on Ports:
    1099 0.0.0.0 RMI Naming
    1389 0.0.0.0 Apache Directory LDAP
    1527 0.0.0.0 Derby Connector
    4201 0.0.0.0 ActiveIO Connector EJB
    4242 0.0.0.0 Remote Login Listener
    8009 0.0.0.0 Tomcat Connector AJP
    8080 0.0.0.0 Tomcat Connector HTTP
    8443 0.0.0.0 Tomcat Connector HTTPS
   61616 0.0.0.0 ActiveMQ Message Broker Connector

  Started Application Modules:
    EAR: geronimo/daytrader-derby-tomcat/1.0/car
    EAR: geronimo/uddi-tomcat/1.0/car
    EAR: geronimo/webconsole-tomcat/1.0/car
    RAR: geronimo/activemq/1.0/car
    RAR: geronimo/system-database/1.0/car
    WAR: geronimo/jmxdebug-tomcat/1.0/car
    WAR: geronimo/jsp-examples-tomcat/1.0/car
    WAR: geronimo/ldap-demo-tomcat/1.0/car
    WAR: geronimo/remote-deploy-tomcat/1.0/car
    WAR: geronimo/servlets-examples-tomcat/1.0/car
    WAR: geronimo/welcome-tomcat/1.0/car

  Web Applications:
    http://A074LTP:8080/
    http://A074LTP:8080/console
    http://A074LTP:8080/console-standard
    http://A074LTP:8080/daytrader
    http://A074LTP:8080/debug-tool
    http://A074LTP:8080/jsp-examples
    http://A074LTP:8080/juddi
    http://A074LTP:8080/ldap-demo
    http://A074LTP:8080/remote-deploy
    http://A074LTP:8080/servlets-examples
Geronimo Application Server started
```

Figure 1-13. *Geronimo server startup*

You can also start Geronimo by using one of the following two commands: geronimo.bat start or startup.bat. This starts the server in a new command window.

You can get the help listing, shown in Figure 1-14, by issuing this command:

```
geronimo.bat --help
```

You can also give as parameters to the following command a list of configurations that you want to start:

```
geronimo.bat start --override geronimo/j2ee-system/1.0/car
```

This command will load and start only the System configuration. In the default mode, when no configurations are explicitly given as command parameters, Geronimo will load all known configurations. This list of configurations is obtained from the file var/config/config.xml. Geronimo keeps this list up-to-date with all last-known configurations.

```
C:\geronimo-tomcat-j2ee-1.0\geronimo-1.0\bin>geronimo.bat --help
Using GERONIMO_BASE:    C:\geronimo-tomcat-j2ee-1.0\geronimo-1.0
Using GERONIMO_HOME:    C:\geronimo-tomcat-j2ee-1.0\geronimo-1.0
Using GERONIMO_TMPDIR: C:\geronimo-tomcat-j2ee-1.0\geronimo-1.0\var\temp
Using JRE_HOME:         C:\j2sdk1.4.2_05
Usage:  geronimo command [args]
commands:
   debug               Debug Geronimo in jdb debugger
   jpda start          Start Geronimo under JPDA debugger
   run                 Start Geronimo in the current window
   start               Start Geronimo in a separate window
   stop                Stop Geronimo

args for debug, jpda start, run and start commands:
      --quiet          No startup progress
      --long           Long startup progress
   -v --verbose        INFO log level
   -vv --veryverbose   DEBUG log level
      --override       Override configurations. USE WITH CAUTION!
      --help           Detailed help.

args for stop command:
      --user           Admin user
      --password       Admin password
      --port           RMI port to connect to

C:\geronimo-tomcat-j2ee-1.0\geronimo-1.0\bin>
```

Figure 1-14. *Geronimo startup help*

You can also specify verbose options as command parameters when you start the server. To start Geronimo in silent mode, use the following command:

`geronimo.bat start --quiet`

For verbose mode, use the following command:

`geronimo.bat start -v`

This option will print all log messages with priority greater than or equal to INFO. To print all log messages (including the DEBUG messages) use the following command:

`geronimo.bat start -vv`

Once the Geronimo J2EE server starts, you can test the installation by using a browser to access `http://localhost:8080/`. This should bring up the default home page, as shown in Figure 1-15.

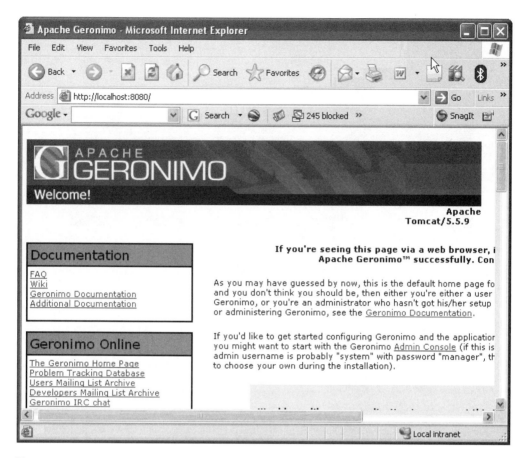

Figure 1-15. *Geronimo default page*

You can access the administration console, shown in Figure 1-16, at `http://host:port/ console`. Log in by using the user name "system" and the password "manager."

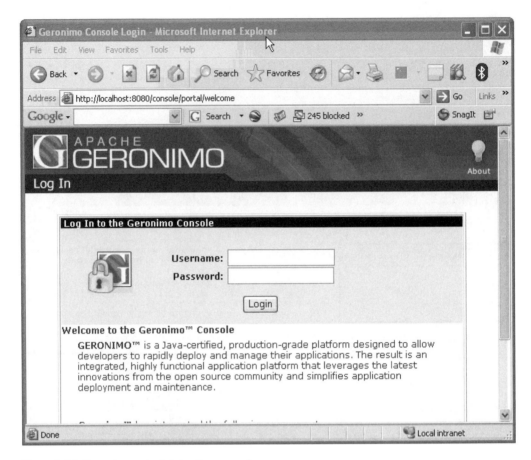

Figure 1-16. *Geronimo administration console*

Stopping the Server

To stop the server, press Ctrl+C in the console window. You can also use one of the following commands from the command window to stop the server: `geronimo.bat stop` or `shutdown.bat`.

Summary

In this chapter, you learned about the features of the Geronimo application server. You also saw how to install and use Geronimo. In the next chapter, you'll examine Geronimo's architecture.

■■■

CHAPTER 2

Geronimo Architecture

Geronimo has a lightweight, modular architecture. At its core, it is an IOC framework for components called GBeans, and it offers the following capabilities:

- Provides a framework and platform for building applications

- Defines components (GBeans) that you can configure and deploy in the platform to extend the functionality of the platform

- Manages the components' life cycle behavior

- Manages the dependencies between the components

- Provides a mechanism for serializing GBeans into a persistent store and later deserializing and loading them back into the platform

- Facilitates intercomponent communication

The Geronimo J2EE server is implemented as a prebuilt set of GBean components that can be deployed into the Geronimo platform.

In this chapter, you'll explore details of Geronimo's architecture. You'll also learn how to create a simple GBean and deploy it into Geronimo.

Architecture Components Overview

The Geronimo platform framework, also called the kernel, is a J2EE-agnostic container for GBeans. It is built on the fundamental concepts of IOC and Dependency Injection.

As an IOC container, the Geronimo platform manages the life cycle of GBeans. You can deploy one or more GBeans into the Geronimo platform, and the platform injects dependencies into the GBeans.

A configuration is a grouping of related GBeans that you can deploy, start, stop, and manage as an entity. A configuration is itself a GBean, and this makes it a deployable entity into the Geronimo kernel. When you deploy a configuration, you deploy all the GBeans it contains.

Figure 2-1 depicts a high-level overview of Geronimo functioning as a J2EE server.

INVERSION OF CONTROL

IOC (also known as the Hollywood principle) is what differentiates a library from a framework. Consider a simple menu-driven application in which the main program presents the user with input prompts (like Enter the numbers:) to collect user inputs. Here, the main control logic is coded within the application. In the case of a GUI application, you need to code only the event handlers, and the main control flow is hidden within the GUI framework. The framework calls your event handlers when appropriate GUI events happen. However, when you use a library, the control still lies within the calling program. In short, IOC is a mechanism by which the main control logic is encapsulated within a framework. You extend the functionality of the framework by deploying suitable extension points like plugins or event handlers, depending on the platform.

Apart from the main application control logic, other application aspects can be shifted to the framework code. Dependency Injection is one such aspect. Most objects have dependencies with other objects, like a service object having a dependency with a Data Access Object to access the database. You can hard-code this dependency within the service object or use a service locator design pattern to resolve the dependency at runtime. With both of these approaches, the logic of dependency resolution lies within the application logic. An alternative to this is to have the container resolve this dependency by injecting the actual dependency (Data Access Object) at runtime when the target object (service object) is created. You can configure this dependency engine in a container-specific mechanism that can be configuration file based.

There are two kinds of commonly used Dependency Injection techniques: constructor based and setter based. With a constructor-based Dependency Injection, the IOC container provides all the object dependencies to the constructor of the target object. With a setter-based Dependency Injection, the IOC container uses setter methods to inject dependencies. PicoContainer is an open source IOC container that uses constructor-based Dependency Injection, and the Spring framework IOC container supports both techniques.

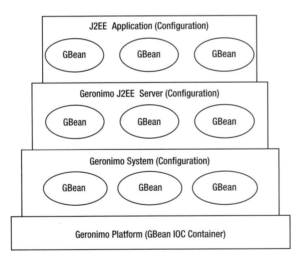

Figure 2-1. *Geronimo functioning as a J2EE server*

As mentioned, the Geronimo System configuration is J2EE agnostic, and it defines all the basic services (as GBeans) required for any server, like the registry service and the logging service. The J2EE server configuration defines GBeans that provide services that are required

by the J2EE specification. When you deploy a J2EE application, Geronimo deployer components create a configuration GBean (containing one or more GBeans to represent the various
application components) corresponding to your application and deploy it into the kernel.
When this configuration is started, the J2EE application starts.

In the following sections, you'll learn about the various Geronimo components in more
detail. I'll also present further details about certain components later in this chapter.

GBeans

A GBean is the smallest manageable element in Geronimo. In fact, everything in Geronimo
is a GBean: containers, connectors, applications, and so on. The GBean acts like a facade to
service implementations (and even to simple POJOs), thereby injecting manageability aspects
into them. A system might comprise many GBean components as well as many non-GBean
components. Only those components that need to participate in life cycle activities and to expose
their attributes and operations to JMX clients must be deployed as GBeans. A GBean can have
multiple instances. The Geronimo platform assigns a unique name to each of these instances
at runtime.

In sum, a GBean has the following characteristics:

- It wraps a service implementation.

- It can hold either persistent or nonpersistent state information.

- It provides manageability aspects to the service it wraps.

- Relationships and dependencies with other GBeans can be defined within the GBean
  itself.

- It is deployed and run on the Geronimo platform.

When you deploy an enterprise application into Geronimo, Geronimo internally creates a
number of GBeans and deploys them to represent the following components of the application:

- The enterprise application

- Each module in the application (web, EJB, and so forth)

- Each servlet in the web application

- Each EJB in the EJB JAR

- Each connection factory or admin object configured

As mentioned, GBean instances can be serialized and saved to a persistent store, and
Geronimo can later deserialize them to reconstruct the GBeans.

Configurations

A configuration, as noted previously, is a logical grouping of GBeans that you can deploy and
manipulate (deploy, start, stop, or undeploy) as a unit. A configuration defines the library
dependencies and a set of related GBeans. When you load and start a configuration, the
kernel (Geronimo platform) loads and starts all the GBeans defined in that configuration.

The XML serialization of a configuration is called a deployment plan. A configuration builder can build a configuration instance from a plan and deploy it into Geronimo.

Configurations are hierarchical. All configurations—except the geronimo/j2ee-system/1.0/car configuration—have a parent configuration. A configuration cannot be loaded until its parent configuration is loaded, and, similarly, a configuration cannot be started until its parent configuration is started.

What is the relation between a GBean and a configuration? You've learned that a configuration defines one or more related GBeans. In addition, a configuration is also a GBean. So, when you load a configuration into a Geronimo system, you are loading the configuration GBean, which in turn loads all the GBeans it contains. These GBeans are then marked as dependent on the configuration GBean. Likewise, when the configuration GBean is started, it starts all the GBeans within it.

A configuration is associated with a separate classloader. This classloader is used to load the GBeans that are defined by this configuration.

Configuration Manager

The configuration manager is a central service that manages Geronimo configurations. It uses a configuration store to deserialize stored configurations and load them into the Geronimo kernel. You can also use it to unload configurations from the kernel.

Dependency Manager

The dependency manager records dependencies between the GBeans. A GBean can be started only if all the GBeans that it depends on (parent GBeans) are started. Similarly, when a GBean is stopped, all the dependent GBeans are also stopped. A configuration GBean is dependent on all the GBeans it contains, and you can explicitly specify this inside the configuration deployment plan, as shown here:

```
<configuration ... >
...
    <gbean name="properties-login" ➡
class="org.apache.geronimo.security.jaas.JaasLoginModuleUse">
        <attribute name="controlFlag">REQUIRED</attribute>
        <reference name="LoginModule">
            <name>properties-login</name>
        </reference>
    </gbean>

    <gbean name="JMX" ➡
class="org.apache.geronimo.security.jaas.ServerRealmConfigurationEntry">
        <attribute name="applicationConfigName">JMX</attribute>
        <attribute name="realmName">
            geronimo-properties-realm
        </attribute>
    </gbean>
...
</configuration>
```

This deployment plan defines a configuration that contains one or more dependent GBeans. When a configuration is loaded, it registers all its dependent GBeans (as being dependent) with the dependency manager. Geronimo uses this information when it starts and stops the GBeans.

Blocker (Start Holds) GBeans are also part of this process. Before Geronimo starts a GBean, it checks for any blocker GBeans that are registered with the dependency manager against this GBean. If any are present, Geronimo will not start this GBean until all the blocker GBeans are dead or removed.

The relationships between the dependency manager, GBeans, and the Geronimo kernel are shown in Figure 2-2.

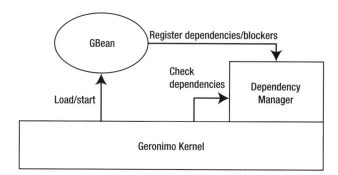

Figure 2-2. *Relationships between the dependency manager, GBeans, and the kernel*

Note I'll discuss the life cycle of a GBean in detail later in this chapter.

Configuration Store

Prebuilt, ready-to-start configurations are stored in the configuration store. Geronimo's configuration store is a simple, local file system–based implementation. This configuration store (LocalConfigStore) stores the serialized form of configuration instances that come with Geronimo. Figure 2-3 depicts the LocalConfigStore directory structure.

The config-store directory stores configurations in subdirectories with numeric names. When you add a new configuration, the highest directory number is incremented, and a new directory is created with this name. The config.ser file contains a serialized configuration instance. The index.properties file maintains a map between the configuration ID (such as geronimo/j2ee-system/1.0/car) and the numeric name of the subdirectory where the configuration is unpacked and stored.

When Geronimo starts, it does not load and start all configurations that are deployed and available in the configuration store. You can specify the configurations you want to start by passing them as startup arguments to the Geronimo kernel; otherwise, Geronimo uses the LocalAttributeManager GBean to decide which configurations need to be loaded from the configuration store.

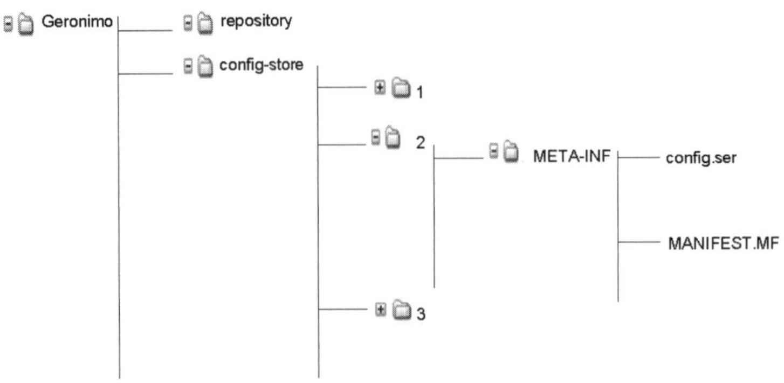

Figure 2-3. *LocalConfigStore directory structure*

Persistent Configuration List

As you've just learned, you can start Geronimo by providing a list of configurations as startup arguments. In this case, Geronimo will load (from the configuration store) and start only these configurations. When you don't specify any configurations as startup arguments, Geronimo loads a preknown list of configurations. Geronimo updates this configuration list every time it loads and unloads a configuration. Hence, this list contains all last-known loaded configurations.

Geronimo includes a simple implementation, the LocalAttributeManager GBean, that maintains this configuration list in a config.xml file in the var/config directory. (This GBean is contained in the geronimo/j2ee-system/1.0/car configuration.) You can plug in your own persistent configuration list by deploying a GBean that implements the Persistent➥ ConfigurationList interface and is named AttributeManager.

Repository

The repository is a container for all shared libraries. When a configuration is loaded, any configured dependencies are resolved relative to the repository root. Geronimo's built-in repository service (FileSystemRepository) maintains the libraries in a directory called repository in the Geronimo root directory.

You can specify a dependency reference within your deployment plan, as shown here:

```
<configuration ... >
    <dependency>
        <uri>geronimo/jars/geronimo-core.jar</uri>
    </dependency>
...
</configuration>
```

Registry

Geronimo comes with a simple registry implementation called the BasicRegistry service. The registry service manages a map of GBeans instances. All GBeans known to the kernel are registered with the registry. The registry service stores GBean JMX ObjectNames and implements a JMX-compliant algorithm to match GBean name patterns.

Kernel

The Geronimo platform core is the kernel. It is a container for GBeans. The kernel is responsible for managing the life cycle and dependencies of all loaded GBeans. In addition, it manages the interaction between the GBeans. GBeans cannot directly interact, but the kernel provides a proxy-based communication channel for facilitating their interactions. The kernel uses a registry to store GBeans, a dependency manager to record GBean dependencies, and a configuration manager to load and manage configurations. Geronimo's kernel implementation is called BasicKernel.

Figure 2-4 depicts the Geronimo kernel hosting some of the services loaded as GBeans.

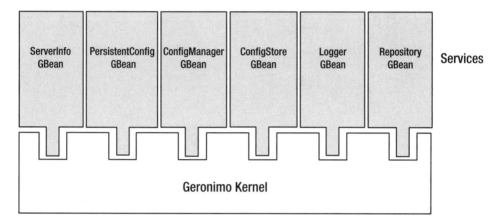

Figure 2-4. *Geronimo with GBeans loaded from the System configuration*

The figure shows the services that are loaded from the geronimo/j2ee-system/1.0/car configuration. This kernel state is achieved when you start Geronimo by using the following command:

```
java -jar bin/server.jar --override geronimo/j2ee-system/1.0/car
```

The geronimo/j2ee-system/1.0/car configuration is the parent configuration for all other configurations.

More About GBeans

The concept of a GBean is central to Geronimo. GBeans are the primary building blocks of a Geronimo system. As you have already seen, Geronimo is just a simple IOC platform, and without any deployed GBeans, it does not do anything. You add new services by adding one or more GBeans into the Geronimo platform. This section discusses in detail the design features of a GBean that enable it to extend the capabilities of the Geronimo platform.

The general architecture of a GBean is shown in Figure 2-5.

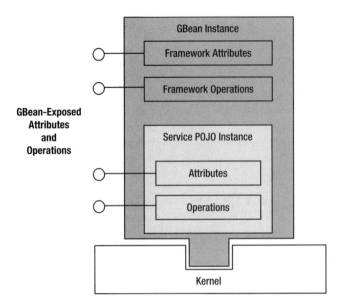

Figure 2-5. *A GBean instance*

The kernel wraps every POJO-based service implementation by using a GBeanInstance object. The GBeanInstance object provides the GBean with the necessary kernel pluggability and controls the GBean life cycle. It also defines certain framework attributes (like startTime and eventTypes) and framework operations (like start and stop) that are common to all GBeans.

A GBean POJO is a simple Java bean. Every attribute that needs to be exposed, and hence manageable, requires a getter and a setter according to Java bean syntax. You can make an attribute nonreadable or nonwritable by not defining a getter or setter method accordingly. GBeans can also define operations. You need to explicitly define attributes and operations that need to be exposed by using a GBeanInfo object, as shown here:

```
Static {
        GBeanInfoBuilder infoFactory = new ➥
GBeanInfoBuilder(LocalConfigStore.class, "ConfigurationStore");

        infoFactory.addAttribute("kernel", Kernel.class, false);
        infoFactory.addAttribute("objectName", String.class, false);
        infoFactory.addAttribute("root", URI.class, true);

        infoFactory.addReference("GeronimoServerInfo", ➥
ServerInfo.class, "GBean");

        infoFactory.addInterface(ConfigurationStore.class);

        infoFactory.setConstructor(new String[]{"kernel", ➥
"objectName", "root", "GeronimoServerInfo"});

        GBEAN_INFO = infoFactory.getBeanInfo();
}
```

A GBeanInfoBuilder is a helper class you can use to build a GBeanInfo object that describes a GBean to the kernel. This static code block in the LocalConfigStore class defines a GBean and exposes three attributes: kernel, objectName, and root. The last parameter in the addAttribute() method defines whether or not this attribute is a persistent attribute (we will discuss persistent attributes in a subsequent section). The LocalConfigStore GBean also defines a reference (we will also discuss GBean references in a later section) to ServerInfo GBean. The addInterface() method of GBeanInfoBuilder takes an interface type as a parameter and uses reflection to add all methods in this interface (and its parent types) as operations of GBeans that should be exposed. All getter and setter methods are treated as GBean attributes that should be exposed to other GBeans.

After you define a GBeanInfo, you need to define a getGBeanInfo() method in your class to expose the GBeanInfo instance to Geronimo. The following command is all Geronimo needs to convert your POJO class to a GBean:

```
public static GBeanInfo getGBeanInfo(){
        return GBEAN_INFO;
}
```

GBean Names

GBean names are similar in syntax to JMX ObjectNames. This simplifies the deployment of GBeans as MBeans in a JMX-compliant server. The general syntax of a GBean name is domainName:name=value[,name=value]*, where * represents zero or more occurrences of the name-value pair. The Geronimo kernel itself has an object name, geronimo:role=Kernel. A GBean representing a loaded configuration has a name like geronimo.config:name= geronimo/j2ee-system/1.0/car. Also, most of the GBeans defined in a configuration have names similar to this:

```
geronimo.server:J2EEServer=geronimo,J2EEApplication=null, ➥
J2EEModule=geronimo/j2ee-system/1.0/car,j2eeType=GBean, ➥
name=RMIRegistry
```

A GBean name assumes that every component that is deployed into Geronimo has a server, an application, a j2eeType, a module, and a module-specific name associated with it. One or more of these can be empty (null) if they are not applicable to that component. This naming convention is in accordance with the JSR 77 object names syntax for J2EE-managed objects. For example, the name of the GBean that represents a JVM is as follows:

```
geronimo.server:J2EEServer=geronimo,j2eeType=JVM,name=JVM
```

GBean Attributes

GBeans can have attributes that are exposed to other GBeans and to the management and monitoring clients. These attributes can be either persistent or nonpersistent, and the framework supports storing and restoring GBeans. Persistent attributes are saved as the GBean state when the GBeans are unloaded from the kernel and are made available when they are loaded back into the kernel.

Certain GBean attributes, like objectName and kernel, are known as special, or magic, attributes. These attributes represent kernel runtime-specific and environment-specific values. They are never persistent and are injected into every GBean when it is loaded into the kernel. In fact, they cannot be persistent since they hold runtime-specific environment details.

Certain other attributes of GBeans are known as framework attributes. These common attributes are available to every GBean and are not GBean specific (service POJO specific). Figure 2-5 showed that every GBean is wrapped within a GBeanInstance object that defines the framework attributes like startTime and state. Framework attributes are also nonpersistent.

All other attributes that the GBean defines are GBean specific and are attributes that this GBean wants to expose to other GBeans. These attributes can be either persistent or nonpersistent. The kernel injects all persistent attributes' values into the GBeans when they are loaded.

GBean References

GBeans might need to communicate with other GBeans that are available and loaded in the kernel. You accomplish this by declaring a reference that specifies which GBean another GBean should interact with. You can declare a GBean reference by issuing the following code fragment from within your GBean code:

```
GBeanInfoBuilder infoFactory = new ➡
GBeanInfoBuilder(LocalConfigStore.class, "ConfigurationStore");

infoFactory.addReference("GeronimoServerInfo", ServerInfo.class, ➡
"GBean");

infoFactory.setConstructor(new String[]{"kernel", "objectName", ➡
"root", " GeronimoServerInfo "});

GBEAN_INFO = infoFactory.getBeanInfo();
```

This declares a GBean reference to the ServerInfo GBean. The addReference() method requires a name and the reference type as parameters. Your GBean either should declare a constructor that accepts the reference type as a parameter or should declare a setter method for the reference type. In the preceding example, the kernel uses the constructor to inject this dependency since the GBeanInfo declares a constructor that accepts a ServerInfo reference type.

When the kernel loads and starts your GBean, it will initialize your GBean with a valid reference to the ServerInfo GBean. However, the kernel needs to know the target GBean(s) to satisfy the reference link. You need to define the target GBean(s) for every reference, and one way to do this is to define the target GBean in the deployment plan file, as shown here:

```
<configuration xmlns=" http://geronimo.apache.org/xml/ns/deployment-1.0"➡
 configId="MySystem" domain="geronimo.server" server="geronimo" >
...
  <gbean name="ServerInfo" ➡
class="org.apache.geronimo.system.serverinfo.ServerInfo"/>
```

```
<gbean name="LocalStore" ➥
class="org.apache.geronimo.system.configuration.LocalConfigStore">
    <attribute name="root">config-store</attribute>
    <reference name=" GeronimoServerInfo>
      <name>ServerInfo</name>
    </reference>
  </gbean>

...
</configuration>
```

This defines the MySystem configuration, which in turn defines the LocalStore GBean. The GBean definition provides an initial value for one of its persistent attributes, root. (The other two attributes, objectName and kernel, as declared by the GBeanInfo of this GBean [see the preceding code listing], are special attributes that the kernel initializes and injects.) It also defines a target for the GeronimoServerInfo reference. The kernel satisfies this reference link by using all GBeans that match the target GBean name (also called a reference pattern).

A GBean reference injected by the kernel is actually a proxy for a direct reference to the original GBean. In this way, Geronimo does not allow direct interaction between GBeans. Figure 2-6 depicts how GBeans interact.

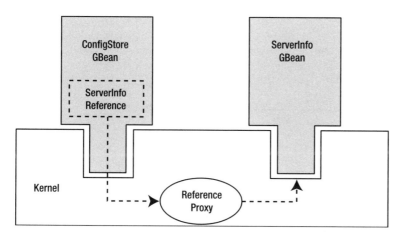

Figure 2-6. *Proxy-based GBean interactions*

Geronimo uses cglib (or JDK Proxy) for implementing reference proxies. Cglib (http:// cglib.sourceforge.net) is a code-generation library. Depending on the reference parameter type, the proxy can be a single GBean reference or a collection GBean reference. A single GBean reference requires the reference to match a single target GBean, and for a collection GBean reference, the reference pattern can match one or more target GBeans. The collection reference will contain a list of proxies corresponding to every match.

Every reference has the following states: initial, online, started, stopped, and offline. When the reference is created, it is in the initial state. When the kernel loads a GBean, it brings all its references to the online state. In this state, the reference queries the kernel for all known target GBeans that match its reference patterns. Additionally, it starts a life cycle listener to listen for all GBean life cycle events from the kernel and thereby updates its target list when new GBeans that match the reference pattern are loaded. When the kernel brings the reference offline, it stops the life cycle listener and clears its known target lists. The kernel starts a reference after it creates the GBean target instance (GBean POJO instance), and then the reference creates the proxy to the target reference and makes it available for use. Finally, when the kernel stops the reference, it destroys the reference proxy.

GBean Life Cycle

Geronimo implements the JSR 77 managed-object life cycle for all its GBean instances. You can save and store a GBean in a configuration store, in which case the GBean is in the stored state. After being loaded into the Geronimo platform, a GBean instance goes through the soloing states and transitions, as depicted in Figure 2-7.

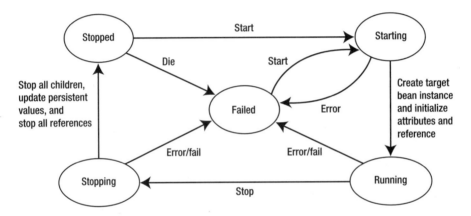

Figure 2-7. *GBean life cycle*

A GBean is a kernel component that wraps a target bean (POJO). When the GBean is created, it is initially in the stopped state, with all the references in the online state. When the kernel starts the GBean, it creates the target GBean instance (the POJO), initializes the persistent and special attributes, and starts its GBean references (creates the reference proxy and makes it ready for use). When the kernel stops a GBean, it stops all dependent GBeans, updates the GBean persistent values, and stops all the GBean references by destroying the proxy objects. A GBean moves to the failed state when an error occurs or when it is made to fail explicitly. Also, when a stopped GBean is made to die, it destroys the target instance and brings all the references offline.

The target bean (POJO) can implement the GBeanLifecycle interface to receive life cycle callbacks from the kernel.

```
public class MyBean implements GBeanLifecycle {

        public void doStart throws Exception {
                // do something
        }

        public void doStop throws Exception {
                // do something
        }

        public void doFail() {
                // do something
        }

        public GBeanInfo getGBeanInfo(){
                // return the GBeanInfo object
        }

        static {
                // create the GBean Info using GBean Info Builder
        }
}
```

The doStart() method will be called before the GBean goes into the running state, and the doStop() method will be called before the GBean goes into the stopped state.

Since a configuration is also internally represented as a GBean, it undergoes a similar life cycle. When the kernel starts a configuration GBean, in addition to going through the normal process of starting a GBean, it loads and starts all the GBeans defined by this configuration and marks them as dependents with the kernel dependency manager. Also, when the configuration GBean is stopped, the kernel stops all the GBean's dependent GBeans, unloads and unregisters them with the kernel, and stores the GBean state (and the configuration state) in the configuration store.

More About the Geronimo Kernel

The Geronimo kernel is a container for GBeans. Additionally, it is an IOC framework since it can inject GBean dependencies (special attributes, persistent attributes, and references) at runtime. The kernel itself is available as a GBean called the KernelGBean.

The following events happen when the kernel boots:

1. The kernel registers the kernel instance with the kernel registry. The kernel registry contains a map of all available kernels.

2. The kernel starts the GBean registry. The GBean registry contains a map of all GBeans that are loaded in the kernel.

3. It creates a GBean life cycle monitor. A life cycle monitor is a central place that collects GBean life cycle event notifications and broadcasts the events to all registered listeners.

4. It creates a dependency manager, which records all GBean dependencies.

5. It creates a proxy manager. A proxy manager is responsible for creating proxies that are used to satisfy GBean references.

6. Finally, it creates a KernelGBean and loads this GBean into the kernel.

Geronimo Server Startup

After the Geronimo kernel boots, it loads the System configuration, followed by the one or more configurations that were loaded by the server when it was last run. The System configuration defines all the basic services, and every other configuration loaded introduces new services into the Geronimo platform. This section details the complete startup process of the Geronimo server.

During server startup, Geronimo does the following:

1. Reads the serialized server configuration from META-INF/config.ser (loaded from bin/server.jar). This is actually the serialized form of the geronimo/j2ee-system/1.0/car configuration.

2. Creates an MBean server.

3. Creates a kernel instance named geronimo.

4. Boots the kernel. This initializes the kernel and makes it ready to load GBeans into it.

5. Loads the geronimo/j2ee-system/1.0/car configuration into the kernel.

6. Loads and starts the MBeanServerKernelBridge GBean. From this point, for every GBean that is loaded into the kernel, the MBeanServerKernelBridge creates a corresponding MBean and registers it with the MBean server.

7. Starts the geronimo/j2ee-system/1.0/car configuration and all GBeans defined from this configuration. This loads and starts all the basic services, like configuration store, repository, and logger.

8. Checks with all registered PersistentConfigurationList providers to get the list of configurations that need to be loaded and started, if no configurations are explicitly given as startup parameters. The geronimo/j2ee-system/1.0/car configuration, which is already loaded and started, has registered an XML file-based PersistentConfigurationList provider that stores a list of configurations in the var/config/config.xml file. Hence, the server collects all known configurations from this PersistentConfigurationList provider. However, if a list of configurations is provided as startup arguments, the PersistentConfigurationList providers are not used and the server loads and starts only the given list of configurations.

9. Loads and starts (recursively) all the configurations.

10. Waits in an infinite loop.

Some of the key configurations available with the Geronimo 1.0 release are as follows:

geronimo/j2ee-system/1.0/car: Contains the basic services, like logging and configuration store. This configuration should always be run, and it is the first configuration to start during server startup. It serves as the parent configuration (directly or indirectly) for all other configurations.

geronimo/j2ee-server/1.0/car: Defines GBeans that implement all the services required for a J2EE server. It contains GBeans that start a web container, an EJB container, and a J2EE connector service.

geronimo/rmi-naming/1.0/car: Defines the RMI and naming services.

geronimo/j2ee-security/1.0/car: Defines all the Geronimo security features and services and defines security realms for the administration console.

geronimo/geronimo-gbean-deployer/1.0/car: Defines the basic deployment services required to deploy configurations and GBeans.

geronimo/j2ee-deployer/1.0/car: Defines the J2EE-specific deployment services required to deploy J2EE application components except for web applications. Another configuration handles deployment of web applications since Geronimo needs to support both Jetty and Tomcat separately and out of the box.

geronimo/tomcat-deployer/1.0/car: Defines services to deploy web applications for the Tomcat container.

geronimo/tomcat/1.0/car: Defines the Tomcat web container along with default network listeners.

geronimo/online-deployer/1.0/car: Should not be started by default since the deployer JAR uses it under the covers.

geronimo/hot-deployer/1.0/car: Defines the hot-deployment feature.

geronimo/directory/1.0/car: Defines an embedded Apache Lightweight Directory Access Protocol (LDAP) server. An application can define security realms that use this LDAP server.

geronimo/javamail/1.0/car: Defines the JavaMail features and provides a basic SMTP transport.

geronimo/ldap-realm/1.0/car: Defines a sample LDAP-based security realm.

geronimo/j2ee-corba/1.0/car: Defines the services required to support CORBA connectivity.

geronimo/client-corba/1.0/car: Defines the services required for CORBA connectivity from the J2EE application client container. This should not be started and is used internally by the client container.

geronimo/client-system/1.0/car: Defines the J2EE application client container. This should not be started and is used internally.

geronimo/client/1.0/car: Should not be started and is used internally by the J2EE application client container.

geronimo/client-security/1.0/car: Should not be started and is used internally by the J2EE application client container.

geronimo/system-database/1.0/car: Defines GBeans that start an embedded Derby database. This service is required to support EJB timer and JMS persistence functionality.

geronimo/activemq-broker/1.0/car: Defines GBeans that start an ActiveMQ messaging service.

geronimo/activemq/1.0/car: Starts a JMS connection factory and two JMS queues for internal server use. This configuration depends on the geronimo/activemq-broker/1.0/car configuration.

Table 2-1 details the web applications provided with Geronimo.

Table 2-1. *Web Applications Provided with Geronimo*

Configuration	Description
geronimo/welcome-tomcat/1.0/car	Geronimo welcome application accessible at `http://hostname:8080/`
geronimo/webconsole-tomcat/1.0/car	Geronimo administration console accessible at `http://hostname:8080/console`
geronimo/servlets-examples-tomcat/1.0/car	Servlet examples accessible at `http://hostname:8080/servlets-examples`
geronimo/jsp-examples-tomcat/1.0/car	JSP examples accessible at `http://hostname:8080/jsp-examples`
geronimo/jmxdebug-tomcat/1.0/car	Debug tool for JMX objects; accessible at `http://hostname:8080/debug-tool`
geronimo/remote-deploy-tomcat/1.0/car	Web application that services remote deployment requests; accessible at `http://hostname:8080/remote-deploy`
geronimo/uddi-tomcat/1.0/car	JAXR UDDI implementation accessible at `http://hostname:8080/juddi`
geronimo/ldap-demo-tomcat/1.0/car	LDAP demo web application accessible at `http://hostname:8080/ldap-demo`
geronimo/daytrader-derby-tomcat/1.0/car	Sample application that can be used for performance testing; accessible at `http://hostname:8080/daytrader`

MBeanServerKernelBridge

All GBeans loaded and registered with the kernel (GBean container) are also loaded and registered as corresponding MBeans with an MBean server. The MBeanServerKernelBridge registers with the kernel for all GBeans' life cycle events, and for every GBean that is loaded into the kernel, it creates a corresponding MBeanGBeanBridge instance (this is a dynamic MBean) and registers this instance with the MBean server. This MBean also registers with the kernel for all life cycle events of the GBean that it represents so that it can send corresponding MBean notifications.

Figure 2-8 shows the relationship between GBeans and their corresponding MBeans.

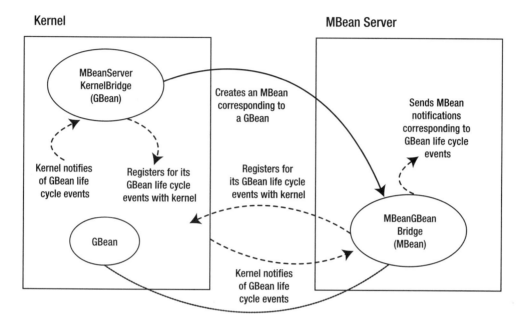

Figure 2-8. *GBean-MBean relationship*

Deployment Architecture

Since the kernel is a container for GBeans, everything that needs to be loaded into the kernel should be a GBean. Thus, a system component, like a web container, or an application component, like a web application, is deployed into the kernel as a GBean. A configuration, which is also a GBean, defines the smallest deployable unit that defines one or more GBeans that need to be deployed. For example, when you deploy a web application, you are actually deploying a configuration that defines many GBeans (like a GBean for every servlet) within it.

You can deploy a configuration into the kernel in one of three ways:

- *Using a deployment plan*: A configuration builder component (already deployed and registered with the kernel) can parse the deployment plan, create a GBean serialized representation (GBeanData instance) of the configuration (containing a serialized representation of all its dependent GBeans), serialize the configuration, and store it in the configuration store. This can be later deserialized, loaded into the kernel, and started. (To deploy using a deployment plan, use this command: `java -jar bin/deployer.jar deploy my-deployment-plan.xml`.)

- *Using a J2EE module (like a WAR file)*: A deployer component (an EAR configuration builder or a web module builder) creates GBeans to represent a configuration for that module and for various application components, like servlets, and serializes the configuration to the configuration store. You can also give a module-specific Geronimo deployment plan along with the module (like a geronimo-web.xml plan along with a WAR module). In this case, a module builder parses the module-specific deployment plan and creates GBeans accordingly. (To deploy a configuration by using a J2EE module, use these commands: `java -jar bin/deployer.jar deploy my-web-app.war` and `java -jar bin/deployer.jar deploy my-web-app.jar my-web-plan.xml`.)

- *Programmatically creating a configuration*: You can create a configuration programmatically and load it into the kernel. However, this is the least commonly used option.

Geronimo Deployer

The geronimo/geronimo-gbean-deployer/1.0/car configuration defines the deployer GBean that performs deployments at kernel runtime. Figure 2-9 depicts the various components of the deployer.

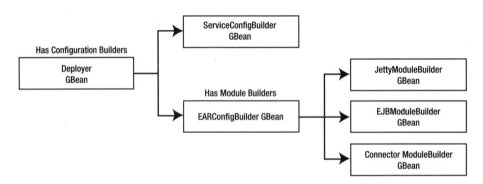

Figure 2-9. *Deployer components*

The deployer uses configuration builder components to build a configuration from a deployment plan. The serviceConfigBuilder component can parse and build a configuration from an XML deployment plan file that conforms to the service configuration Document Type Definition (DTD). A sample service configuration file is shown here:

```
<configuration ...>

  <gbean name="EJBBuilder" ➥
class="org.openejb.deployment.OpenEJBModuleBuilder">
    <attribute name="defaultParentId">
      geronimo/j2ee-server/1.0/car
    </attribute>
```

```
  <reference name="Repository">
    <gbean-name>*:name=Repository,*</gbean-name>
  </reference>
...
  </gbean>

</configuration>
```

The EARConfigBuilder component can build a configuration for a J2EE application EAR component or for other J2EE application components, like a web application. It requires a JAR module file and an optional module-specific deployment plan. The EARConfigBuilder uses a list of module builders, like TomcatModuleBuilder (or JettyModuleBuilder), for handling web applications, EJBModuleBuilder for handling EJB modules, and so on, to create a configuration that can be stored in the configuration store.

Deploy Tool

Geronimo has a deploy tool that can deploy both application modules and services. The general syntax for using the deploy tool is as follows:

```
java -jar deployer.jar [options] command [command options]
```

Alternatively, you can use this syntax:

```
deploy.bat [options] command [command options]
```

Common options include the following:

- `--uri uri`: This Uniform Resource Identifier (URI) is used to connect to the server. This URI should be in the JSR 88 format like this: deployer:geronimo:jmx:rmi:///jndi/rmi://host:port/JMXConnector.

- `--driver jarfile`: This tool can connect to any JSR-compliant server. This option specifies the JSR 88–compliant driver JAR file that can be used to connect to the server.

- `--user username`: The user name for connecting to the server.

- `--password password`: The password for connecting to the server.

Tip For a detailed help listing, type `deploy.bat help` in the command window.

Now let's look at the commands you can use with the deploy tool.

Deploy Command

You can use this command to deploy a service or an application component, like a web application, to the server and start it.

```
java -jar deployer.jar deploy my-web-app.war
java -jar deployer.jar deploy web-app.war web-app-deployment-plan.xml
```

The second command specifies both an application module and a module-specific deployment plan. This command works only when the server is running.

Undeploy Command

This command stops the configuration if it is running and removes the configuration from the server environment.

```
java -jar deployer.jar undeploy my-web-app
```

You can specify a list of configurations that need to be undeployed. Once you undeploy them, you cannot restart them unless you deploy (or distribute) the configuration to the server. This command requires the server to be running.

Distribute Command

This command is similar to the deploy command in that it also installs the configuration to the server. The difference is that this command can work in offline mode and does not start it.

```
java -jar deployer.jar distribute my-web-app.war
```

This command works whether or not the server is running.

Redeploy Command

The redeploy command replaces an existing configuration with a new one.

```
java -jar deployer.jar redeploy new-web-app.war web-app-config-id
```

This replaces the configuration my-web-app-config-id with the my-new-web-app.war application. This command requires the server to be running.

Start Command

The start command starts an already installed application.

```
java -jar deployer.jar start my-web-app-config-id
```

Here, you specify the configuration ID of the web application that you want to start. This command requires the server to be running.

Stop Command

The stop command stops an already running configuration. It does not uninstall the configuration from the server.

```
java -jar deployer.jar stop my-web-app-config-id
```

This command requires the server to be running.

List Modules Command

This command lists all configurations that are installed and available on the server.

```
java -jar deployer.jar list-modules
```

You can specify the `--started` or `--stopped` option to restrict the output to either started or stopped configurations. This command requires the server to be running.

List Targets Command

The list targets command lists all available targets. A target is a configuration store on a server. A Geronimo server can contain one or more configuration stores.

```
java -jar deployer.jar list-targets
```

This command requires the server to be running.

Help Commands

You can use these commands to display help for the deploy tool.

- `java -jar deployer.jar help`: Displays general help.

- `java -jar deployer.jar help options`: Displays help about common options.

- `java -jar deployer.jar help [command]`: Displays help about a specific command.

- `java -jar deployer.jar help all`: Displays help about all commands.

You can also use all of these options with the deploy script (deploy.bat).

Classloader Architecture

For any J2EE application server, its classloader design is very critical. It should be flexible enough to accommodate J2EE application component needs and at the same time efficient. Geronimo has a very elegant and simple classloader design, and this section discusses its architecture.

The classloader hierarchy follows the same structure as that of a configuration. Each configuration has its own separate classloader. This classloader is actually a Uniform Resource Locator (URL) classloader, with all dependencies (library dependencies defined by this configuration in the deployment plan file) added as target URLs, and will have the classloader of the parent configuration as its parent classloader.

Figure 2-10 depicts the classloader hierarchy for an application EAR containing EJBs, resource adapters (RARs), and a web application (WAR).

Here, the geronimo/j2ee-server/1.0/car configuration has the geronimo/j2ee-system/ 1.0/car configuration as its parent, and their classloaders follow the same hierarchy. All web applications loaded from an application EAR will have the EAR classloader as the parent classloader for the web application classloader. The EAR classloader loads all EJBs and RAR classes. In this way, invoking EJBs from a web application from the same EAR is easier.

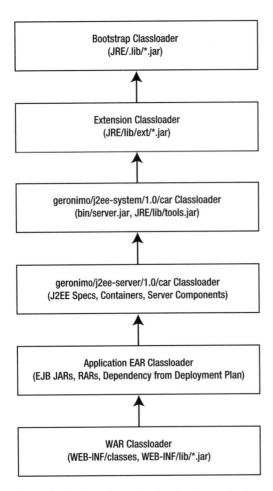

Figure 2-10. *Geronimo classloader hierarchy for an application EAR*

Building and Deploying a Sample GBean

Now that you've familiarized yourself with Geronimo's architecture, let's discuss how to build and deploy a GBean. Here's a summary of the steps you'll follow to develop a service (in our example, echo service) as a GBean and deploy it to Geronimo:

1. Develop the GBean.

2. Compile and package the GBean.

3. Add the JAR to the Geronimo repository.

4. Develop the deployment plan.

5. Deploy and start the service.

Let's look at these steps in more detail.

Develop the GBean (Echo Service)

To develop our sample GBean, we need to use this code:

```
public class EchoServer implements GBeanLifecycle {

  private static final GBeanInfo GBEAN_INFO;
  private final String objectName;

  private int port;
  private ServerSocket serversocket;
  private boolean started = false;

  static {
  ..GBeanInfoBuilder infoFactory = new ➡
GBeanInfoBuilder(EchoServer.class.getName(), EchoServer.class);
    ..infoFactory.addAttribute("objectName", String.class, false);
    ..infoFactory.addAttribute("port", int.class, true);

    ..infoFactory.setConstructor(new String[] { ➡
"objectName", "port" });
    ..GBEAN_INFO = infoFactory.getBeanInfo();
  }

  public EchoServer(String objectName, int port) {
    this.objectName = objectName;
    this.port = port;
  }

  public GBeanInfo getGBeanInfo(){
    return GBEAN_INFO;
  }

  public void doStart() throws WaitingException, Exception {
    // Start a thread that opens a server socket on the
    // given port and listens for client connections.
  }

  public void doStop() throws WaitingException, Exception {
    // Stop the listener thread
  }
}
```

The preceding code defines a GBean with two attributes: objectName and port. The attribute objectName is a special attribute, and its value will be injected into the GBean when it is loaded into Geronimo. The attribute port is a persistent attribute, and hence you can give an initial value (let us say 9999) by using a deployment plan file. The static code block creates a GBeanInfo object and exposes it to Geronimo through a getter method. Since this GBean implements the GBeanLifecycle interface, Geronimo invokes the doStart() method just as the GBean goes into the running state. Here, this EchoServer GBean starts a thread that opens a server socket listening on the given port. It echoes back any text that a client sends to it. Before Geronimo takes the GBean out of service, it invokes the doStop() method, and the EchoServer GBean stops the listener thread.

Compile and Package the GBean

Compile this class, and package it as a JAR file.

Add the JAR to the Geronimo Repository

Create the subdirectories echoserver/jars in the repository folder, and place the JAR file there.

Develop the Deployment Plan

Create a deployment plan, an XML file with the schema geronimo-config.xml in the schema subdirectory of the Geronimo installation, by issuing the following command:

```
<?xml version="1.0" encoding="UTF-8"?>
<configuration xmlns="http://geronimo.apache.org/xml/ns/deployment-1.0" ➥
configId="sample/echoserver">
  <dependency>
    <uri>echoserver/jars/echoserver.jar</uri>
  </dependency>
  <gbean name="geronimo.apps:name=echoserver" class="EchoServer" >
    <attribute name="port" type="int">4545</attribute>
  </gbean>
</configuration>
```

The dependency URI defines the echo server JAR in the repository. Also, the GBean element defines an initial value for the persistent attribute port.

Deploy and Start the Service

You can deploy and start the echo server service by using the following command:

```
java -jar deployer.jar deploy echo-server-plan.xml
```

Summary

Geronimo utilizes a base IOC platform for building a J2EE server. It provides a runtime environment for Geronimo components called GBeans. A GBean wraps a service implementation to extend the capability of the core platform. In this sense, every function— the web container, the EJB container, and so on—of the J2EE server is implemented as a set of GBean components. Moreover, every user-deployed J2EE application is also represented as one or more managed GBean objects. In this chapter, you explored the Geronimo architecture and its internals in detail. You also saw how to create a simple GBean and deploy it into Geronimo. In Chapter 3, you'll discover how to use the Geronimo J2EE server for web application development.

CHAPTER 3

■ ■ ■

Web Application Development with Geronimo

Using Apache Geronimo, you can deploy and run various application components, like web applications, EJB components, J2EE connectors, J2EE client application components, and J2EE enterprise application components. Geronimo provides a web application container to host your web applications. It also enables your web application to connect to any EIS, including relational databases and messaging middleware systems. Additionally, your applications can utilize the web security infrastructure Geronimo provides.

In this chapter, we will discuss how to use Geronimo to deploy and run your web applications. You'll consider the steps involved by looking at the development of a sample application. Next, you'll learn how to configure database connectivity from a web application. Finally, we'll discuss connection pools and web application security.

J2EE Web Applications

J2EE web applications consist of one or more servlets, JSPs, and resource files (including static HTML pages, images, and JavaScript pages). In addition, a J2EE web application must provide a standard deployment descriptor file to describe the application parameters to the hosting container. Optionally, it can provide a container-specific deployment descriptor to define container-specific application parameters.

Servlets are Java classes that provide dynamic extension capabilities to the web server. JSPs are template files that provide a convenient mechanism for creating dynamic content. They are ultimately run as servlets by the container.

Geronimo supports the Servlet 2.4 and JSP 2.0 specifications. The open source web containers Jetty and Apache Tomcat provide Geronimo's web application support. As of this writing, Geronimo is preconfigured to work with the Jetty and Tomcat web containers, and each is available in a separate download of Geronimo.

Developing and Running a Sample Application

The general steps involved in creating a J2EE web application are as follows:

1. Develop the web application (servlets, JSPs, filters, Java helper classes, and resource files).

2. Develop the web application standard deployment descriptor (web.xml).

3. Develop the optional Geronimo-specific deployment descriptor (geronimo-web.xml).

4. Compile the web application (including helper classes).

5. Package the application to a standard deployable unit (a WAR file).

6. Deploy the application by using the Geronimo deployer tool.

7. Access the application by using its URL.

Let's consider these steps in more detail by creating a sample Hello World application.

Develop the Web Application

Let's say our sample application has the following components and features:

- It has a front controller servlet that accepts the user requests, executes a command, and forwards to the next view to be displayed back to the user.

- Dynamic logic that needs to be executed is implemented as a command class (in this case, a WelcomeCommand class).

- When the command class is executed, it creates and returns a model object (in this case, a String message).

- The welcome.jsp view implements the presentation logic.

The controller servlet is shown here:

```
public class FrontController extends HttpServlet {
  public void doGet(HttpServletRequest request, HttpServletResponse ➥
response) throws ServletException, IOException{
    String commandName=request.getParameter("command");
    Command command=null;
    if("welcome".equals(commandName)){
      command=new WelcomeCommand();
    } else {
      // handle this case - maybe use a default command
    }
    Object msg=command.execute(request);
    request.setAttribute("message",msg);
    String nextView=command.getNextView(request,msg);
    RequestDispatcher rd=getServletContext().➥
getRequestDispatcher(nextView);
    rd.forward(request,response);
  }
}
```

The controller servlet instantiates an appropriate command instance, depending on the request parameter, and executes it. The WelcomeCommand returns the welcome message as the execution result. The controller uses the command to find the next view and then dispatches the control to this view.

Create the WelcomeCommand class as shown here:

```
public class WelcomeCommand implements Command {
  public Object execute(HttpServletRequest request){
    return "Hello World !!!";
  }
  public String getNextView(HttpServletRequest request, Object ➥
result){
    return "/welcome.jsp";
  }
}
```

The WelcomeCommand class implements the Command interface, which defines the execute method.

You implement the view (welcome.jsp) as a JSP page, as shown here:

```
<html> <head><title>Hello World</title></head><body>
<h1>This is a sample application.</h1>
Message is: <%=request.getAttribute("message")%>
</body></html>
```

Develop the Standard Deployment Descriptor

A J2EE web application is required to have a standard deployment descriptor that defines the web application details to the web container. This deployment descriptor is an XML file named web.xml. The deployment descriptor for our sample application is given here:

```
<!DOCTYPE web-app PUBLIC   "-//Sun Microsystems, Inc.//DTD Web ➥
Application 2.3//EN"  "http://java.sun.com/dtd/web-app_2_4.dtd">
  <web-app>
    <display-name>Hello World</display-name>
    <description>Hello World Web Application</description>
    <servlet>
      <servlet-name>frontControllerServlet</servlet-name>
      <servlet-class>FrontController</servlet-class>
    </servlet>

    <servlet-mapping>
      <servlet-name>frontControllerServlet</servlet-name>
      <url-pattern>*.htm</url-pattern>
    </servlet-mapping>

  </web-app>
```

This web deployment descriptor defines the servlets (the front controller servlet) and specifies a servlet mapping to invoke the front controller servlet for all requests having a URL that ends in an .htm extension.

Develop the Geronimo-Specific Deployment Descriptor

A J2EE web application can have an optional vendor-specific deployment descriptor to define vendor-specific application parameters. Geronimo uses Jetty as its web container and requires a deployment descriptor file geronimo-web.xml. This file is defined by the geronimo-web.xsd schema file in the schema subdirectory of the Geronimo installation. In our example, since we do not need any vendor-specific configurations, this file is trivial and simple.

```
<?xml version="1.0" encoding="UTF-8"?>
  <web-app xmlns="http://geronimo.apache.org/xml/ns/web" ➥
configId="welcome" parentId="geronimo/j2ee-server/car/1.0">
    <context-root>welcome</context-root>
    < context-priority-classloader>true</context-priority-classloader>
  </web-app>
```

The configId attribute is a unique name that identifies this module (also called a configuration in Geronimo). You can use this name to identify (or refer to) this module wherever required (especially when you use the deploy tool to manage this module). The parentId attribute refers to a parent configuration. Every configuration in Geronimo can have a parent configuration. If we had an EJB module that our web module depended on, we could have it as the parent configuration of the web configuration. This way, the web application could see all the classes from the EJB application. This is because their classloaders would follow the same structure as their respective configurations, and hence the EJB module's classloader would be the parent classloader for the web module's classloader. By default, the parent configuration for all J2EE components should be geronimo/j2ee-server/car/1.0, which is the configId for the Geronimo J2EE server configuration.

The context-root element specifies the context root of the application. Every web application is deployed in the web container in a different context root, and the container makes the application available at the URL http://[host-name][:port]/[context-Root]. The context-priority-classloader element defines whether the web application classloader loads classes from the web application before loading classes from its parent classloader.

Compile and Package the Web Application

Next, you need to compile the servlets and the helper classes.

J2EE web applications have a standard structure. The top-level directory of the web application (web module) is called the document root. This is where the static HTML pages, resource files (like images and JavaScript pages), JSP pages, and so on are stored. The document root directory contains a WEB-INF subdirectory, which contains the following files and subdirectories:

- *web.xml*: The web application standard deployment descriptor

- *Geronimo-specific deployment descriptor*: In our case, geronimo-web.xml

- *Compiled classes*: A subdirectory (WEB-INF/classes) where all the Java classes (including servlet and helper classes) are placed

- *lib*: A subdirectory (WEB-INF/lib) where the external JARs on which this application depends are placed

Figure 3-1 shows the web application directory structure.

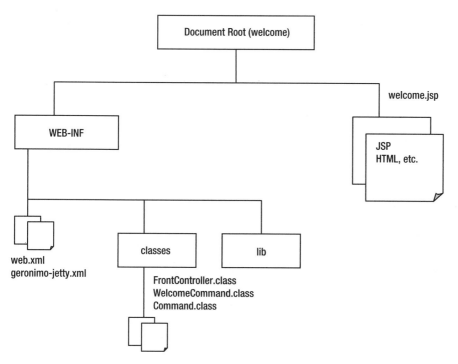

Figure 3-1. *Web application standard structure*

You can deploy web applications as an unpacked file structure (exploded directory format) or as a packaged JAR known as a Web Archive, or WAR, file. WAR files have a .war file extension.

From the document root directory (welcome) JAR, you create a WAR file by issuing the command shown here:

```
jar -cvf welcome.war
```

You can also use an IDE-like NetBean to create the WAR file and to deploy the application by clicking a single button.

Deploy the Application

You can deploy applications (and services) into Geronimo by using the Geronimo deployer JAR. To deploy a WAR file, use the following command:

```
java -jar bin/deployer.jar deploy welcome.war
```

This command requires the Geronimo server to be running. You can start the server by issuing the following command:

```
java -jar bin/server.jar
```

The application will be deployed with the context root as welcome (specified in the geronimo-web.xml file) and will then be started. You can also deploy applications into Geronimo by using any JSR 88–compliant IDE.

Access the Application

You can access the welcome application by using this URL:

```
http://localhost/welcome/welcome.htm?command=welcome
```

The context root, welcome, tells the container which web application should handle this request. This sample web application has a servlet mapping specified in its web.xml file that tells the container to execute the FrontController servlet for all URLs ending with the .htm extension. This servlet will be executed, and finally, the welcome.jsp displays a response page back to the user.

Configuring Database Connectivity

Geronimo comes with an embedded Derby database (http://db.apache.org/derby/) for its internal use. Derby is a pure Java Apache project. We will use this database as an example to explore database connectivity from a web application.

The following three steps are required to configure database connectivity from a web application:

1. Add a resource reference entry in the web deployment descriptor (web.xml).

2. Add a resource reference entry in the Geronimo web deployment descriptor (geronimo-web.xml).

3. Use JNDI to look up a data source and to create a JDBC connection.

Add a Resource Reference Entry in the Web Deployment Descriptor

Add the following resource reference entry in the web.xml web application deployment descriptor:

```
<web-app>
  <!-- other elements -->

  <resource-ref>
    <res-ref-name>jdbc/sampleResource </res-ref-name>
    <res-type>javax.sql.DataSource</res-type>
    <res-auth>Container</res-auth>
    <res-sharing-scope>Shareable</res-sharing-scope>
  </resource-ref>

</web-app>
```

This declares a resource reference named jdbc/sampleResource and of the type javax.sql.DataSource. The web application needs to use this resource reference name when querying the JNDI server for the data source instance that can be used to create JDBC connection instances, as shown in the following code fragment:

```
Context ic =  new InitialContext();
Context envContext = (Context)ic.lookup("java:comp/env");

DataSource ds = envContext.lookup("jdbc/sampleResource");
Connection con = ds.getConnection();
```

The res-auth element specifies that the container, not the user application, will perform the database authentication. The res-sharing-scope element specifies that the connection instances this resource obtains are shareable among components of the same transaction.

Add a Resource Reference Entry in the Geronimo Web Deployment Descriptor

The resource reference entry in the web deployment descriptor declares a resource that can be referenced in a container implementation–independent manner. This allows the application code to be totally independent of the container. You need to specify all container-specific details through corresponding vendor-specific deployment descriptor entries, as shown here:

```
<web-app xmlns="http://geronimo.apache.org/xml/ns/web" ➥
  xmlns:naming="http://geronimo.apache.org/xml/ns/naming" ➥
configId="welcome" parentId="geronimo/j2ee-server/car/1.0">

  <naming:resource-ref>
    <naming:ref-name>jdbc/sampleResource</naming:ref-name>
    <naming:resource-link>SystemDatasource</naming:resource-link>
  </naming:resource-ref>

</web-app>
```

The resource-ref entry maps the resource reference name used in the application (and as specified in the corresponding resource-ref/res-ref-name element of web.xml) to the actual data source. The resource-link element should match the name of the Derby system database deployment plan.

To see whether the Derby system database configuration is available and started, list all the configIds on the current (running) server by using the following command:

```
java –jar bin/deployer.jar --user userName --password password ➥
list-modules --started
```

Use JNDI to Look Up the Data Source

The last step in configuring database connectivity is to use JNDI to look up the data source and to create JDBC connections to the database. From your web application, you can access the data source as shown here:

```
Context ic =  new InitialContext();
Context envContext = (Context)ic.lookup("java:comp/env");

DataSource ds = envContext.lookup("jdbc/ sampleResource");
Connection con = ds.getConnection();
```

Here, note that we use the resource reference name to look up the JNDI tree under the component environment context to obtain the reference to the data source.

Configuring a New Connection Pool

With Geronimo, you can configure a connection pool at the server level, the application level, or the module level. Resources you configure at the server level are visible and available to all applications and services. Resources you configure at the application level are available only to all the modules in a particular application. Module-level resources can be used only by a particular module.

To configure and use a new connection pool, you need to do the following:

1. Add the JDBC driver to the Geronimo repository.

2. Configure the connection pool.

3. Deploy the connection pool.

Add the JDBC Driver to the Repository

Common libraries that need to be shared across applications are generally stored in the Geronimo repository. Geronimo's architecture supports pluggable repository implementations, and the default repository implementation provided is a read-only local repository (SERVER_HOME/repository). Figure 3-2 shows the repository's directory structure.

Figure 3-2. *Repository directory structure*

The libraries are stored under the repository folder in the repository/library-name/jars folder. So, for example, if you want to add the postgreSQL JDBC driver to the repository, you need to add it to the repository/postgreSQL/jars folder.

Configure the Database Pool

You configure database pools and other resources as J2EE connectors that provide the connection pool functionality for a particular database. The TranQL RAR (repository/tranql/rars/tranql-connector-1.0xxx.rar) provides the resource adapter module that implements the J2EE connector functionality. You can configure and deploy different instances of the RAR module to access different resources, like database pools and external systems.

To configure the connector RAR, we need to create a connector deployment plan. The code that follows shows a sample connector deployment plan:

```
<connector xmlns="http://geronimo.apache.org/xml/ns/j2ee/connector" ➥
 version="1.5"  configId="MyPostgreSQLDbPool" ➥
parentId="geronimo/j2ee-server/car/1.0">

<dependency>
  <uri>postgresql/jars/ postgresql.jar </uri>
</dependency>

<resourceadapter>
  <outbound-resourceadapter>

    <connection-definition>
      <connectionfactory-interface>
        javax.sql.DataSource
      </connectionfactory-interface>

        <connectiondefinition-instance>
          <name>PostgreSQLDataSource</name>
          <config-property-setting name="UserName">
            Dbuser
          </config-property-setting>
          <config-property-setting name="Password">
            Dbpw
          </config-property-setting>
          <config-property-setting name="Driver">
            org.postgresql.Driver
          </config-property-setting>
          <config-property-setting name="ConnectionURL">
            jdbc:postgresql://localhost/mydb
          </config-property-setting>
          <config-property-setting name="CommitBeforeAutocommit">
            true
          </config-property-setting>
          <config-property-setting name="ExceptionSorterClass">
            org.tranql.connector.NoExceptionsAreFatalSorter
          </config-property-setting>
```

```
        <connectionmanager>
          <local-transaction/>
          <single-pool>
            <max-size>10</max-size>
            <min-size>0</min-size>
            <blocking-timeout-milliseconds>
              5000
            </blocking-timeout-milliseconds>
            <idle-timeout-minutes>
              30
            </idle-timeout-minutes>
            <match-one/>
          </single-pool>
        </connectionmanager>

        <global-jndi-name>
          jdbc/MyPostgresDatabase
        </global-jndi-name>
      </connectiondefinition-instance>

    </connection-definition>
   </outbound-resourceadapter>
  </resourceadapter>
</connector>
```

The key elements of this connector deployment plan are described in Table 3-1. (I will cover resource adapters in detail in a later chapter.)

Table 3-1. *Connector Deployment Plan Elements*

Element	Description
configId	This is the configuration identifier for the connection pool.
parentId	This is the parent configuration. The default value is geronimo/ j2ee-server/car/1.0.
dependency	One or more dependency elements denote the external JARs that the resource adapter requires. These libraries should be available in the repository. In our case, the resource adapter is dependent only on the PostgreSQL JDBC driver JAR.
connectionfactory-interface	For JDBC connection pools, this needs to be javax.sql.DataSource. The connection factory interface should specify a fully qualified name of the connection factory interface supported by the resource adapter.
name	This is the name used for all references to this connection pool. This value is used in the resource-link element of the geronimo-web deployment descriptor to reference this connection pool from a web application.
config-property-setting	This specifies a value for one of the configuration settings for the connector.

Element	Description
max-size	This specifies the maximum number of simultaneous connection instances in the pool.
min-size	This indicates the minimum number of connection instances in the pool. If the pool size falls below this limit, the pool will be refilled to the size specified here. The default value is 0.
blocking-timeout-milliseconds	The caller will wait this long for a connection to be available before throwing an exception back. If all the available connections (as set by max-size) are currently in use, the caller needs to wait until a connection is freed. This value sets a timeout for this waiting period.
idle-timeout-minutes	The connection pool periodically checks for idle connections and removes them. This entry specifies the interval between these checks.
global-jndi-name	This is the JNDI name a J2EE client application uses to look up this connection pool. It should not be used by any server components. This name should be unique for every resource deployed in Geronimo.

Deploy the Connection Pool

Once the deployment plan is available, you can deploy the connection pool with one of three visibility options: server, application, or module. To deploy a connection pool, you need both the deployment plan (connection pool configuration) and the resource adapter TranQL RAR.

Deploying a Server-Scoped Connection Pool

As mentioned, a server-scoped connection pool is available to all applications and services in Geronimo. To deploy a server-scoped connection pool, create a deployment plan file (let's call it postgreSQLPlan.xml) and use the following command with the server running:

```
java -jar   bin/deployer.jar   deploy   postgreSQLPlan.xml ➡
repository/tranql/rars/ tranql-connector-1.0-xxx.rar
```

The general syntax is shown here:

```
java -jar bin/deployer.jar [command-name] [plan-name] ➡
[tranql-module-rar-file-name]
```

If the server is not running, you can use the distribute command instead of the deploy command. Then, you need to explicitly start the connection pool configuration after the server is started, as shown here:

```
java -jar bin/deployer.jar start [configId]
```

This configId value should match the configId value in the connection pool deployment plan.

Deploying an Application-Scoped Connection Pool

An application-scoped connection pool is visible only to the application that deployed it.
To deploy an application-scoped connection pool, you need to follow these steps:

1. Specify the connector module in the application deployment descriptor.

2. Specify the connector deployment plan in the Geronimo-specific application deployment descriptor.

3. Package the application EAR.

Specify the Connector Module in the Application Deployment Descriptor

The application deployment descriptor (META-INF/application.xml) should define the
TranQL connector module, as shown here:

```
<application xmlns="http://java.sun.com/xml/ns/j2ee" ➥
xmlns:xsi="http://www.w3.org/2001/XMLSchema-instance" ➥
xsi:schemaLocation="http://java.sun.com/xml/ns/j2ee ➥
http://java.sun.com/xml/ns/j2ee/application_1_4.xsd" version="1.4">
  <module>
    <ejb>ejbs.jar</ejb>
  </module>
  <module>
    <web>
      <web-uri>my-web-app.war</web-uri>
      <context-root>/my-web-app</context-root>
    </web>
  </module>
  <module>
    <connector> tranql-connector-1.0-xxx.rar </connector>
  </module>
</application>
```

You should package the connector RAR file along with the application EAR file.

Specify the Connector Deployment Plan in the Geronimo Application Deployment Descriptor

Specify the connector deployment plan file in the Geronimo application deployment descriptor (META-INF/geronimo-application.xml), as shown here:

```
<application ➥
xmlns="http://geronimo.apache.org/xml/ns/j2ee/application" ➥
configId="MyApplication">
  <module>
    <connector> tranql-connector-1.0-xxx.rar </connector>
    <alt-dd> postgreSQLPlan.xml</alt-dd>
  </module>
</application>
```

The alt-dd element specifies which deployment plan to use for deploying the connector module. This is a convenient way to override the Geronimo deployment plan. If the alt-dd element is not present, the file META-INF/geronimo-ra.xml, which is packaged within the RAR file, is used as the Geronimo deployment plan.

Package the Application EAR

In this case, you need to package the TranQL RAR and the connection pool deployment plan within an application EAR. Figure 3-3 depicts this arrangement.

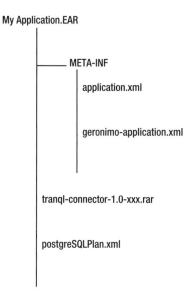

My Application.EAR

Figure 3-3. *Application EAR packaged with a connector RAR*

Deploying a Module-Scoped Connection Pool

Module-scoped connection pools can be used from within only the module that defined the connection pool. To deploy a module-scoped connection pool, specify the connection deployment plan inline with the Geronimo module-specific deployment descriptor. For a web application, you need to specify this in the geronimo-web.xml file, as shown here:

```
<web-app xmlns="http://geronimo.apache.org/xml/ns/web" ➥
xmlns:naming="http://geronimo.apache.org/xml/ns/naming" ...>
...
  <resource>

    <external-rar>
      tranql/rars/ tranql-connector-1.0-xxx.rar
    </external-rar>
```

```
    <connector ➥
xmlns="http://geronimo.apache.org/xml/ns/j2ee/connector" ➥
version="1.5"configId=" MyPostgreSQLDbPool ">
        <!-- Same as the connector deployment plan (postgreSQLPlan.xml) ➥
contents -->
    </connector>

  </resource>

</web-app>
```

The external-rar element should point to the common RAR file in the Geronimo repository.

Securing Your Web Application

Now that you've seen how to use Geronimo to develop and run a web application, we'll discuss providing security for your application. You configure web application security in the web deployment descriptor. J2EE containers are required to provide security services to J2EE components. Containers provide both declarative security and programmatic security. With declarative security, application components specify access control security needs in an external file such as the deployment descriptor. Using programmatic security, the components can programmatically use security features to implement custom security requirements.

A J2EE application can consist of both protected and unprotected resources. Application security generally involves two different processes: authentication and authorization. Authentication is the process of identifying the user (usually through a user login) to the system, and authorization is the process by which the system restricts access to protected resources to authorized users.

Let's examine the authentication process in more detail. Then, you'll learn how to configure web application security in Geronimo.

J2EE Authentication Methods

J2EE web containers are required to support the following authentication schemes:

- HTTP basic authentication

- Form-based authentication

- Digest authentication

- Client-side/server-side certification–based authentication

HTTP Basic Authentication

Figure 3-4 shows how the HTTP basic authentication mechanism works.

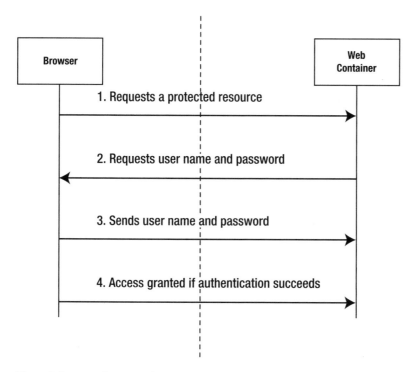

Figure 3-4. *HTTP basic authentication*

When the client requests any of a web application's protected resources, the container intercepts the request and presents the client with a login dialog box. The container allows access only if the user name and password are valid. The main disadvantage of HTTP basic authentication is that it transmits user names and passwords as clear text data (base64-encoded form) through the network. However, you can use HTTPS transport to secure the data transported between the client and the server.

Form-Based Authentication

Form-based authentication allows you to use custom login pages and login error pages. With the basic authentication method, when the server challenges the browser for authentication information, it shows the user a login dialog box. With form-based authentication, the container displays a custom login page to the user. Figure 3-5 depicts the form-based authentication mechanism.

Here, also, the authentication information is sent as clear text data unless it is using the HTTPS protocol.

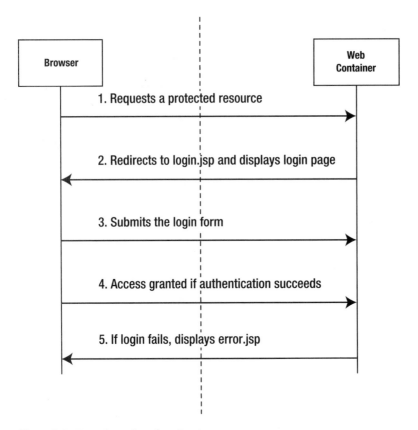

Figure 3-5. *Form-based authentication*

Digest Authentication

This method is more secure than the basic- and form-based mechanisms. When the user tries to access a protected resource, the browser shows a login dialog box similar to the one shown for basic authentication. It sends the authentication details in an encrypted form that is more secure than the base64 encoding in the basic authentication scheme. Also, with this approach, the integrity of the URL data is certified. This method is not widely used.

Client-Side/Server-Side Certification–Based Authentication

This is the most secure authentication mechanism. Here, the client and the server use HTTPS protocol to transfer data to each other. When the client requests access to a protected resource, the server sends a digital certificate to the client. The client verifies the certificate, and if it is valid, the client uses the server-supplied public key to encrypt the data (login information) and sends it to the server. By verifying the server certificate, the client ensures it is securely sending data to the right server. You can increase security by having the client present a certificate to the server to verify the authenticity of the client.

■**Note** We will discuss authentication methods in more detail, including how to set up Geronimo for HTTPS connections, in Chapter 10.

Web Application Security Configuration

In this section, you will explore how to configure web application security with Geronimo by using an available security realm. In a later chapter, we will discuss how to create a custom security realm in Geronimo. The steps required to configure web application security in Geronimo are as follows:

1. Specify the protected resource list (web.xml).

2. Specify the login configuration (web.xml).

3. Specify security roles (web.xml).

4. Define security role mapping (geronimo-web.xml).

Specify the Protected Resource List

To specify the list of resources in the web application that need to be protected, you can use a security constraint element in the web deployment descriptor, as shown here:

```
<security-constraint>
  <web-resource-collection>
    <web-resource-name>My Protected Resources</web-resource-name>
      <url-pattern>/admin/*</url-pattern>
    </web-resource-collection>

    <auth-constraint>
      <role-name>appUser</role-name>
    </auth-constraint>
</security-constraint>
```

This configuration specifies that only users belonging to the appUser role can access resources with the URL pattern /admin/*. With this configuration, the URL http://hostname: port/webAppContext/admin/index.jsp will be protected, but the resource http://hostname:port/ webAppContext/index.jsp will not be.

Specify the Login Configuration

Next, you need to specify the authentication method and the security realm (in web.xml) that should be used to authenticate a user. The authentication method can be any one of the methods described earlier (indicate the mechanism as follows: BASIC, FORM, DIGEST, or CLIENT_CERT). A security realm is a collection of user and group definitions that are controlled by the same authentication policy.

```
<login-config>
  <auth-method>BASIC</auth-method>
  <realm-name>geronimo-properties-realm</realm-name>
</login-config>
```

In the case of form-based authentication, you need to specify the login and login error pages.

```
<login-config>
  <auth-method>FORM</auth-method>
  <realm-name>geronimo-properties-realm</realm-name>
  <form-login-config>
    <form-login-page>/logon.jsp</form-login-page>
    <form-error-page>/logonError.jsp</form-error-page>
  </form-login-config>
</login-config>
```

The realm name specified here should be a valid realm on the Geronimo server.

Specify Security Roles

Specify the security role used in the security constraint configuration in the web deployment descriptor, as shown here:

```
<security-role>
  <role-name>appUser</role-name>
</security-role>
```

Map Security Roles to Physical Roles in the Geronimo Deployment Descriptor

The final step is to map security roles to physical roles in a security realm defined on the Geronimo server. (We will discuss the details of defining and configuring a security realm in the chapter about J2EE security.) To complete this step, use the code shown here:

```
<?xml version="1.0" encoding="UTF-8"?>
<web-app xmlns="http://geronimo.apache.org/xml/ns/web" ➡
xmlns:naming="http://geronimo.apache.org/xml/ns/naming"  ➡
xmlns:sec="http://geronimo.apache.org/xml/ns/security"  ➡
configId="HelloWorldWebApp" parentId="geronimo/j2ee-security/car/1.0">

  <context-root>welcome</context-root>
  <context-priority-classloader>true</context-priority-classloader>

  <security-realm-name>geronimo-properties-realm</security-realm-name>
  <sec:security>
    <sec:default-principal realm-name="geronimo-properties-realm">
      <sec:principal ➡
class="org.apache.geronimo.security.realm.providers. ➡
GeronimoUserPrincipal"  name="metro"/>
    </sec:default-principal>
```

```
    <sec:role-mappings>
      <sec:role role-name="appUser">
        <sec:realm realm-name="geronimo-properties-realm">
          <sec:principal ➥
class="org.apache.geronimo.security.realm.providers. ➥
GeronimoGroupPrincipal" name="it" designated-run-as="true"/>
          <sec:principal ➥
class="org.apache.geronimo.security.realm.providers. ➥
GeronimoUserPrincipal" name="metro"/>
        </sec:realm>
      </sec:role>
    </sec:role-mappings>
  </sec:security>

</web-app>
```

The Geronimo web deployment descriptor defines the geronimo/j2ee-security/car/1.0 configuration as the parent configuration. This configuration defines the realm geronimo-properties-realm. I've included this realm in our example only for demonstration purposes—you need to create a new realm for use in your applications. The geronimo-properties-realm uses two property files (var/security/ users.properties and var/security/ groups.properties) for configuring users and user groups. The security element defines a default principal and a role-to-principal mapping for the logical role appUser defined in the web application. The role appUser is mapped to the group named "it" and the user named "metro" in the geronimo-properties-realm. To configure a new user to the realm, add the line username=password to the users.properties file, and to configure a new group, add the line groupName=userName1, userName2 to the groups.properties file.

You can access the application by using the URL http://localhost:8080/welcome. When you are prompted to enter a user name and password, enter the user name and password as configured in your users.properties file.

Summary

In this chapter, we discussed how to use Geronimo to deploy and run web applications. We also looked at configuring, deploying, and using a database connection pool, and you saw how to configure a web application to utilize Geronimo's security features. In the next chapter, you will explore developing and using EJBs with Geronimo.

CHAPTER 4

■ ■ ■

Session Beans

It is a common practice—and a universally accepted best practice—to have a clear separation between presentation logic and business logic in a web application. You could achieve this separation by defining appropriate business interfaces and moving all your business logic into Java implementation classes. While this would result in a logical separation, you would not be able to host your business implementation in a physically different machine from the one that runs your presentation logic. In many cases, however, physical separation is required to scale up an application to meet increasing client demands. To meet client demand, you can have a web application hosted in a server farm that contains several machines (a cluster) hosting the business logic and several others hosting the presentation logic. Additionally, to achieve this physical separation, you can use Enterprise JavaBeans.

This chapter focuses on a type of EJB called a session bean. First, you'll learn about the general characteristics of EJBs, and then we'll discuss session beans in particular. Our discussion will include examples of creating session beans.

EJB Overview

An EJB is a distributed component that implements the business logic of an enterprise application. EJBs have the following characteristics and functions:

- They define a component-oriented architecture for distributed applications.

- They are used to implement transaction-oriented business logic of an enterprise application.

- EJBs live and run in a container called the EJB container.

- The container provides enterprise-level services, like security and transactions, to the EJB.

- They can be customized at deployment time by editing their deployment descriptor.

In short, an EJB represents a powerful, component-oriented model for implementing business logic in a transactional enterprise application. The key aspect of an EJB is the separation of concerns that it provides. The bean developer can focus on the business logic of the application and not get bogged down in the complexities of the enterprise application and its system-level services. Typically, the container that runs the EJB intercepts client invocations and injects the required enterprise-level system services at runtime into the bean.

Figure 4-1 depicts the high-level architecture of Enterprise JavaBeans.

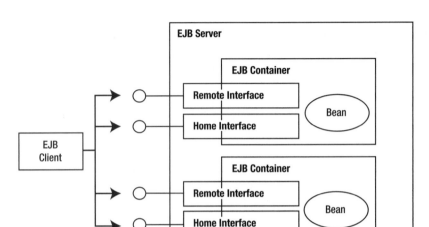

Figure 4-1. *Enterprise JavaBean architecture overview*

EJB clients do not access the bean implementation directly. The remote interface presents a client view of the EJB object that the clients use to connect to the bean. The home interface defines factory methods that the clients use to create and destroy the EJB object.

An EJB developer creates the following components:

- An EJB remote interface that declares all the methods that the client can access

- An EJB home interface that declares all the EJB factory methods

- The bean implementation that implements every remote interface method

The container must provide implementation classes for the remote and home interfaces, and this is one place where the container can place logic to intercept client calls and execute container-specific code before executing the actual bean implementation (provided by the developer). A container can use code generation as a technique to create the implementation classes for the remote and home interfaces. This code generation happens during the deployment process.

EJB Types

Enterprise JavaBeans can be broadly classified into three types: session beans, entity beans, and message-driven beans. The behavior you require of the bean determines which type to use.

A session bean executes requests on behalf of a client. It is a client-specific object, and multiple clients cannot use the same instance at the same time. You can use a session bean in the following scenarios:

- To represent an object that implements a stateless service

- To represent an object that implements a stateless service that is exposed as a web service endpoint to web service clients

- To represent an object that represents the conversational state of a client

- To update or access shared data, like data in the database

You use a message-driven bean to represent an object that implements a stateless service that is invoked asynchronously when an event occurs (such as the arrival of a message in a queue).

An entity bean represents shared data in a persistent store. Use it in the following scenarios:

- To represent an object that implements shared business logic that is either stateless or stateful

- To represent a shared object that is an object-oriented view of persistent data, like an object containing the data of a row in a table

More About Session Beans

Session beans can be classified as stateless or stateful session beans. A stateless session EJB does not hold client state information and is generally used to implement stateless services. The container maintains a pool of session EJB instances and selects any one of them to execute a client request. After the request is processed, the container returns the instance to the pool so that it can be used to service another client request. A stateless session bean instance is not dedicated to servicing any specific client, and hence the client cannot assume that it is executing the same instance for every request that it makes. By contrast, a stateful session bean holds client-specific conversational state information and joins the client in a one-to-one relationship. Hence, a dedicated session object instance is used to service all requests from a particular client.

For example, if you need to implement a credit card authorization service, you can consider using a stateless session bean, and if you need to implement a wizardlike checkout process, you'll need a stateful session bean. A checkout process needs to store the information that it collects from all the wizard pages until it commits the changes to the back-end data store. A stateful session bean can hold these as values in its instance variables and finally save the checkout information collected from the user to the data store in a transaction context.

Remote and Local EJB Objects

Both session and entity EJBs can be either remote or local. A remote EJB can be accessed from a remote client, and a local EJB can be accessed only by a client running in the same JVM as that of the EJB. This way, a local EJB does not have the overhead of a remote call and can be used for fine-grained interfaces. A remote EJB is used only when distributed access is required, and hence for better performance, you should create coarse-grained interfaces and thus reduce the number of round trips. Another difference between remote and local EJBs is that for a local EJB, method parameter objects are passed by reference, whereas for a remote EJB, they are passed by value mechanism.

Stateless Session Bean Example

Now let's look at how to create a stateless session bean. Our example will focus on a user management service. To implement this as a stateless session bean, you need to follow these steps:

1. Create the remote interface (or a local interface for a local EJB object).

2. Create the home interface (or a local home interface for a local home EJB).

3. Create the bean implementation Java class.

4. Create the EJB standard deployment descriptor.

5. Create the Geronimo-specific EJB deployment descriptor.

6. Compile, package, and create the EJB JAR.

7. Deploy the EJB JAR into Geronimo.

Create the Remote (or Local) Interface

The remote interface defines a client view of the EJB to remote clients. It lists all the business methods that the EJB exposes to its clients. The code for this step is shown here:

```
package samples.usermgmt.sl;

// imports

public interface UserManagement extends EJBObject {
  public User addUser(String userName)throws RemoteException, ➥
        UserMgmtException;
  public List listUser(String userNamePattern) throws RemoteException, ➥
        UserMgmtException;
  public void deleteUser(long userId) throws RemoteException, ➥
        UserMgmtException;

}
```

A remote interface should extend from the EJBObject interface. As stated, it needs to declare all the methods that the EJB exposes to its clients. Each of these methods should throw the RMI RemoteException, and, optionally, it can throw one or more application-specific exceptions. Here, we have all the UserManagement interface methods throw a custom exception called UserMgmtException. Since, in this case, this is a simple wrapper class over the java.lang.Exception class, the details of this class are not shown.

If you need to create a local EJB object, create a local interface, as shown here:

```
package samples.usermgmt.sl;

// imports

public interface UserManagementLocal extends EJBLocalObject {
  public User addUser(String userName)throws UserMgmtException;
  public List listUser(String userNamePattern) throws UserMgmtException;
  public void deleteUser(long userId) throws UserMgmtException;

}
```

A local interface should extend from EJBLocalObject interface. The local interface's methods, unlike the remote interface's, need not throw the RMI RemoteException.

Create the Home (or Local Home) Interface

The home interface serves as a factory for EJB objects. It contains methods for creating and destroying EJB objects. Create the home interface as shown here:

```
package samples.usermgmt.sl;
// imports
public interface UserManagementHome extends EJBHome {
  public UserManagement create() throws RemoteException, CreateException ;
}
```

The home interface should extend the EJBHome interface. For a stateless session bean, there should be only one create() method (no argument), and it should return the remote interface type.

If you need local EJB objects, you need to create a local home interface, as shown here:

```
package samples.usermgmt.sl;

// imports

public interface UserManagementLocalHome extends EJBLocalHome {
  public UserManagement create() throws CreateException ;
}
```

A local home interface should extend from EJBLocalHome. Its methods need not throw the RMI RemoteException.

Create the EJB Bean Implementation

The bean implementation contains the actual logic that needs to be executed for the bean interface methods. To complete this step, use this code:

```
package samples.usermgmt.sl;

//imports

public class UserManagementBean implements SessionBean {
  private Users users;
  private SessionContext context;

  public void ejbCreate() { users=Users.getInstance();}

  public void ejbRemove() { users=null;}

  public void ejbActivate() { }

  public void ejbPassivate() { }

  public void setSessionContext(SessionContext ctx) { this.context=ctx; }

  public User addUser(String userName) throws RemoteException,➥
UserMgmtException {
    return users.addUser(userName);
  }

  public List listUser(String userNamePattern) throws RemoteException, ➥
UserMgmtException {
    return users.listUser(userNamePattern);
  }

  public void deleteUser(int userId) throws RemoteException, UserMgmtException {
    users.deleteUser(userId);
  }

}
```

The Users class is a singleton, in-memory database of User objects. This class is shown here:

```
package samples.usermgmt.sl;

// imports

// A simple in-memory database of users--works for single-JVM cases only
public class Users {

  private List users;
  private static Users instance;
```

```
static { instance=new Users(); }

private Users(){
  users=new ArrayList();
}

public static Users getInstance(){
  return instance;
}

public User addUser(String userName) throws UserMgmtException {

  if(null==userName){
    throw new UserMgmtException("Invalid User name");
  }

  User user=new User(userName);
  user.setId(users.size());
  users.add(user);
  return user;
}

public List listUser(String userNamePattern) throws  UserMgmtException {
    List results=new ArrayList();
    for(int i=0;i<users.size();i++){
      User user=(User)users.get(i);
      if (user.getName().matches(userNamePattern)){
        results.add(user);
      }
    }
    return results;
}

public void deleteUser(int userId) throws  UserMgmtException {
    users.remove(userId);
}

}
```

The methods ejbActivate(), ejbPassivate(), ejbRemove(), and setSessionContext() are methods declared in the SessionBean interface. In addition, a valid EJB bean implementation must provide corresponding ejbCreate() methods for every create() method declared in the EJB home interface. For a stateless session bean, ejbCreate() is a method with no arguments.

Since we do not have anything to clean up, we have an empty ejbRemove() method. The ejbCreate() method is called by the container during the EJB creation process, and the ejbRemove() method is invoked by the container before it destroys the EJB.

The ejbActivate() and ejbPassivate() methods are not used for a stateless session EJB, and we will discuss these methods later in this chapter, in the section about stateful session EJB objects.

The container provides the EJB with session context by invoking the setSessionContext() method. The SessionContext instance acts like a container callback mechanism.

We also have implementations for all the business methods (every method declared in the remote or local EJB interface)—addUser(), listUser(), and deleteUser().

For remote EJB objects, all method parameter types and return types need to be valid RMI types. In our example, the User object needs to be a Java serializable object, as shown here:

```
package samples.usermgmt.sl;

// imports

public class User implements Serializable {

  private int id;
  private String name;
  private String address1;
  private String address2;
  private String city;
  private String state;
  private String country; // Add getters and setters

  public User(String userName){
    this.name=userName;
  }

  public void setId(int id){
    this.id=id;
  }

  public int getId(){
    return id;
  }

  public void setName(String name){
    this.name=name;
  }

  public String getName(){
    return name;
  }

}
```

Create the EJB Standard Deployment Descriptor

A deployment descriptor defines deployment-level instructions to the deployer and the container. Its main purpose is to capture declarative information that is not provided in the EJB code. A deployment descriptor consists of mandatory structural information and optional assembly instructions. The structural information defines the structure of the bean, and the assembly information defines how the bean is composed, along with other components, to create a complete application. The bean provider (bean developer) provides structural information in the deployment descriptor, and an application assembler provides the assembly information.

The EJB standard deployment descriptor is an XML file named ejb-jar.xml in the META-INF directory in the EJB JAR (see the section on packaging for more information). Figure 4-2 depicts the structure of the standard deployment descriptor.

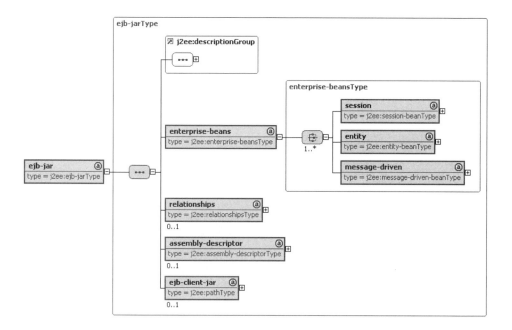

Figure 4-2. *EJB standard deployment descriptor*

Table 4-1 describes the standard deployment descriptor's elements.

Table 4-1. *EJB Standard Deployment Descriptor Elements*

Element	Description
descriptionGroup	This is an XSD type for elements used for describing the contents of the package. This is optional and is not shown in Figure 4-2.
enterprise-beans	This element is required and can contain definitions for one or more EJB types (session, entity, or message driven).
relationships	This element is optional and is used to define relationships between EJB objects. We will discuss this in detail in Chapter 5.
assembly-descriptor	This element is optional and is used to define security, transaction, and related information.
ejb-client-jar	This element is optional and is used to specify a path for the EJB client JAR. The bean provider can specify this information for the assembler so that the assembler can include the right client classes wherever required.

The following code shows a deployment descriptor for our sample application:

```xml
<?xml version="1.0" encoding="UTF-8"?>

<ejb-jar xmlns="http://java.sun.com/xml/ns/j2ee"
xmlns:xsi="http://www.w3.org/2001/XMLSchema-instance"
xsi:schemaLocation="http://java.sun.com/xml/ns/j2ee
http://java.sun.com/xml/ns/j2ee/ejb-jar_2_1.xsd"
version="2.1">
  <enterprise-beans>
    <session>
      <ejb-name>UserMgmt</ejb-name>
      <home>samples.usermgmt.sl.UserManagementHome</home>
      <remote>samples.usermgmt.sl.UserManagement</remote>
      <local-home>samples.usermgmt.sl.UserManagementLocalHome</local-home>
      <local>samples.usermgmt.sl.UserManagementLocal</local>
      <ejb-class>samples.usermgmt.sl.UserManagementBean</ejb-class>
      <session-type>Stateless</session-type>
      <transaction-type>Container</transaction-type>
    </session>
  </enterprise-beans>
</ejb-jar>
```

If our EJB were a local EJB, then instead of using the home and remote elements, we would use the following local elements:

```xml
<local-home>samples.usermgmt.sl.UserManagementLocalHome</local-home>
<local>samples.usermgmt.sl.UserManagementLocal</local>
```

The session element and its subelements are shown in Figure 4-3.

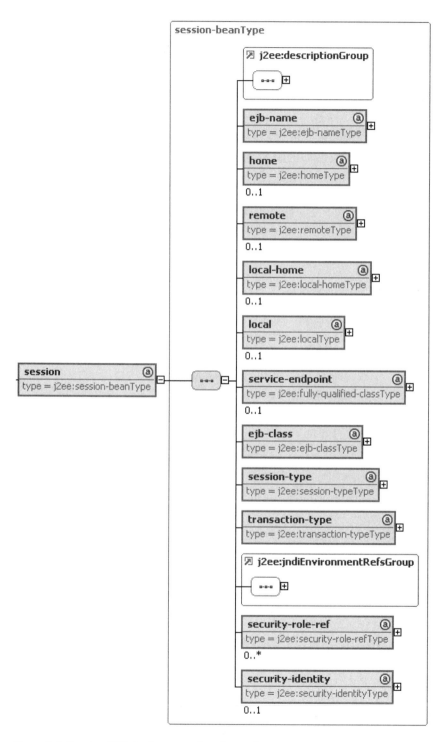

Figure 4-3. *Session EJB deployment descriptor elements*

Table 4-2 describes the session EJB deployment descriptor elements.

Table 4-2. *Session EJB Deployment Descriptor Elements*

Element	Description
ejb-name	Assigns a name to the EJB.
home	Specifies a fully qualified class name for the home interface.
remote	Specifies a fully qualified class name for the remote interface.
local-home	Specifies a fully qualified class name for the local home interface.
local	Specifies a fully qualified class name for the local interface.
service-endpoint	Specifies a fully qualified class name for the web service endpoint interface. This can be specified only if the bean is a stateless session bean.
ejb-class	Specifies the fully qualified class name for the session bean's implementation class.
session-type	Denotes the session bean type. This value should be either Stateless or Stateful.
transaction-type	Denotes the transaction type. This value should be either Bean or Container.
jndiEnvironmentRefsGroup	Specifies an XSD type to denote elements and subelements to specify environment-specific settings, like references to other EJBs and references to message destination references. We will discuss these topics later in this chapter.

security-role-ref	Specifies references to security role definitions specified in the same deployment descriptor. These are logical names used in the bean code, and if required, they can be linked to common security role definitions:
	`<security-role-ref>`
	`<description>`
	`Administration role for user management functions`
	`</description>`
	`<role-name>userAdmin<role-name>`
	`<role-link>appAdmin<role-link>`
	`</security-role-ref>`
	The role-link element should specify a valid role name defined in the same file.

security-identity	Specifies whether to use the caller's identity or a run-as identity to execute EJB methods. This contains an optional description and a specification of the security identity to be used.

Create the Geronimo-Specific Deployment Descriptor

You also need to create a Geronimo-specific deployment descriptor to specify Geronimo-specific items. Using the Geronimo-specific deployment descriptor, you can do the following:

- Specify external dependencies and libraries relative to the Geronimo repository.

- Specify a connection factory for entity beans that use container-managed persistence.

- Specify the EJB query language compiler to be used. This is used for entity beans.

- Specify a database syntax factory to provide database-specific syntax functions. This is used for entity beans that use container-managed persistence.

- Specify whether the container should enforce foreign-key constraints. This is also used for entity beans that use container-managed persistence.

- Define enterprise bean–specific items like the JNDI name and details for resolving environment references.

- Define EJB relationships.

- Define security role mappings to a security realm.

- Define new services (GBeans) that can be deployed, started, and stopped along with the EJB package.

Figure 4-4 depicts the elements and the structure of the Geronimo deployment descriptor (also called the Geronimo deployment plan).

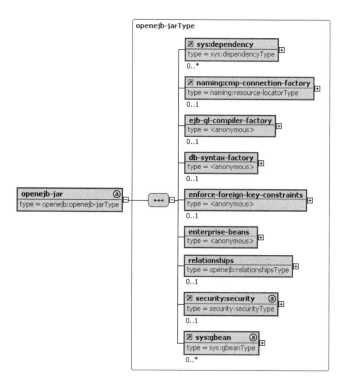

Figure 4-4. *Geronimo deployment plan*

Note We will discuss the cmp-connection-factory, db-syntax-factory, enforce-foreign-key-constraints, and relationships elements in Chapter 5.

The Geronimo deployment plan is an XML file named openejb-jar.xml in the META-INF directory in the EJB JAR (for more details, see the section on packaging). The deployment plan for our example is shown here:

```
<?xml version="1.0" encoding="UTF-8"?>
<openejb-jar
xmlns="http://www.openejb.org/xml/ns/openejb-jar"
xmlns:naming="http://geronimo.apache.org/xml/ns/naming"
xmlns:security="http://geronimo.apache.org/xml/ns/security"
xmlns:sys="http://geronimo.apache.org/xml/ns/deployment"
configId="UserManagement"
parentId="geronimo/j2ee-server/1.0/car">
  <enterprise-beans>
    <session>
      <ejb-name>UserMgmt</ejb-name>
      <jndi-name>ejb/UserMgmt</jndi-name>
    </session>
  </enterprise-beans>
</openejb-jar>
```

This plan specifies a JNDI name for the UserMgmt EJB as defined in the standard deployment descriptor. The details of the structure of the session element and its subelements in the Geronimo deployment plan are shown in Figure 4-5.

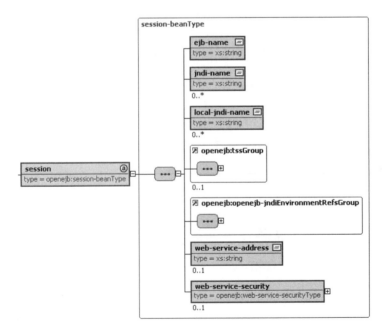

Figure 4-5. *Session element in the Geronimo deployment plan*

Table 4-3 describes the Geronimo deployment plan's session element.

Table 4-3. *Session Element in the Geronimo Deployment Plan*

Element	Description
ejb-name	The name of the EJB. It should match an ejb-name entry in the standard deployment descriptor.
jndi-name	The JNDI name with which the home interface of the EJB is registered with the naming service. Remote clients can use this name to connect to the EJB. This element is relevant only for a remote EJB.
local-jndi-name	The JNDI name with which the local home interface of the EJB is registered. This element is relevant only for a local EJB.
tssGroup	Security settings for EJBs that are exposed to CORBA clients.
openejb-jndiEnvironmentRefsGroup	An XSD type with elements to resolve references declared by the current session bean (including EJB references, resource references, and web service references). We will discuss these references later in this chapter.
web-service-address	A URL where the web service endpoint can be accessed, if this EJB exposes one.
web-service-security	Security configuration for the web service.

Compile, Package, and Create the EJB JAR

EJBs are packaged as a JAR archive. You need to create the following directories and place the files in them, as shown here:

```
samples/usermgmt/sl/UserManagement.class
samples/usermgmt/sl/UserManagementHome.class
samples/usermgmt/sl/UserManagementBean.class
META-INF/MANIFEST.MF
META-INF/ejb-jar.xml
META-INF/openejb-jar.xml
```

The MANIFEST file is the JAR MANIFEST file where you can define external library dependencies. If a MANIFEST file is not provided, the JAR utility can automatically produce a MANIFEST file with default values. After you create the required directories and place the files in them, archive the files by using the command shown here:

```
jar -cvf usermanagement.jar
```

You can either package the Geronimo deployment descriptor within the EJB JAR, as shown previously, or supply it directly to the deploy tool during deployment. In the latter case, you need not name this file openejb-jar.xml.

Deploy the EJB into Geronimo

You can deploy the EJB JAR as a stand-alone JAR or package it as part of an enterprise application archive (an EAR). (We'll discuss J2EE enterprise applications in detail in Chapter 7.) To deploy the EJB JAR into Geronimo, use the following command:

```
java -jar deployer.jar deploy usermanagement.jar
```

As noted, if you do not package the Geronimo-specific deployment descriptor within the EJB JAR, you can provide it directly to the deploy tool, as shown here:

```
java -jar deployer.jar deploy usermanagement.jar ➥
user-Mgmt-deployment-plan.xml
```

You can also deploy the EJB by using the Geronimo console application (`http://hostname:8080/console`). Select Applications ➤ Deploy New from the menu on the left, and Geronimo displays the screen shown in Figure 4-6.

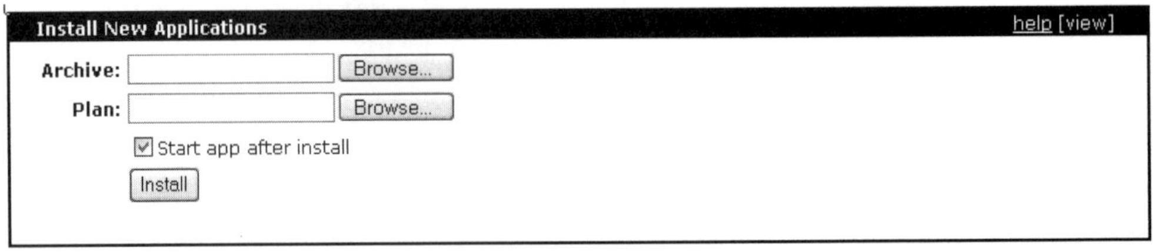

Figure 4-6. *Install applications screen*

Browse and select the EJB JAR file and the deployment plan file, and click Install to deploy the EJB into Geronimo.

Stateful Session Bean Example

A stateful session bean is closely associated with a client. Once the container assigns a bean instance to a client, every request from that client will be handled by the same bean instance. This way, the bean can be coded to store state information in its member variables.

Let us consider a sample bean that implements checkout logic. To use Geronimo to create, package, and deploy this stateful session bean, you'll follow these steps:

1. Create the remote interface (or a local interface for a local EJB object).

2. Create the home interface (or a local home interface for a local EJB object).

3. Create the bean implementation Java class.

4. Create the EJB standard deployment descriptor.

5. Create the Geronimo-specific EJB deployment descriptor.

6. Compile, package, and create the EJB JAR.

7. Deploy the EJB JAR into Geronimo.

Most of these steps are very similar to the steps you used to create a stateless session bean. Steps 3 and 4 (creating the bean implementation class and creating the J2EE standard deployment descriptor) involve differences, however.

Create the Remote (or Local) Interface

This step is identical to the corresponding step in the stateless session bean example.

Create the Home (or Local Home) Interface

This step is identical to the corresponding step in the stateless session bean example.

Create the EJB Bean Implementation

As noted, this step is significantly different from the corresponding step in the process of creating a stateless session bean. Complete this step as shown here:

```
package samples.usermgmt.sf;

// imports

public class UserManagementBean implements SessionBean {

  private List users;
  private SessionContext context;
  public void ejbCreate() { users=new ArrayList();}

  public void ejbRemove() { users=null;}

  public void ejbActivate() { }

  public void ejbPassivate() { }

  public void setSessionContext(SessionContext context) {
    this.context=context ;
  }

  public User addUser(String userName) throws RemoteException,
  UserMgmtException {
```

```
  if(null==userName){
    throw new UserMgmtException("Invalid User name");
  }

  User user=new User(userName);
  user.setId(users.size());
  users.add(user);
  return user;
}

public List listUser(String userNamePattern) throws RemoteException,
UserMgmtException {

  List results=new ArrayList();
  for(int i=0;i<users.size();i++){
    User user=(User)users.get(i);
    if (user.getName().matches(userNamePattern)){
      results.add(user);
    }
  }
  return results;
}

public void deleteUser(int userId) throws RemoteException, UserMgmtException {
  users.remove(userId);
}

}
```

The addUser() method adds a new User to the users list instance variable. A stateful session bean can retain its instance member values between method invocations from the same client. This is the primary difference between a stateful and a stateless session bean. The ejbPassivate() method will be called when the container decides to passivate the bean instance and temporarily store its state in a secondary store. You need to make sure that after this method is invoked, the bean is in a state such that the standard Java serialization mechanism can be used to serialize it. EJB passivation is triggered by an interval of user inactivity. Once the container decides to make the bean available again to the user, it calls the ejbActivate() method. You need to make sure that after the method is invoked, the bean instance is in a state ready to accept user requests. For instance, if you had closed a socket connection in the ejbPassivate() method, you would need to open the socket in the ejbActivate() method.

Create the EJB Standard Deployment Descriptor

Use this code to create the standard deployment descriptor:

```xml
<?xml version="1.0" encoding="UTF-8"?>

<ejb-jar xmlns="http://java.sun.com/xml/ns/j2ee"
xmlns:xsi="http://www.w3.org/2001/XMLSchema-instance"
xsi:schemaLocation="http://java.sun.com/xml/ns/j2ee
http://java.sun.com/xml/ns/j2ee/ejb-jar_2_1.xsd"
version="2.1">
  <enterprise-beans>
    <session>
      <ejb-name>sfUserMgmt</ejb-name>
      <home>samples.usermgmt.sf.UserManagementHome</home>
      <remote>samples.usermgmt.sf.UserManagement</remote>
      <local-home>samples.usermgmt.sf.UserManagementLocalHome</local-home>
      <local>samples.usermgmt.sf.UserManagementLocal</local>
      <ejb-class>samples.usermgmt.sf.UserManagementBean</ejb-class>
      <session-type>Stateful</session-type>
      <transaction-type>Container</transaction-type>
    </session>
  </enterprise-beans>
</ejb-jar>
```

You can package the checkout bean as a separate EJB JAR or include it in the same EJB JAR that contains the user management bean we created in the previous section.

Create the Geronimo-Specific Deployment Descriptor

You create the Geronimo-specific deployment descriptor by completing the step shown here:

```xml
<?xml version="1.0" encoding="UTF-8"?>
<openejb-jar
xmlns="http://www.openejb.org/xml/ns/openejb-jar"
xmlns:naming="http://geronimo.apache.org/xml/ns/naming"
xmlns:security="http://geronimo.apache.org/xml/ns/security"
xmlns:sys="http://geronimo.apache.org/xml/ns/deployment"
configId="StatefulUserManagement"
parentId="geronimo/j2ee-server/1.0/car">
  <enterprise-beans>
    <session>
      <ejb-name>sfUserMgmt</ejb-name>
      <jndi-name>ejb/StatefulUserMgmt</jndi-name>
    </session>
  </enterprise-beans>
</openejb-jar>
```

Compile, Package, and Create the EJB JAR

This step is very similar to the corresponding step in the stateless session bean example. You can either package the EJB as a separate EJB JAR or include both your beans in one package. In the latter case, you will have only one standard deployment descriptor and one Geronimo-specific deployment descriptor. Otherwise, you will have two JAR files, one for each bean containing their classes and deployment descriptors.

Deploy the EJB into Geronimo

Assuming you packaged both the beans in the same JAR, you can deploy both the beans by using this command:

```
java -jar deployer.jar deploy mybeans.jar
```

You can also use the Geronimo console to deploy the EJB. This process is very similar to the corresponding step in the stateless session bean example.

EJB Clients

A typical EJB client uses the RMI over IIOP protocol to access the EJB. To connect to and use the EJB, the client needs to do the following:

1. Look up a home object

2. Create the remote object reference

3. Invoke business methods

4. Remove the EJB object

Look Up an EJB Home Object

EJB home references are registered with the Geronimo naming service. They are registered with a name that is provided in the Geronimo-specific deployment descriptor of an EJB. For any of the J2EE server components (like a servlet), you can look up the home reference, as shown here:

```
InitialContext context=new InitialContext();
Object home=context.lookup("java:comp/env/ejb/StatefulUserMgmt");
UserManagementHome userMgmtHome=PortableRemoteObject.narrow(home,➡
UserManagementHome.class);
```

If your client is a non-J2EE component or is a component that is not running in the same server environment, you need to specify the JNDI connection properties when you create an InitialContext object, as shown here:

```
Hashtable properties=newHashtable();
properties.put("java.naming.factory.initial", ➥
org.openejb.client.RemoteInitialContextFactory
properties.put("java.naming.security.principal",
"username");
properties.put("java.naming.security. credentials", "passwd");

properties.put("java.naming.provider.url", " localhost:4201");

InitialContext context=new InitialContext(properties);
```

Here, we specify the InitialContextFactory, the security credentials, and the provider URL.
Once you obtain an initial context reference, you can look up the EJB. You need to give the
value of the element session/jndi-name (for local EJBs, use the value of the element session/
local-jndi-name) specified in the Geronimo deployment plan of the EJB. Finally, you need to
narrow down the reference by using the RMI PortableRemoteObject to make sure that it works
for both RMI and RMI over IIOP protocols (RMI over IIOP is a technology that enables CORBA
clients to invoke Java remote objects and allows Java clients to invoke CORBA services).

Create the Remote Object Reference

Use the EJB home reference to create the remote object reference, as shown here:

```
UserManagement userMgmt = PortableRemoteObject.narrow (➥
userMgmtHome.create(user),UserManagement.class);
```

Invoke Business Methods

Next, you must invoke the business methods, as shown here:

```
userMgmt.addUser("user1");
List users=userMgmt.listUser("user.");
```

Remove the EJB Object

Use the following code to remove the session EJB:

```
userMgmt.remove()
```

Environment References

When EJBs need to use a resource manager, like a database connection, connect to other EJBs,
use a message destination, and so on, they use environment references. For every reference
you create, you must follow these two distinct steps:

1. Declare a reference in the EJB JAR deployment descriptor. Use this logical name in
   the code.

2. Define and resolve the logical reference to an actual resource in the Geronimo-specific
   deployment descriptor.

By using environment references, you can make your EJB code application server–environment independent. All you must do to run it in a different environment is relink the references in the deployment plan. For instance, an EJB can directly connect to another EJB, on the same server, by directly looking up its home interface using its JNDI name. However, this means that the EJB code has references to the other EJB's JNDI name. This is not the recommended approach; instead, you should use an EJB reference entry in the deployment descriptor. In the following sections, you'll learn how to create references to various resources.

Resolving EJB References

If an EJB needs to connect to another EJB, the first EJB must declare a reference to the second EJB in the standard deployment descriptor, as shown here:

```
<ejb-ref>
  <ejb-ref-name>ejb/user</ejb-ref-name>
  <ejb-ref-type>Entity</ejb-ref-type>
  <home>sample/usermgmt/UserHome</home>
  <remote>sample/usermgmt/User</remote>
  <ejb-link>user</ejb-link>
</ejb-ref>
```

You need to reference the EJB in your code by using the logical JNDI name ejb/user. The ejb-link element can be used to specify a target EJB in the same application. You can also specify the link by using a relative path name specifying the EJB JAR containing the EJB, as shown here:

```
<ejb-link>../product/product.jar#product</ejb-link>
```

The ejb-link element is optional, and if it is not provided, the EJB reference should be resolved in the Geronimo deployment plan. The relevant elements for resolving EJB references in the Geronimo deployment plan are shown in Figure 4-7.

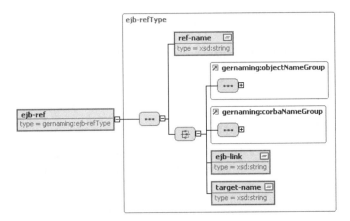

Figure 4-7. *Structure of ejb-ref elements in the Geronimo deployment plan*

Table 4-4 provides descriptions of these elements.

Table 4-4. *Elements of ejb-ref in the Geronimo Deployment Plan*

Element	Description
ref-name	A name matching the ejb-ref/ejb-ref-name element in ejb-jar.xml.
objectNameGroup	An XSD type defining a JSR 77 object name of the referenced EJB.
corbaNameGroup	An XSD type defining CORBA settings that are required to connect to a remote EJB that uses CORBA.
ejb-link	A name (or relative path name) matching an EJB name in the current application.
target-name	The fully expanded Geronimo name of the referenced EJB. You can use this element to map an EJB in a different application.

Let's look at objectNameGroup in more detail. The elements of objectNameGroup are shown in Figure 4-8.

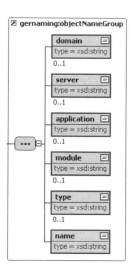

Figure 4-8. *Elements of objectNameGroup*

Table 4-5 describes these elements.

Table 4-5. *Elements of objectNameGroup*

Element	Description
domain	The domain name portion. Its default value is `geronimo.server`.
server	The server name portion. Its default value is `geronimo`.
application	The application name portion. For instance, if this EJB is deployed as a stand-alone unit, the application name is null; otherwise, if the EJB is part of a J2EE application, this element should be the applicationId name of that application that is specified in the application's Geronimo deployment plan. If no applicationId is specified, this value should be the configId of the J2EE application as specified in its Geronimo deployment plan.
module	The configId of the module (the EJB JAR).
type	The module type. For an EJB, this should be `StatelessSessionBean`, `StatefulSessionBean`, `EntityBean`, or `MessageDrivenBean`.
name	The name of the component. In this case, it should be the name of the EJB.

You can use the objectNameGroup element anywhere to refer to any J2EE component deployed in Geronimo. Alternatively, you can use the target-name element to specify a J2EE component deployed in Geronimo. A sample target name is shown here:

```
geronimo.server:J2EEServer=geronimo,J2EEApplication=ear-name, ➥
EJBModule=ejb-jar-name.jar,j2eeType=StatelessSessionBean, name=EJBName
```

Resolving local EJB references is very similar to resolving remote EJB references. The code snippets shown in Listings 4-1 and 4-2 demonstrate this.

Listing 4-1. *EJB Local Reference Definition in ejb-jar.xml*

```
<ejb-local-ref>
  <ejb-ref-name>ejb/user</ejb-ref-name>
  <ejb-ref-type>Entity</ejb-ref-type>
  <home-home>sample/usermgmt/UserHomeLocal</local-home>
  <local>sample/usermgmt/UserLocal</local>
  <ejb-link>user</ejb-link>
</ejb-local-ref>
```

Listing 4-2. *EJB Local Reference Definition in openejb-jar.xml*

```
<ejb-local-ref>
  <ref-name>ejb/user</ejb-ref-name>
  <ejb-link>user</ejb-link>
</ejb-local-ref>
```

(This step is not required if an ejb-link is already present in ejb-jar.xml.)

Resolving Resource Manager References

You need to define a resource manager reference in order to connect to a database. First, declare a logical name for the resource manager by specifying a resource reference in the ejb-jar.xml file, as shown here:

```
<resource-ref>
  <resource-ref-name>jdbc/mydb</resource-ref-name>
  <ref-type>javax.sql.DataSource </ref-type>
  <res-auth>Container</res-auth>
  <res-sharing-scope>Shareable</res-sharing-scope>
</resource-ref>
```

You need to use the name specified in the resource-ref-name element in your EJB code. The res-auth element should be either Application or Container. If you specify the value as Application, you need to authenticate in your application code, and if you specify this value as Container, the container will perform the necessary authentication. The res-sharing-scope element specifies whether a connection obtained from this resource could be shared.

Next, you need to resolve this logical resource name in the Geronimo deployment plan, as shown here:

```
<resource-ref>
  <ref-name>jdbc/mydb</ref-name>
  <resource-link>myDataSource </resource-link>
</resource-ref>
```

You can use the resource-link element to specify a database connection pool or a JMS connection factory resource deployed as a J2EE connector. The given value should match the connectiondefinition/name element in the Geronimo deployment plan for that resource.

Alternatively, you can specify a JSR 77 ObjectNameGroup element or an equivalent target-name element identifying the target resource, as shown here:

```
geronimo.server:J2EEServer=geronimo,J2EEApplication=null,➥
JCAModule=db-conn-pool,j2eeType=JCAManagedConnectionFactory,➥
name=myDataSource
```

Resolving Resource Environment References

A resource environment reference is used to refer to administered objects, like a JMS queue or a JMS topic. Listings 4-3 and 4-4 show how to create this type of reference.

Listing 4-3. *Resource Environment Reference Declaration in ejb-jar.xml*

```
<resource-env-ref>
  <resource-env-ref-name>jms/myQueue</resource-env-ref-name>
  <resource-env-ref-type>javax.jms.Queue</resource-env-ref-type>
</resource-env-ref>
```

Listing 4-4. *Resource Environment Reference Linked to an Administered Object in the Geronimo Deployment Plan*

```
<resource-env-ref>
  < ref-name>jms/myQueue</ ref-name>
  <message-destination-link>myQueue</message-destination-link>
</resource-env-ref>
```

The message-destination-link element is used to specify an administered object that is deployed as a J2EE connector. The value specified here should match the message-destination-name value mentioned in the admin object section of the Geronimo deployment plan for the connector. Alternatively, you can use a JSR 77 object name group or an equivalent target-name element to link the administered object, as shown here:

```
geronimo.server:J2EEServer=geronimo,J2EEApplication=null, ➡
JCAModule=jms-plan,j2eeType=JCAAdminObject,name=MyQueue
```

Resolving Message Destination References

J2EE 1.4 allows you to configure references to JMS queues and JMS topics by using an EJB JAR message-destination-ref entry. As explained in the previous section, you can connect to a JMS queue or topic by using a resource-env-ref definition. However, by using a message-destination-ref entry, you can completely specify the reference in the EJB JAR and do not need any entry in the Geronimo deployment plan. Listing 4-5 shows how to create a message destination reference.

Listing 4-5. *The ejb-jar.xml File with Message Destination Reference Declaration from a Session Bean*

```
<enterprise-beans>
  <session>
    <message-destination-ref>
      <message-destination-ref-name>
        jms/myQueue
      </message-destination-ref-name>
      <message-destination-type>
        javax.jms.Queue
      </message-destination-type>
      <message-destination-usage>Consumes</message-destination-usage>
      <message-destination-link>MyQueue</message-destination-link>
    </message-destination-ref>
  </session>

</enterprise-beans>
```

```
<assembly-descriptor>
  <message-destination>
    <message-destination-name>MyQueue</message-destination-name>
  </message-destination>
</assembly-descriptor>
```

This completely defines a message destination. The only requirement is that a J2EE connector with the adminobject/message-destination-name element name (in its Geronimo deployment plan) MyQueue is already deployed in Geronimo and available for use. We will discuss deploying an administered object in Chapter 6.

Summary

Using Enterprise JavaBeans is an effective and efficient way to write your business logic. As you have seen in this chapter, you can use a session EJB to implement stateless services or stateful client-oriented business logic. You also explored packaging session beans and deploying them into Geronimo. In the next chapter, we will discuss entity beans.

CHAPTER 5

Entity Beans

An entity bean is an Enterprise JavaBean that represents an object-oriented view of a persistent entity. For database storage, each entity bean is associated with a database table, and each instance is associated with a row in that table. An entity bean instance can also represent an external EIS application that performs the actual persistence mechanism of the entities that it represents.

In this chapter, you'll learn about developing and running entity beans in Geronimo by working through two examples. This process will include creating a sample database that you will use for the examples. Before you begin the entity bean examples, you'll also review the basic characteristics of entity beans.

Entity Bean Overview

The characteristics of an entity bean are as follows:

- It represents a persistent entity.

- Its instance is sharable among multiple clients.

- Every instance has a unique identifier called the primary key.

- It supports relationships with other entity beans.

The values of the member fields (persistent fields) of an entity bean instance represent its state and are stored in a persistent storage. An entity bean supports two kinds of persistence mechanisms: bean-managed persistence (BMP) and container-managed persistence (CMP). With BMP, the bean developer uses JDBC to store the entity object state in the persistent store, whereas with CMP, the container transparently provides the persistence of the state with the storage. I will cover both types of persistence mechanisms in this chapter's examples.

A session bean instance, whether it's a stateless bean or a stateful bean, is tied to a particular client instance. The container guarantees that the same instance is not shared among multiple clients. By contrast, since an entity bean represents an entity in the persistent storage, it is shared by multiple clients. For instance, if an entity bean instance represents a row in a database table, multiple clients can access the same entity bean instance and hence the same row in the table.

Every instance of an entity bean has a unique identifier, called a primary key, that distinguishes it from other instances. A primary key needs to be a valid RMI type.

Entity beans support relationships with other entity beans by using the following two mechanisms: bean-managed relationships (BMRs) and container-managed relationships (CMRs). With BMRs, you need to provide code to manage the bean relationships, and with CMRs, the container will manage the relationship for you.

With this overview, let's create the database we'll use in this chapter's entity bean examples.

Sample Derby Database

The examples in this chapter use the Apache Derby database bundled with Geronimo. Derby is an open source Java relational database that has a very small memory footprint. It supports common Structured Query Language (SQL) syntax and provides JDBC drivers that let you embed Derby in your application or use it in a client/server mode. Derby is particularly easy to install and use.

First, you need to create the following table:

```
CREATE TABLE STUD ( fname varchar(40), lname varchar(40), marks int)
```

Additionally, you need to configure a database connection pool named mydbpool and deploy it into Geronimo as a serverwide resource. I have used the Geronimo console to set up the database (embedded Derby database) and deploy the connection pool, as described in the following sections.

Create the Database and the Tables

Open the Geronimo console application (http://localhost:8080/console), and choose Misc ➤ Embedded DB ➤ DB Manager from the Console Navigation menu on the left. The embedded Derby database manager screen appears, as shown in Figure 5-1.

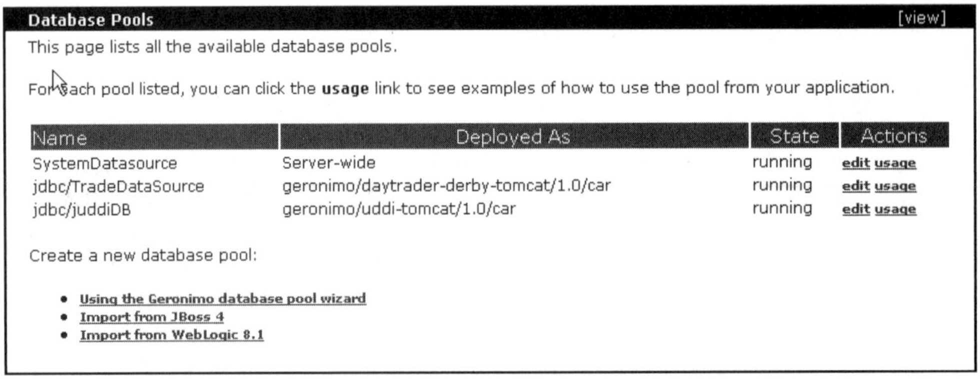

Figure 5-1. *Embedded database manager*

Use this tool to create a database named EJBDatabase, and run the following query:

```
CREATE TABLE STUD ( fname varchar(40), lname varchar(40), marks int)
```

Using the View Tables section of the DB Viewer (shown in Figure 5-2), you can view the contents of both application and system tables of all available databases.

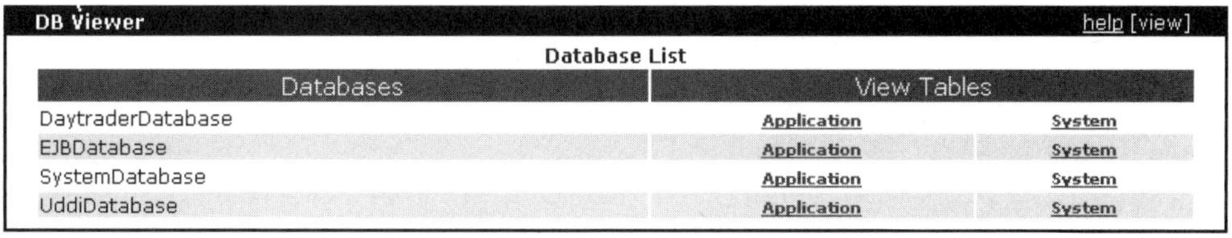

Figure 5-2. *DB Viewer*

If you select the STUD table in EJBDatabase, you will see the screen shown in Figure 5-3.

Figure 5-3. *STUD table*

Configure and Deploy a Connection Pool

Now, choose the Database Pools link (from the Console Navigation menu, select Services ➤ Database Pools) to display all the currently available database connection pools, as shown in Figure 5-4.

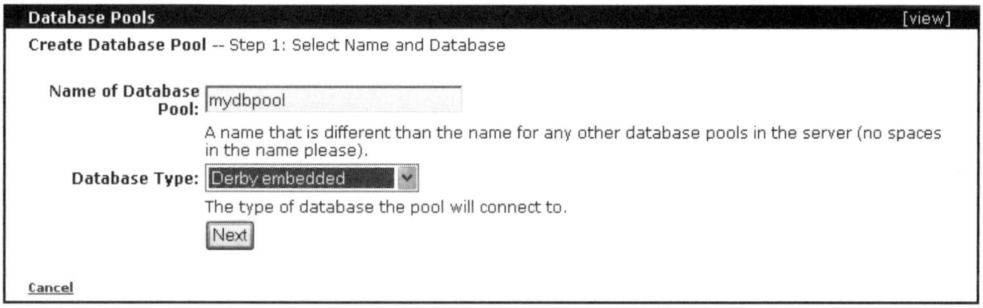

Figure 5-4. *Available database pools*

Click the top link, using the Geronimo database pool wizard, to start creating a new database pool. The screen shown in Figure 5-5 appears.

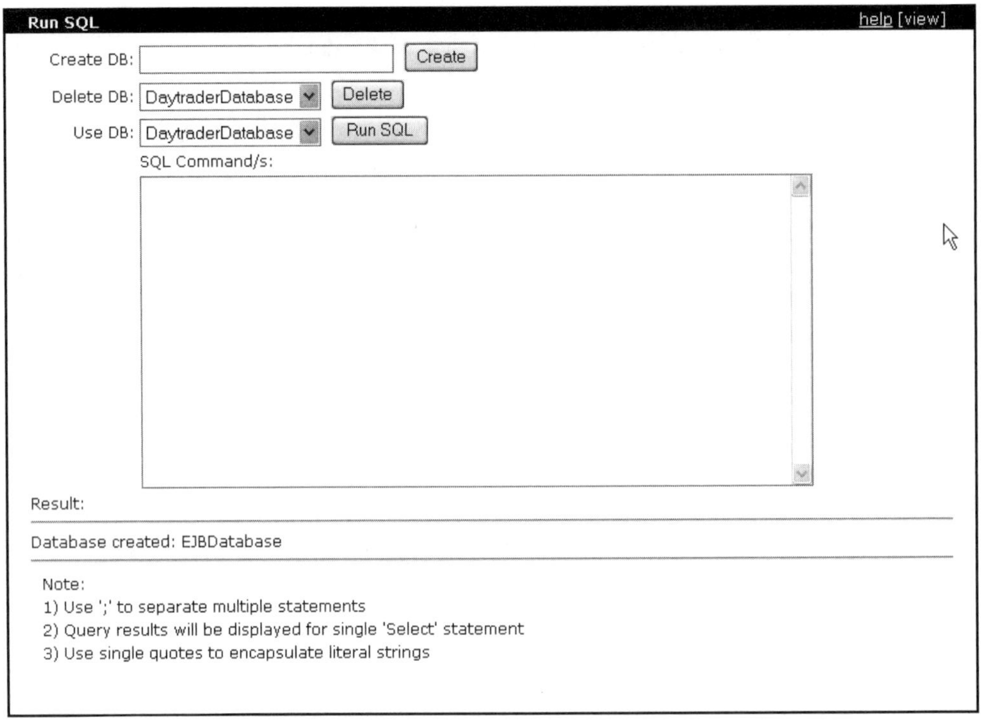

Figure 5-5. *Database pool name and database type*

Provide the name mydbpool as the database pool name, select the Derby embedded database for the database type, and click Next. You will see the screen shown in Figure 5-6.

Select the Derby database driver JAR (loaded from the Geronimo repository), and enter the database name as EJBDatabase. The driver JAR selection shown in Figure 5-6, org.apache. derby/derby/10.1.1.0/jar, specifies derby-10.1.1.0.jar in the GERONIMO-HOME/repository/ org.apache.derby/jars directory. If the database driver is not available in the Geronimo repository, you can download the driver from the Internet by clicking the Download a Driver button. Click Next, and the console will display the screen shown in Figure 5-7.

You can modify the connection pool parameters or use the default settings by leaving these fields blank. To test the connection, click Test Connection, or to skip the test and deploy right away, click Skip Test and Deploy. You can also view the configuration plan before deploying by clicking the Skip Test and Show Plan button. Additionally, you can copy the plan and save it as a text file and later use the command-line deploy tool (GERONIMO-HOME/bin/deploy.bat) to deploy the pool. In our example, we'll click Skip Test and Deploy to deploy the connection pool into Geronimo.

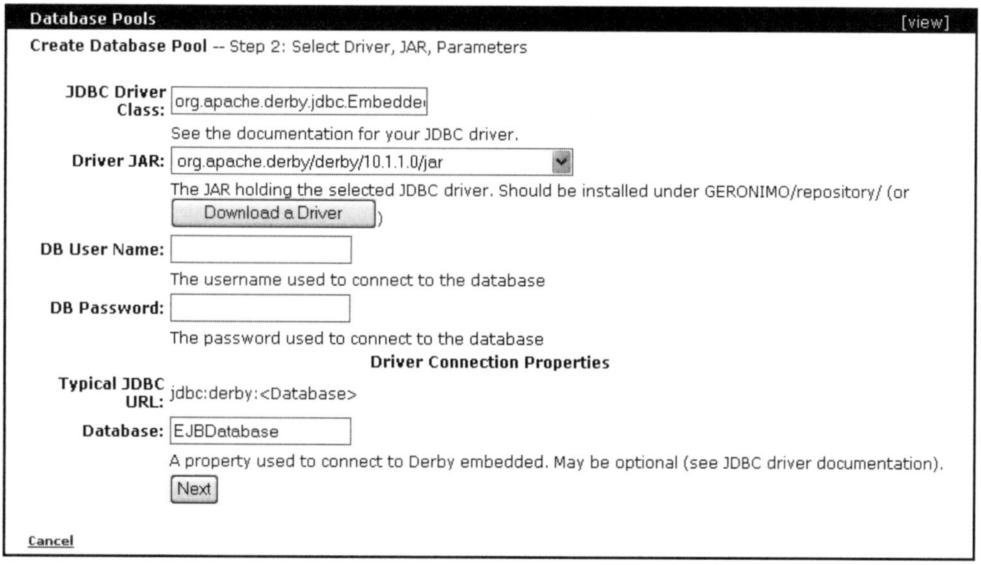

Figure 5-6. *Database pool settings*

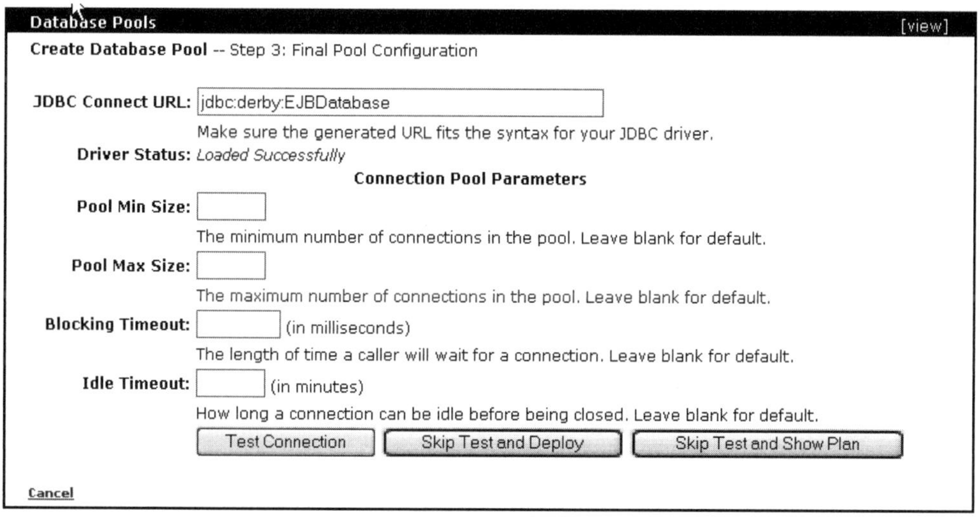

Figure 5-7. *Connection pool settings*

Create a Directory Structure

Create two separate directories: bmp and cmp, for our bean-managed and container-managed entity bean examples, respectively. Under each of these directories, create three subdirectories: src, dd, and build. The src subdirectory will contain the Java source files, the dd subdirectory will contain the deploy descriptors, and the build subdirectory will contain the build outputs.

Now let's turn to our first example, a bean-managed entity bean. Later in the chapter, you'll explore container-managed entity beans.

Bean-Managed Entity Bean

An entity bean with bean-managed persistence manages the persistence of the bean state directly in the bean implementation. For instance, in the case of a relational database, you can use JDBC to code the logic of the bean state persistence in the bean implementation in a relational database store.

Let's create a sample bean-managed entity bean to represent a student. You need to follow these steps:

1. Write the home interface.

2. Write the EJB component interface.

3. Write the primary key class.

4. Write the bean implementation.

5. Create the standard deployment descriptor (ejb-jar.xml).

6. Create the Geronimo-specific deployment descriptor (openejb-jar.xml).

7. Package and deploy the entity bean.

Write the Home Interface

The home interface for an entity bean can define methods to create and find entity bean instances. You can define one or more create methods (overloaded) to correspond to all available options to create a new entity bean instance. In the case of a relational database store, a create method corresponds to executing a SQL INSERT statement to create a new row in the database table. The new entity bean instance will represent the values of this new row. The home interface of an entity bean can also define one or more finder methods to search for existing entities. A finder method corresponds to executing a SQL SELECT statement against a relational database. In addition to defining create and finder methods, the home interface of an entity bean can define home business methods. These methods are not specific to any entity bean instance but apply to all entity instances belonging to the same home instance.

To define a home interface for a remote entity bean, use this code:

```
package samples.bmp.student;

// imports

public interface StudentHome extends EJBHome {
  // create methods
  public Student create(String firstName) throws CreateException, RemoteException;
  public Student create(String firstName, String lastName) ➥
throws CreateException, RemoteException;

  // finder methods
  public Student findByPrimaryKey(StudentPKey pk) ➥
throws FinderException,RemoteException;
  public Collection findAll() throws FinderException,RemoteException;

  // home business methods
  public int getPassPercentage() throws RemoteException;
}
```

For a local entity bean, the home interface should extend from the EJBLocalHome interface, as shown here. (Please note that methods in the local home interface do not throw the RemoteException.)

```
public interface StudentLocalHome extends EJBLocalHome {
  // create methods
  public StudentLocal create(String firstName) throws CreateException;
  public StudentLocal create(String firstName, String lastName) ➥
throws CreateException;

  // finder methods
  public StudentLocal findByPrimaryKey(StudentPKey pk) ➥
throws FinderException;
  public Collection findAll() throws FinderException;

  // home business methods
  public int getPassPercentage() throws RemoteException;
}
```

The create methods need to throw the EJB CreateException and return the EJB object interface type as a return type. Also, an entity bean can define one or more finder methods, but it needs to define a method named findByPrimaryKey() that returns the EJB object interface type as its return type. The name of a finder method starts with the word "find," and the finder method needs to throw the EJB FinderException.

Create the EJB Component Interface

The EJB component interface for an entity bean defines methods that this entity exposes to its clients. If you want to create the Student entity bean as a remote EJB, use the following code to create the remote interface:

```
package samples.bmp.student;

// imports

public interface Student extends EJBObject {

  public String getFirstName() throws RemoteException;
  public String getLastName() throws RemoteException;
  public void setLastName(String name)throws RemoteException;
  public int getMarks() throws RemoteException;
  public void setMarks(int marks)throws RemoteException;
  public boolean passed() throws RemoteException;

}
```

To create a local EJB type, you should extend this interface from EJBLocalObject, as shown here:

```
public interface StudentLocal extends EJBLocalObject {

  public String getFirstName();
  public String getLastName();
  public void setLastName(String name);
  public int getMarks();
  public void setMarks(int marks);
  public boolean passed();

}
```

Create the Primary Key Class

A primary key class is required for an entity bean. This is a simple serializable JavaBean, as shown here:

```
package samples.bmp.student;

// imports

public class StudentPKey implements Serializable {
  public String firstName;

  public StudentPKey(){}
  public StudentPKey(String firstName){this.firstName=firstName;}
```

```
  public int hashCode(){return firstName.hashCode();}
  public boolean equals(Object obj){
    boolean ret=false;
    if(obj instanceof StudentPKey){
      ret=((StudentPKey)obj).equals(firstName);
    }
    return ret;
  }

}
```

This primary key class is a wrapper around the simple primary key field (id). A primary key class is required to implement the hashCode() and equals() methods so that the container can internally maintain a hash table to store entities with the corresponding primary key objects as their key values.

Create the Bean Implementation Class

The bean implementation class is required to implement the EJB EntityBean interface and provide an implementation for the following methods:

- An ejbCreate() method for every create method defined in the home interface

- A matching ejbPostCreate() method for every ejbCreate() method

- An ejbFind() method for every finder method defined in the home interface

- All the home business methods defined in the home interface

- All the client interface methods defined in the EJB object interface (remote or local)

- EJB entity bean–required methods

The code listing for the Student bean is shown here:

```
package samples.bmp.student;

// imports

public class StudentBean implements EntityBean{

  protected EntityContext context;
  private static final int PASS_MARK=40;

  // BEAN MANAGED PERSISTENT FIELDS
  private String firstName; // primary key field
  private String lastName;
  private int marks;

  public StudentBean(){ }
```

```
// CREATE METHODS
public StudentPKey ejbCreate(String firstName) throws CreateException {

  insertStudent(firstName,null);
  this.firstName=firstName;
  this.lastName=null;
  StudentPKey pk=new StudentPKey(firstName);
  return pk;
}

public void ejbPostCreate(String firstName){}

public StudentPKey ejbCreate(String firstName, String lastName) ➡
throws CreateException{
  insertStudent(firstName,lastName);
  this.firstName=firstName;
  this.lastName=lastName;
  StudentPKey pk=new StudentPKey(firstName);
  return pk;
}

public void ejbPostCreate(String firstName, String lastName){}
```

The ejbCreate() method executes an SQL INSERT statement to insert a new row into the STUD table, sets the persistent field values, and returns the primary key object. For every ejbCreate() method, you must have a corresponding ejbPostCreate() method. The container invokes this method soon after the EJB object is created but before the entity bean is available for clients to use, and you can implement any postcreation logic here.

The getters, setters, business methods, and home business methods are shown here:

```
// GETTERS FOR PERSISTENT FIELDS
public String getFirstName(){return firstName;}
public String getLastName() {return lastName;}
public int getMarks(){return marks;}

// SETTERS FOR PERSISTENT FIELD
public void setLastName(String name){lastName=name;}
public void setMarks(int marks){this.marks=marks;}

// BUSINESS METHOD
public boolean passed(){return (marks>=PASS_MARK);}

// HOME BUSINESS METHODS
public int ejbHomeGetPassPercentage()throws EJBException{
  Connection conn=null;
```

```
    try {
        conn=getConnection();
        int totalCount=getTotalCount(conn);
        int passCount=getPassCount(conn);
        return (int)(((float)passCount/(float)totalCount)*100);
    }catch (Exception e){
        throw new EJBException("Failed:"+e.getMessage());
    }finally {
        close(conn);
    }
}
```

You can implement accessor methods for all persistent fields. In addition, you need to implement all the EJB object interface methods (business logic methods) and all business methods defined in the home interface.

The finder methods are shown here:

```
// FINDER METHOD IMPLEMENTATIONS
public StudentPKey ejbFindByPrimaryKey(StudentPKey pk) throws FinderException{
    Connection conn=null;
    PreparedStatement ps=null;
    ResultSet rs=null;

    try{
        conn=getConnection();
        ps=conn.prepareStatement("
            select fname,lname,marks from stud where fname=?");
        ps.setString(1,pk.firstName);
        rs=ps.executeQuery();
        rs.next();
        // no error return the primary key
        return pk;
    }catch(Exception e){
        // handle exception
    }finally{
        // close resources
    }

}

public Collection ejbFindAll() throws FinderException{
    Connection conn=null;
    PreparedStatement ps=null;
    ResultSet rs=null;
```

```
    try{
        conn=getConnection();
        ps=conn.prepareStatement("select fname from stud");
        rs=ps.executeQuery();
        Collection list=new ArrayList();
        while(rs.next()){
            list.add(new StudentPKey(rs.getString(1)));
        }
        return list;
    }catch(Exception e){
        // handle exception
    }finally{
        // close resources
    }
}
```

All finder methods declared in the home interface should have a corresponding ejbFind() implementation method here. Finder methods are required to return a primary key instance (or a collection of primary key instances) of the matching entity (or entities).

The EJB required methods are shown here:

```
// EJB REQUIRED METHODS
public void ejbPassivate() {}
public void ejbActivate() {}
public void ejbRemove() throws RemoveException{
   StudentPKey pk=(StudentPKey)context.getPrimaryKey();
   deleteStudent(pk.firstName);
}

public void ejbLoad(){
   Connection conn=null;
   PreparedStatement ps=null;
   ResultSet rs=null;
   try{
       StudentPKey pk=(StudentPKey)context.getPrimaryKey();
       conn=getConnection();
       ps=conn.prepareStatement ➥
       ("select fname,lname,marks from stud where fname=?");
       ps.setString(1,pk.firstName);
       rs=ps.executeQuery();
       while(rs.next()){
           this.firstName=rs.getString(1);
           this.lastName=rs.getString(2);
           this.marks=rs.getInt(3);
       }
```

```
   }catch(Exception e){
       // handle exception
   }finally{
       // close resources
   }
}

public void ejbStore(){
  updateStudent();
}

public void setEntityContext(EntityContext context){
  this.context=context;
}

public void unsetEntityContext(){
  this.context=null;
}
```

The bean implementation must also implement the EJB-required methods for an entity bean. The container calls the ejbPassivate() method before it serializes the instance to a secondary store and calls the ejbActivate() method after it has deserialized the instance from the secondary store and before the instance is made ready for use. The container invokes ejbRemove() when the client has invoked the remove() method on the home or EJB object. The methods ejbLoad() and ejbStore() are invoked by the container for loading values from the persistent store to the instance persistent fields and for writing the persistent field values back into the persistent store. In the preceding example, the ejbRemove() method has code to delete the matching row from the STUD table, the ejbLoad() method has code to load the row to the instance fields, and the ejbStore() method stores the field values back in the STUD table.

The utility methods, like updateStudent(), insertStudent(), and deleteStudent(), are shown here:

```
private Connection getConnection() throws Exception{
  InitialContext ic=new InitialContext();
  DataSource ds=(DataSource)ic.lookup("java:comp/env/jdbc/mydbpool");
  return ds.getConnection();
}

private void insertStudent(Connection connection,String firstName) ➡
  throws Exception {
  insertStudent(firstName,null);
}
```

```
private void insertStudent(String firstName, String lastName) ➡
    throws CreateException {
    Connection conn=null;
    PreparedStatement ps=null;
    try {
        conn=getConnection();
        ps=conn.prepareStatement(
        "INSERT INTO stud (fname,lname) values (?,?)");
        ps.setString(1,firstName);
        ps.setString(2,lastName);
        ps.executeUpdate();
    } catch(Exception e){
        // handle exception
    }finally {
        // close resources
    }
}

private void updateStudent() throws EJBException {
    Connection conn=null;
    PreparedStatement ps=null;
    try {
        conn=getConnection();
        ps=conn.prepareStatement( ➡
            "update stud set lname=?, marks=? where fname=?");
        ps.setString(1,lastName);
        ps.setInt(2,marks);
        ps.setString(3,firstName);
        ps.executeUpdate();
} catch(Exception e){
        // handle exception
    }finally {
        // close resources
    }
}

private void deleteStudent(String firstName) throws RemoveException {
    //execute 'delete from stud where fname=?' to delete student record
}

..private int getPassCount(Connection connection)throws Exception{
    // execute 'select count(*) from stud where marks >="+PASS_MARK'
    // and return count
}
```

```
  private int getTotalCount(Connection connection)throws Exception{
    // execute 'select count(*) from stud' and return count
  }

  private void close(ResultSet rs){
    // close result set
}

  private void close(Statement st){
    // close statement
}

private void close(Connection conn){
    // close connection
  }

}
```

Create the Standard Deployment Descriptor

The standard deployment descriptor for an entity bean is the same as that of a session bean, and it is an XML document named ejb-jar.xml. Create the standard deployment descriptor as shown here:

```xml
<?xml version="1.0"?>
<ejb-jar xmlns="http://java.sun.com/xml/ns/j2ee"
xmlns:xsi="http://www.w3.org/2001/XMLSchema-instance"
xsi:schemaLocation="http://java.sun.com/xml/ns/j2ee
http://java.sun.com/xml/ns/j2ee/ejb-jar_2_1.xsd"  version="2.1">
<enterprise-beans>
    <entity>
          <ejb-name>StudentBMPEJB</ejb-name>
          <home>samples.bmp.student.StudentHome</home>
          <remote>samples.bmp.student.Student</remote>
          <ejb-class>samples.bmp.student.StudentBean</ejb-class>
          <persistence-type>Bean</persistence-type>
          <prim-key-class>samples.bmp.student.StudentPKey</prim-key-class>
          <reentrant>false</reentrant>
          <resource-ref>
                <res-ref-name>jdbc/mydbpool</res-ref-name>
                <res-type>javax.sql.DataSource</res-type>
                <res-auth>Container</res-auth>
          </resource-ref>
    </entity>
</enterprise-beans>
```

```
<assembly-descriptor>
    <container-transaction>
        <method>
                <ejb-name>Account</ejb-name>
                <method-intf>Remote</method-intf>
                <method-name>*</method-name>
        </method>
        <trans-attribute>Required</trans-attribute>
    </container-transaction>
</assembly-descriptor>

</ejb-jar>
```

The enterprise-beans/entity element defines the entity bean by specifying the remote and local interfaces, the bean implementation class, and the primary key class. The persistence-type element value of Bean specifies that the bean will use the BMP mechanism. The deployment descriptor also defines a resource reference that it uses to get a connection to the database (from the getConnection() method).

The enterprise-beans element can define one or more EJBs (including both session and entity bean types) that are contained in the same EJB JAR. The assembly-descriptor element defines assembly-time definitions, like transaction and security attributes, for the EJBs defined in the enterprise-beans section. In the preceding example, it defines a Required transaction attribute for both its local and remote interface methods.

Create the Geronimo-Specific Deployment Descriptor

The Geronimo-specific deployment plan (descriptor) is an XML file named openejb-jar.xml if you package it within the EJB JAR file. You can provide many environment- and Geronimo-specific values in this file, and you can use it to specify a configuration name for the EJB. This name is required for you to identify this configuration from, for instance, tools like the deploy tool. Hence, even if you don't need to provide any Geronimo-specific settings, you still need to create this file. Figure 5-8 depicts the structure of the Geronimo-specific deployment descriptor for EJBs.

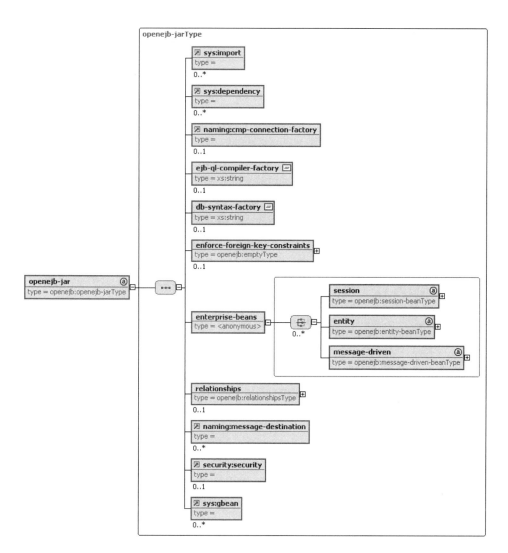

Figure 5-8. *Geronimo-specific deployment descriptor for EJBs*

You already learned about many of these elements in Chapter 4, when we discussed session beans. The elements described in Table 5-1 are applicable to container-managed entity beans.

Table 5-1. *Deployment Descriptor Elements*

Element	Description
cmp-connection-factory	This element specifies the data source to be used for container-managed persistence. You can specify the connection factory like you resolve a resource reference; that is, by providing either the Geronimo object name or a resource-link or a target-name.
ejb-ql-compiler-factory	This element specifies the EJB-QL compiler factory to be used. This setting is applicable to container-managed beans and should specify a fully qualified class name that implements the org.tranql.sql.EJBQLCompilerFactory interface. The default value is for the Derby database, but you can also use this element for other databases.
bb-syntax-factory	This element specifies the name of a class that specializes SQL generation for a particular database. The default value is for the Derby database, but you can also use this element for other databases.
enforce-foreign-key-constraints	If this element is specified, the EJB container will, whenever possible, execute SQL statements in an order that does not violate foreign key constraints.
relationships	This element is used to specify all details about CMRs. We will explore entity relationships later in this chapter.
entity	This element is used to describe the entity bean.

The structure of the entity element is as shown in Figure 5-9.

Many of the fields apply to container-managed entity beans, and hence we will discuss these later in this chapter. A sample deployment descriptor for the Student sample entity bean is shown here:

```
<?xml version="1.0" encoding="UTF-8"?>
<openejb-jar
xmlns="http://www.openejb.org/xml/ns/openejb-jar"
xmlns:naming="http://geronimo.apache.org/xml/ns/naming"
xmlns:security="http://geronimo.apache.org/xml/ns/security"
xmlns:sys="http://geronimo.apache.org/xml/ns/deployment"
configId="StudentBMP"
parentId="geronimo/j2ee-server/1.0/car">
  <enterprise-beans>
        <entity>
                <ejb-name>StudentBMPEJB</ejb-name>
                <jndi-name>ejb/Student</jndi-name>
                <naming:resource-ref>
                        <naming:ref-name> jdbc/mydbpool </naming:ref-name>
                        <naming:resource-link>mydbpool</naming:resource-link>
                </naming:resource-ref>
        </entity>
  </enterprise-beans>
</openejb-jar>
```

This defines a JNDI name for the container to bind this EJB in the JNDI space and resolves the resource references defined in the ejb-jar.xml deployment descriptor.

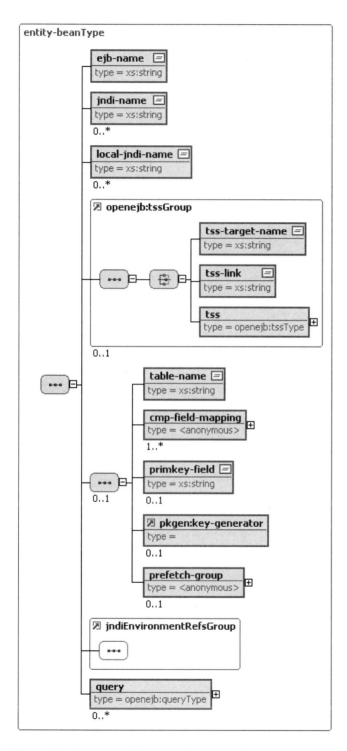

Figure 5-9. *Structure of the entity element in the Geronimo deployment plan*

Compile, Package, and Deploy the Entity Bean

Create the following directory structure and files in the bmp/build subdirectory:

```
samples/bmp/student/Student.class
samples/bmp/student/StudentHome.class
samples/bmp/student/StudentBean.class
samples/bmp/student/StudentPKey.class
META-INF/ejb-jar.xml
META-INF/openejb-jar.xml
```

Create the EJB JAR by issuing the following command from the bmp/build subdirectory:

```
jar -cvf studentBMP.jar
```

You can deploy the EJB by using one of the following commands:

```
java -jar deployer.jar deploy studentBMP.jar
deploy.bat deploy studentBMP.jar
```

You can also deploy the EJB through the console application by selecting Application ➤ Deploy New from the Console Navigation menu and uploading the EJB JAR.

Container-Managed Entity Bean

An entity bean with container-managed persistence does not have persistence code in the bean implementation, and the container automatically generates the code for its persistence. There are many differences between writing a bean-managed entity bean and a container-managed entity bean, and we will discuss them in this section. In addition, a CMP bean offers the following benefits over a BMP bean:

- Bean code is independent of the underlying database. This allows you to change your database product without any change to your bean code.

- It is more object friendly. With CMP, you specify your queries by using EJB Query Language (EJB-QL), a more object friendly query mechanism than SQL, which is a relational query language.

- The container provides better optimization and more efficient execution of queries.

In many cases, these advantages provide more than enough reasons to go with the CMP approach over the BMP approach. For our example, we will create the same Student bean by using a CMP entity bean.

The steps required to create the CMP bean are as follows:

1. Write the home interface.

2. Write the EJB object interface.

3. Write the primary key class.

4. Write the bean implementation.

5. Create the standard deployment descriptor.

6. Create the Geronimo-specific deployment plan.

7. Package and deploy the entity bean.

Write the Home Interface

This step is the same as in the BMP example.

Write the EJB Object Interface

Again, this step is the same as in the BMP example.

Write the Primary Key Class

Here, use java.lang.String as the primary key class.

Write the Bean Implementation

The following list outlines the procedures involved in writing a CMP bean implementation. You'll notice many differences between these procedures and the procedures you used in writing the BMP bean implementation.

The bean implementation class for a CMP entity bean should be an abstract class. The container generates a subclass and provides a concrete implementation for the abstract bean implementation that you provide.

You should not declare the persistent fields in the bean implementation class. Here, also, the container declares these fields in the generated concrete subclass.

You need to declare abstract accessor methods (getter and setter) for all the persistent fields. The container provides the implementation for these methods in the concrete subclass that it generates. You can use these methods in the bean implementation class to access the persistent fields.

For every create method defined in the home interface, you need to define and implement a corresponding ejbCreate() method. This method should set the entity member instance values (by using the abstract accessor methods for persistent fields) from the create parameters and return null.

For every ejbCreate() method, you need a matching ejbPostCreate() method.

You can define one or more ejbSelect() methods. These are helper methods and are very similar to ejbFind() methods, but they are not exposed to the client through the home interface or the EJB object interface. These methods can be called only from other bean implementation methods. You need to declare this method as an abstract method, and like you do for ejbFind() methods, you can provide the necessary SELECT query as an EJB-QL query in the deployment descriptor.

Implement the ejbHome() methods in the bean implementation class. You can use ejbSelect() methods to utilize CMP benefits and invoke them from the ejbHome() methods.

Implement the ejbActivate() method as required.

Implement the ejbPassivate() method as required.

Do not load the database data from your ejbLoad() method. The container loads the data for you before calling the ejbLoad() method, and in this method, you can modify the read-in data if required. Usually, this is an empty implementation.

Do not place data into the database from your ejbStore() method. The container stores the data right after it invokes the ejbStore() method. You can modify the to-be-stored data if required. Usually, this is an empty implementation.

From the ejbRemove() method, do not destroy the data in the database. Instead, perform any operation that needs to be done before the container destroys the data. Usually, this method is an empty implementation.

The following code shows a sample implementation. Note that the amount of code needed to write a CMP bean is considerably reduced.

```
package samples.cmp.student;

// imports

public abstract class StudentBean implements EntityBean{
  protected EntityContext context;
  private static final int PASS_MARK=40;

  // NO DECLARATION OF PERSISTENT FIELDS

  public StudentBean(){ }

  // CREATE METHODS--INITIALIZE USING SETTERS AND RETURN NULL
  public StudentPKey ejbCreate(String firstName) throws CreateException {
    setFirstName(firstName);
    setLastName(null);
    setMarks(0);
    return null;
  }

  public void ejbPostCreate(String firstName){}

  public StudentPKey ejbCreate(String firstName, String lastName) ➡
    throws CreateException{
    setFirstName(firstName);
    setLastName(lastName);
    setMarks(0);
    return null;
  }

  public void ejbPostCreate(String firstName, String lastName){}
```

```
// ABSTRACT GETTERS FOR PERSISTENT FIELDS
public abstract String getFirstName();
public abstract String getLastName();
public abstract int getMarks();

// ABSTRACT SETTERS FOR PERSISTENT FIELD
public abstract void setFirstName(String firstName);
public abstract void setLastName(String lastName);
public abstract void setMarks(int marks);

// BUSINESS METHOD
public boolean passed(){return (getMarks()>=PASS_MARK);}

// HOME BUSINESS METHODS
public int ejbHomeGetPassPercentage(){
  try{
      int totalCount=ejbSelectTotalCount().intValue();
      int passCount=ejbSelectPassCount().intValue();
      return (int)(((float)passCount/(float)totalCount)*100);
  } catch(Exception e){
      // handle Exception
  }
}

// NO FINDER METHOD IMPLEMENTATIONS

// EJB REQUIRED METHODS
public void ejbPassivate() {}
public void ejbActivate() {}
public void ejbRemove() throws RemoveException{ }

// EMPTY EJB LOAD and EJB STORE
public void ejbLoad(){}
public void ejbStore(){}

public void setEntityContext(EntityContext context){
  this.context=context;
}
public void unsetEntityContext(){
  this.context=null;
}

// ABSTRACT SELECTOR METHOD DECLARATION
public abstract Integer ejbSelectPassCount() throws FinderException;
public abstract Integer ejbSelectTotalCount() throws FinderException;
}
```

Create the Standard Deployment Descriptor

The standard deployment descriptor is the ejb-jar.xml file. The deployment descriptor in this example is very similar to the deployment descriptor in the BMP example, except that it also needs to define the CMP-related elements, as shown here:

```xml
<?xml version="1.0"?>
<ejb-jar xmlns="http://java.sun.com/xml/ns/j2ee"
xmlns:xsi="http://www.w3.org/2001/XMLSchema-instance"
xsi:schemaLocation="http://java.sun.com/xml/ns/j2ee
http://java.sun.com/xml/ns/j2ee/ejb-jar_2_1.xsd"  version="2.1">
<enterprise-beans>
    <entity>
        <ejb-name>StudentCMPEJB</ejb-name>
        <home>samples.cmp.student.StudentHome</home>
        <remote>samples.cmp.student.Student</remote>
        <ejb-class>samples.cmp.student.StudentBean</ejb-class>
        <persistence-type>Container</persistence-type>
        <prim-key-class>java.lang.String</prim-key-class>
        <reentrant>false</reentrant>
        <cmp-version>2.x</cmp-version>
        <abstract-schema-name>StudentCMPBean</abstract-schema-name>

        <cmp-field><field-name>firstName</field-name></cmp-field>
        <cmp-field><field-name>lastName</field-name></cmp-field>
        <cmp-field><field-name>marks</field-name></cmp-field>
        <primkey-field>firstName</primkey-field>

        <query>
            <query-method>
                <method-name>findAll</method-name>
                <method-params/>
            </query-method>
            <ejb-ql>
                <![CDATA[SELECT OBJECT(a) from StudentCMPBean AS a]]>
            </ejb-ql>
        </query>

        <query>
            <query-method>
                <method-name>ejbSelectTotalCount</method-name>
                <method-params/>
            </query-method>
            <ejb-ql>
                <![CDATA[SELECT COUNT(a.firstName) from StudentCMPBean AS a]]>
            </ejb-ql>
        </query>
```

```
        <query>
                <query-method>
                    <method-name>ejbSelectPassCount</method-name>
                    <method-params/>
                </query-method>
            <ejb-ql>
                <![CDATA[SELECT COUNT(a.firstName) from StudentCMPBean ➥
    AS a where a.marks>=40]]>
            </ejb-ql>
        </query>
    </entity>

</enterprise-beans>

<assembly-descriptor>
</assembly-descriptor>

</ejb-jar>
```

Table 5-2 outlines the CMP-related elements.

Table 5-2. *CMP-Related Elements in the Standard Deployment Descriptor*

Element	Description
cmp-version	This value can be either 2.x or 1.x, depending on the version of CMP you want to use.
abstract-schema-name	This is a name to denote an abstract schema for this entity bean. You will be using this name in the EJB-QL queries.
cmp-field	This defines all the persistent fields of the entity beans.
field-name	This is the field name for the persistent field.
query	This element defines the query for all your finder and selector methods.
query-method	This element specifies the finder or the selector method.
ejb-ql	This element defines the query in EJB-QL syntax.
method-name, method-params, and method-param	These identify the finder or the selector method.

Create the Geronimo-Specific Deployment Plan

You need to create a Geronimo-specific deployment plan, shown here, to map the abstract schema (and its persistent fields) to a physical table (and columns) in the database. We will use the mydbpool connection pool that we created earlier in the chapter.

```xml
<?xml version="1.0" encoding="UTF-8"?>
<openejb-jar
xmlns="http://www.openejb.org/xml/ns/openejb-jar"
xmlns:naming="http://geronimo.apache.org/xml/ns/naming"
xmlns:security="http://geronimo.apache.org/xml/ns/security"
xmlns:sys="http://geronimo.apache.org/xml/ns/deployment"
configId="StudentCMP"
parentId="geronimo/j2ee-server/1.0/car">

<cmp-connection-factory>
  <resource-link>mydbpool</resource-link>
</cmp-connection-factory>


  <enterprise-beans>
        <entity>
                <ejb-name>StudentCMPEJB</ejb-name>
                <jndi-name>ejb/StudentCMP</jndi-name>

                <table-name>stud</table-name>

                <cmp-field-mapping>
                        <cmp-field-name>firstName</cmp-field-name>
                        <table-column>fname</table-column>
                </cmp-field-mapping>

                <cmp-field-mapping>
                        <cmp-field-name>lastName</cmp-field-name>
                        <table-column>lname</table-column>
                </cmp-field-mapping>

                <cmp-field-mapping>
                        <cmp-field-name>marks</cmp-field-name>
                        <table-column>marks</table-column>
                </cmp-field-mapping>
                <primkey-field>firstName</primkey-field>

        </entity>
</enterprise-beans>

</openejb-jar>
```

Let's look at Geronimo-specific deployment plans in more detail.

Defining CMP Attributes

Table 5-3 describes the elements you use to define CMP attributes.

Table 5-3. *CMP General Fields*

Element	Description
table-name	This is the name of the table this entity is mapped to.
cmp-field-mapping	You use this element to map a persistent field that is defined in the ejb-jar.xml file to a physical column in the table.
cmp-field-name	This is the persistent field name. This should match a field-name element in the ejb-jar.xml file.
cmp-field-class	This optional element specifies the fully qualified class name of the field.
table-column	This is the column name that this field should be mapped to.
sql-type	Use this element to specify a java.sql.Types SQL type name for this field. Usually, the defaults are fine—use this element to override the default mapping.
type-converter	Use this element to specify a custom type converter to be used to convert a Java type to a SQL type. A custom converter should implement the org.tranql.sql.TypeConverter interface.

Figure 5-10 shows the details of the cmp-field-mapping element that was described in Table 5-3.

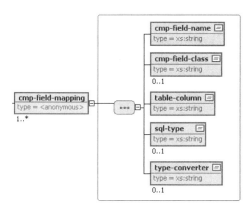

Figure 5-10. *The cmp-field-mapping element*

Specifying a Key Generator

The key-generator element is used to specify the mechanism that the entity uses to generate automatic keys. Our example does not include this element because it does not require automatic key generation. Figure 5-11 depicts the key-generator element and its subelements.

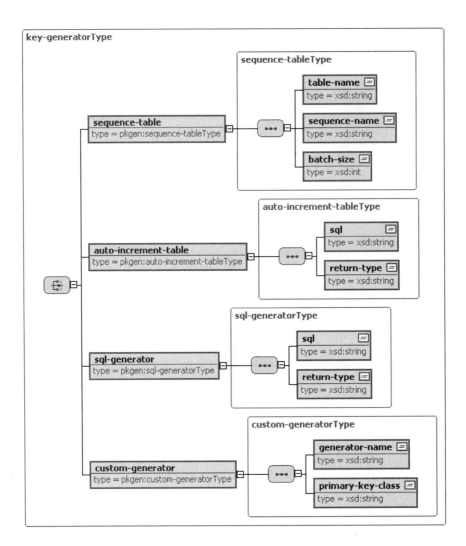

Figure 5-11. *The key-generator element*

Table 5-4 describes the subelements of the key-generator element.

Table 5-4. *Key Generator Elements in the Deployment Descriptor*

Element	Description
sequence-table	Here, you specify a table (by using the table-name subelement) that has a VARCHAR column name and an INTEGER column value to hold several sequences identified by their name.
table-name	This element identifies the table containing the sequences.
sequence-name	This element identifies the sequence name that should be used for this key.
batch-size	Geronimo collects the IDs from this table in batches and stores them in memory so that it need not go back to the table every time a new key needs to be generated. This element specifies the batch size.
auto-increment-table	You use this element to specify to Geronimo that the database will automatically create and populate values for its primary keys. Use this element when you need to use the automatic increment primary key features of your database.
sql-generator	This element uses a provided SQL statement to generate the key.
sql	This is a SELECT SQL statement that generates the next key value when used within the sql-generator element, and it is a SQL INSERT statement that adds a new row to the table when used within the auto-increment-table element.
return-type	This element denotes the Java type returned and is used to get the result from the ResultSet.
custom-generator	You can also use a custom generator if you need custom behavior for key generation. The generator-name element should point to a GBean that implements the org.tranql.pkgenerator.PrimaryKeyGenerator interface.
primary-key-class	This element specifies the fully qualified class name of the primary key class supported by the custom generator.

Specifying a Prefetch Group

When a finder is executed or a CMR field is accessed, only their primary keys, not the actual entities, are loaded. Only when an entity is accessed is its entire data loaded. This often means executing two SQL queries—the first to fetch the primary keys, and the second to fetch the remaining entity data. You can avoid this by specifying a prefetch group. A prefetch group denotes the set of fields that need to be loaded together. If you define a prefetch group to a finder query, it will load all the fields in that group, and hence you can avoid a trip to the database. Figure 5-12 shows the various elements that you can use to define prefetch groups.

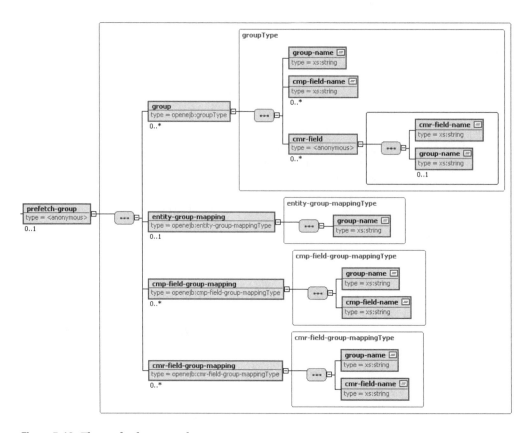

Figure 5-12. *The prefetch-group element*

Table 5-5 describes these elements.

Table 5-5. *The prefetch-group Element and Its Subelements*

Element	Heading
prefetch-group	Use this element to define groups and group mappings to CMP fields and CMR fields. We will discuss CMR later in this chapter.
group	Use this element to define a group. A group contains one or more CMP fields and CMR fields of an entity.
group-name	This is the group name for the defined group. You can use this name to refer to this group from group mappings.
cmp-field-name	This is the CMP field name and should match the field name in the cmp-field-mapping element.
cmr-field	This specifies a group mapping for a CMR field. This will include the cmr-field-name and a group-name identifying the CMP and CMR fields of the entity identified by that CMR field.
cmr-field-name	This identifies the CMR field name.

Element	Heading
entity-group-mapping	This specifies a default group that should be loaded when this entity is accessed. This applies only when no other group definitions apply.
cmp-field-group-mapping	This specifies a group that should be loaded when this CMP field is accessed.
cmr-field-group-mapping	This specifies a group that should be loaded when this CMR field is accessed.

Defining Queries

You can use a query element to define a query that is not defined in the ejb-jar.xml file or to specify a prefetch group for a query that is already defined in the ejb-jar.xml file. Figure 5-13 depicts the query element and its subelements.

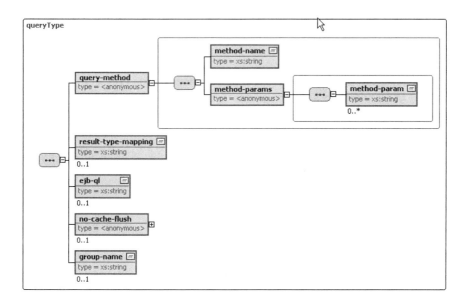

Figure 5-13. *The query element*

Most of these elements are defined in other sections in this chapter.

Package and Deploy the Bean

Create the following directory structure and files in the cmp/build subdirectory:

```
samples/cmp/student/Student.class
samples/cmp/student/StudentHome.class
samples/cmp/student/StudentBean.class
```

```
samples/cmp/student/StudentPKey.class
META-INF/ejb-jar.xml
META-INF/openejb-jar.xml
```

Create the EJB JAR by issuing the following command from the cmp/build subdirectory:

```
jar -cvf studentCMP.jar
```

You can deploy the EJB by using one of the following commands:

```
java -jar deployer.jar deploy studentCMP.jar
deploy.bat deploy studentCMP.jar
```

You can also deploy the EJB through the console application by selecting Application ➤ Deploy New from the Console Navigation menu and uploading the EJB JAR.

Using Container-Managed Relationships

An entity bean can have relationships with other entity beans, like a Student entity bean having a relationship with an Address entity bean. An entity relationship is implemented as a member variable of the appropriate entity type. You can implement this either by using bean-managed relationships, which requires you to manually code the logic of managing the relationship, or by using container-managed relationships, in which case the container transparently manages the relationships for you. In the following sections, you'll learn about the three types of CMRs.

One-to-One Relationship

Let us consider an example in which an Order entity has a one-to-one relationship with the Billing Address entity. The Order entity is shown here:

```
public abstract class OrderBean implements EntityBean {
  // no fields
  public abstract Address getBillingAddress();
  public abstract void setBillingAddress(Address address);

  public void ejbLoad() {} // Empty
  public void ejbStore() {} // Empty
}
```

You also need to define the CMR field (billing address) in your EJB JAR deployment descriptor, as shown here:

```
<ejb-jar>
  <enterprise-beans>
...    </enterprise-beans>
  <relationships>
    <ejb-relation>
        <ejb-relation-name>Order-Shipment</ejb-relation-name>
```

```
            <ejb-relationship-role>
                <ejb-relationship-role-name>
                    order-billing-address
                </ejb-relationship-role-name>
                <multiplicity>One</multiplicity>
                <relationship-role-source>
                    <ejb-name>Order</ejb-name>
                </relationship-role-source>
            <cmr-field><cmr-field-name>billingAddress</cmr-field-name></cmr-field>
            </ejb-relationship-role>
            <ejb-relationship-role>
                <ejb-relationship-role-name>
                    Billing-Address-Of-order
                </ejb-relationship-role-name>
                <multiplicity>One</multiplicity>
                <relationship-role-source>
                    <ejb-name>Address</ejb-name>
                </relationship-role-source>
            </ejb-relationship-role>
        </ejb-relation>
    </relationships>
</ejb-jar>
```

Here, the relationships element defines all relationships (using one or more ejb-relation element definitions) between various entity beans. The ejb-relation element specifies a name for the relation (using the ejb-relation-name element) and defines two ejb-relation-role elements. Each ejb-relation-role element defines one end of the relation, specifies its multiplicity (using the multiplicity element), and maps it to the entity bean type (using the relationship-role-source/ejb-name element) and the CMR field (using the cmr-field element). In the preceding example, at the Address entity bean end of this relationship, there is no CMR field mapping, and hence the relationship is single directional.

The next step is to map the CMR fields to the physical table and columns appropriately in the Geronimo-specific deployment descriptor. Let's consider the following table design for the Order-Address relationship:

```
CREATE TABLE ADDRESS (
ADD_ID INTEGER NOT NULL PRIMARY KEY,
STREET_1 VARCHAR(30),
...
);
CREATE TABLE ORDER (
ORD_ID INTEGER NOT NULL PRIMARY KEY,
ADDRESS_ID INTEGER NOT NULL,
...
CONSTRAINT FK_ORDER_ADDRESS FOREIGN KEY (ADDRESS_ID)
REFERENCES ADDRESS(ADD_ID)
);
```

Use the relationships element of the Geronimo-specific deployment descriptor (openejb-jar.xml) to map the relationship to the physical table and the columns, as shown here:

```
<relationships>
    <ejb-relation>
        <ejb-relationship-role>
            <relationship-role-source>
                <ejb-name>Order</ejb-name>
            </relationship-role-source>
            <cmr-field>
                <cmr-field-name>billingAddress</cmr-field-name>
            </cmr-field>
            <foreign-key-column-on-source />
            <role-mapping>
                <cmr-field-mapping>
                    <key-column>ADD_ID</key-column>
                    <foreign-key-column>ADDRESS_ID</foreign-key-column>
                </cmr-field-mapping>
            </role-mapping>
        </ejb-relationship-role>
    </ejb-relation>

</relationships>
```

The relationships element is very similar to the relationships element in the EJB JAR file. It can specify one or more ejb-relation elements and one or two ejb-relationship-role elements. The preceding example includes only one ejb-relationship-role element since this relationship is single directional. The foreign-key-column-on-source element specifies that the Order entity's foreign key (ADDRESS_ID) refers to the Address entity. The cmr-field-mapping element specifies the key-column and the foreign-key-column elements. Here, since the foreign key is in the source entity (Order), the key-column should be in the Address entity (if the key column were in the Order entity, the foreign key would be in the Address entity).

One-to-Many Relationship

In a one-to-many relationship, an entity has relationships with one or more entities of a different type, like an Order entity having relationships with one or more LineItem entities, as shown in the following example:

```
public abstract class OrderBean implements EntityBean {
  // no fields
  public abstract Collection getLineItems();
  public abstract void setLineItems(Collection lineItems);

  public void ejbLoad() {} // Empty
  public void ejbStore() {} // Empty
}
```

The EJB JAR deployment descriptor defines the relationship, as shown here:

```
<ejb-jar>
    <enterprise-beans>
...
    </enterprise-beans>
    <relationships>
        <ejb-relation>
            <ejb-relation-name>Order-LineItems</ejb-relation-name>
            <ejb-relationship-role>
                <ejb-relationship-role-name>
                    Order-Has-LineItems
                 </ejb-relationship-role-name>
                <multiplicity>One</multiplicity>
                <relationship-role-source>
                    <ejb-name>Order</ejb-name>
                </relationship-role-source>
                <cmr-field>
                    <cmr-field-name>lineItems</cmr-field-name>
                    <cmr-field-type>java util Collection</cmr-field-type>
                </cmr-field>
            </ejb-relationship-role>
            <ejb-relationship-role>
                <ejb-relationship-role-name>
                    LineItems-Belongs-To-Order
                </ejb-relationship-role-name>
                <multiplicity>Many</multiplicity>
                <relationship-role-source>
                    <ejb-name>LineItem</ejb-name>
                </relationship-role-source>
            </ejb-relationship-role>
        </ejb-relation>
    </relationships>
</ejb-jar>
```

Here, the first ejb-relationship-role element defines the relation at the Order end, and the next ejb-relationship-role element defines the relation at the LineItem end. In this case also, only the relation at the Order end has a CMR field, and hence the relationship is single directional. The table design for the Order and LineItem entities is shown here:

```
CREATE TABLE LINEITEM (
ITEM_ID INTEGER NOT NULL PRIMARY KEY,
ORDER_ID INTEGER NOT NULL,
...
CONSTRAINT FK_LINEITEM_ORDER FOREIGN KEY (ORDER_ID)
REFERENCES ORDER(ORD_ID)
);
```

```
CREATE TABLE ORDER (
ORD_ID INTEGER NOT NULL PRIMARY KEY,
...
);
```

You map the relationship to these physical tables by using the relationships element in the Geronimo-specific deployment descriptor, as shown here:

```
<relationships>
    <ejb-relation>
        <ejb-relationship-role>
            <relationship-role-source>
                <ejb-name>Order</ejb-name>
            </relationship-role-source>
            <cmr-field>
                <cmr-field-name>lineItems</cmr-field-name>
             </cmr-field>
            <role-mapping>
                <cmr-field-mapping>
                    <key-column>ORD_ID</key-column>
                    <foreign-key-column>ORDER_ID</foreign-key-column>
                 </cmr-field-mapping>
            </role-mapping>
        </ejb-relationship-role>
    </ejb-relation>

</relationships>
```

Here, the foreign-key-column-on-source element is not present because the foreign key is not defined on the source EJB (Order).

Many-to-Many Relationship

You create a many-to-many relationship by using an intermediate table. Let's consider a sample relationship between a Student entity and a Course entity in which a student can take one or more courses and a course can contain one or more students. Here, an enrollment table will be our intermediate table.

The EJB JAR deployment descriptor defines the relationship, as shown here:

```
<ejb-jar>
<enterprise-beans>
...
</enterprise-beans>
<relationships>
        <ejb-relation>
            <ejb-relation-name> StudentCourseRelation </ejb-relation-name>
```

```
            <ejb-relationship-role>
                <ejb-relationship-role-name>
                    Students-Courses
                 </ejb-relationship-role-name>
                <multiplicity> Many </multiplicity>
                <relationship-role-source>
                    <ejb-name> Student </ejb-name>
                </relationship-role-source>
                <cmr-field>
                    <cmr-field-name> courses </cmr-field-name>
                    <cmr-field-type>java util Collection</cmr-field-type>
                </cmr-field>
            </ejb-relationship-role>
            <ejb-relationship-role>
                <ejb-relationship-role-name>
                    Courses-Students
                </ejb-relationship-role-name>
                <multiplicity>Many</multiplicity>
                <relationship-role-source>
                    <ejb-name> Course </ejb-name>
                </relationship-role-source>
                <cmr-field>
                    <cmr-field-name> students </cmr-field-name>
                    <cmr-field-type>java util Collection</cmr-field-type>
                </cmr-field>
            </ejb-relationship-role>
        </ejb-relation>

</relationships>
</ejb-jar>
```

The table design for realizing this relationship is shown here:

```
CREATE TABLE STUDENT (
STUD_ID INTEGER NOT NULL PRIMARY KEY,
NAME VARCHAR(30),
...
);
CREATE TABLE COURSE (
CRS_ID INTEGER NOT NULL PRIMARY KEY,
COURSE_NAME VARCHAR(30),
...
);
CREATE TABLE ENROLLMENT (
STUDENT_ID INTEGER NOT NULL,
COURSE_ID INTEGER NOT NULL,
```

```
CONSTRAINT FK_STUD_COURSE FOREIGN KEY (STUDENT_ID)
REFERENCES STUDENT(STUD_ID),
CONSTRAINT FK_COURSE_STUDENT FOREIGN KEY (COURSE_ID)
REFERENCES COURSE(CRS_ID)
);
```

The enrollment table is the many-to-many table that maintains the student-to-course mappings. The Geronimo-specific deployment descriptor entries for this many-to-many relationship are shown here:

```
<relationships>

    <ejb-relation>
    <many-to-many-table-name>
        ENROLLMENT
    </many-to-many-table-name>
    <ejb-relationship-role>
        <relationship-role-source>
            <ejb-name>Student</ejb-name>
        </relationship-role-source>
        <cmr-field>
            <cmr-field-name>courses</cmr-field-name>
        </cmr-field>
        <role-mapping>
            <cmr-field-mapping>
                <key-column>STUD_ID</key-column>
                <foreign-key-column>STUDENT_ID</foreign-key-column>
            </cmr-field-mapping>
        </role-mapping>
    </ejb-relationship-role>

        <ejb-relationship-role>
            <relationship-role-source>
                <ejb-name>Course</ejb-name>
            </relationship-role-source>
            <cmr-field>
                <cmr-field-name>students</cmr-field-name>
            </cmr-field>
            <role-mapping>
                <cmr-field-mapping>
                    <key-column>CRS_ID</key-column>
                    <foreign-key-column>COURSE_ID</foreign-key-column>
                </cmr-field-mapping>
            </role-mapping>
        </ejb-relationship-role>
    </ejb-relation>
...
</relationships>
```

The relation defines the mapping for both the entities to the key column in the table representing the entity that contains the key-column and to the foreign key column in the many-to-many table.

Stand-Alone EJB Client

In this section, we will discuss a stand-alone client for the CMP entity bean (you can use similar code for accessing the BMP entity bean). The code fragment you use to access the bean is shown here:

```
package samples.client.student;
public static void main(String[] args){

  try {

    System.out.println("Student EJB Standalone Client ...");

    InitialContext context=getInitialContext();
    StudentHome home=(StudentHome)PortableRemoteObject.narrow(
                context.lookup("ejb/StudentCMP"),StudentHome.class);

    Random generator =new Random();
    Student student=null;
    // create students
    for (int i=1;i<=10;i++){
      student=(Student)PortableRemoteObject.narrow(home.create("f"+i,"l"+i),
              Student.class);
      int marks=generator.nextInt(101);
      student.setMarks(marks);
      System.out.println("Student [f"+i+"][l"+i+"]["+marks+"] created ...");

    }
    System.out.println("Using findByPrimaryKey ... ");

    Object obj = home.findByPrimaryKey("f1");
    student=(Student)PortableRemoteObject.narrow(obj,Student.class);
    System.out.println("Got Student ["+student.getFirstName()+
        "]["+student.getLastName()+"]["+student.getMarks()+"] ... ");
    System.out.println("Using Business Method ...<br>");
    System.out.println("Student Passed:"+student.passed()+":");

    System.out.println("Using Home Business Method...");
    int passPercentage=home.getPassPercentage();
    System.out.println("EJB Home Pass Percentage:"+passPercentage+":");
```

```
    System.out.println("Using findAll ... ");
    Collection list = home.findAll();
    for (Iterator it=list.iterator();it.hasNext();){
      student=(Student)PortableRemoteObject.narrow(it.next(),Student.class);

      System.out.println("Got Student ["+student.getFirstName()+
        "]["+student.getLastName()+"]["+student.getMarks()+"][passed:"+
        student.passed()+"]...");

      student.remove();
      System.out.println("Student Removed... ");
    }


  }catch(Exception e){
    // handle exception
  }

}
```

The getInitialContext() method is shown here:

```
private static InitialContext getInitialContext()throws Exception{
  Properties props = new Properties();

  props.setProperty("java.naming.factory.initial",
            "org.openejb.client.RemoteInitialContextFactory");
  props.setProperty("java.naming.provider.url", "localhost:4201");
  props.setProperty("java.naming.security.principal", "username");
  props.setProperty("java.naming.security.credentials", "passwd");

  return new InitialContext(props);

}
```

Note that since we access the EJB from a non-J2EE component, we need to use the JNDI name specified in the enterprise-beans/entity/jndi-name element of the entity bean's openejb-jar.xml file. Otherwise, if you are accessing the EJB from any J2EE component, like a servlet, you need to use an EJB reference. Another main difference between accessing the EJB from a stand-alone client and accessing it from a J2EE component is how a JNDI Initial-Context is created. For a stand-alone client, you need to specify an initial context factory, a JNDI provider URL, and security credentials.

To run this code, you need to have the following libraries in your classpath: geronimo-kernel-1.0.jar, geronimo-system-1.0.jar, geronimo-security-1.0.jar, geronimo-spec-j2ee-1.4-rc3.jar, openejb-core-2.0.jar, and cglib-nodep-2.1_3.jar. Of course, you will also need the entity EJB home and remote interfaces.

Summary

In this chapter, you learned about entity beans. You explored developing both bean-managed persistence and container-managed persistence beans and deploying and running them in Geronimo server. You also learned how to specify and use various container-managed relationships with entity beans. In the next chapter, we will discuss Java Message Service and message-driven beans.

CHAPTER 6

∎∎∎

JMS and
Message-Driven Beans

Java Message Service is a standard API for developing messaging applications. In a messaging application, which is asynchronous in nature, the components interact by sending and receiving messages. In an application with asynchronous behavior, the message sender need not wait for a response from the other component but can proceed with other tasks. This is the main difference between messaging applications and applications that use other connectivity mechanisms, like RMI and IIOP.

JMS defines two contracts: an application contract and a service provider contract. A JMS provider is a software component that implements these two contracts. Some of the many available JMS providers are IBM's MQSeries, open source ActiveMQ, and JBossMQ. JMS providers are explained in more detail in the next section. The application contract is an API that application components use to interact with the JMS provider, and the service provider contract is for plugging different message broker (or JMS provider) implementations into the application server. A message broker facilitates asynchronous communication between application components.

An enterprise bean can use the JMS API to send and receive messages. Sending messages is easier than receiving messages, which requires much custom coding due to the asynchronous nature of the communication. To simplify messaging, you can configure an EJB type called a message-driven bean (MDB) to receive and process JMS messages.

A typical example of an application that uses JMS is a chat application. You can have your chat clients use JMS to send messages to each other. This way, you can focus on the application logic and leave the message transport and delivery logic to the JMS provider.

In this chapter, we will first discuss JMS concepts and programming. Then, you will learn about Geronimo's support for JMS by creating a JMS client application that sends messages. Later in this chapter, we will discuss MDBs, and we will create a sample MDB to receive messages sent by the JMS client application.

Message-Oriented Middleware

Application components use messaging middleware to send and receive messages. This messaging middleware is external to the application, and in most cases, it is a vendor implementation. Such implementations typically contain mechanisms for application components to register for messages, and they deliver all received messages to their registered destinations.

Any implementation that facilitates message-oriented programming and asynchronous behavior is called Message-Oriented Middleware (MOM), or a message broker. There are many MOM implementations available, including IBM's MQSeries, BEA Tuxedo /Q, and Microsoft's MSMQ. If the MOM supports JMS, it is also known as a JMS provider. Figure 6-1 depicts a MOM.

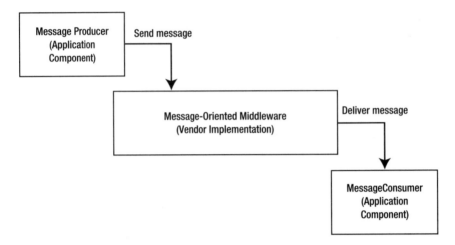

Figure 6-1. *Message-Oriented Middleware*

Java Message Service

Different middleware implementations have different ways for application components to interact with them. Using the JMS API, application components can access the messaging infrastructure in a standard way. Hence, the application components can be programmed in a totally vendor-independent way. You can plug in different messaging implementations without changing your code much, if at all.

JMS supports two types of messaging mechanisms: point-to-point and publish-subscribe. With the point-to-point mechanism, the application component can post a message to a queue, and another application component can pop this message out of the queue. With point-to-point messaging, the message is delivered to only one receiver.

Figure 6-2 depicts a queue. A queue implements a first in, first out (FIFO) model, in which the first message put in the queue is delivered first.

In a publish-subscribe model, one or more application components can register for messages with the messaging middleware. When an appropriate message arrives, the messaging middleware publishes it to all registered receivers. The messaging infrastructure used for this model is called a topic. Application components post messages to a topic, which are sent to all registered receivers for that topic. Figure 6-3 depicts a topic.

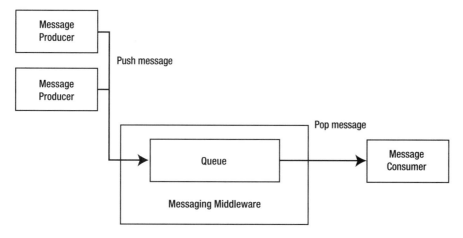

Figure 6-2. *A message queue*

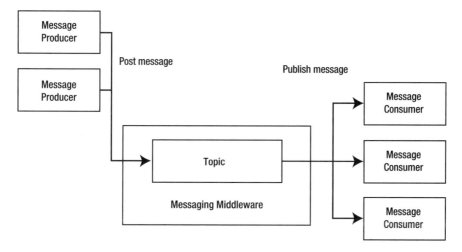

Figure 6-3. *A message topic*

Geronimo fully supports JMS 1.1, and hence you can send and receive JMS messages by using both queues and topics. Geronimo comes with the open source ActiveMQ JMS provider. This provides, among other messaging capabilities, the capability for clustering. Later in this chapter, you will learn more about Geronimo's JMS support by developing a sample JMS application to send JMS messages to a queue and to receive messages from the queue by using an MDB.

JMS Programming Model

You perform the following steps to enable an application client to use the JMS API to interact with a messaging service:

1. Locate the connection factory.

2. Create a JMS connection.

3. Create a JMS session.

4. Locate a JMS destination.

5. Create a JMS producer or a JMS consumer.

6. Send or receive a message.

Locate the JMS Connection Factory

A JMS connection factory is analogous to the JDBC data source and is a factory for JMS connection objects. You need to set up and configure a JMS connection factory in the application server before you can use it. I will explain how to do this in the next section. To access the connection factory from code, you need to perform a JNDI lookup, as shown here:

```
InitialContext ic=new InitialContext();
Object obj=Ic.lookup("jms/myJCAConnectionFactory");
QueueConnectionFactory qcf=(QueueConnectionFactory) ➥
PortableRemoteObject.narrow(obj, QueueConnectionFactory.class);
```

For a topic, use this code:

```
Object obj=ic.lookup("jms/myJCAConnectionFactory");
TopicConnectionFactory tcf=( TopicConnectionFactory) ➥
PortableRemoteObject.narrow(obj, TopicConnectionFactory.class);
```

Create a JMS Connection

To create a JMS connection to a queue, use this code:

```
QueueConnection qConnection=qfc.createQueueConnection();
```

To create a JMS connection to a topic, use this code:

```
TopicConnection tConnection=tcf.createTopicConnection();
```

Create a JMS Session

A JMS session is a factory for message consumers and message producers. In the following code, the first parameter indicates that we do not want transactions, and the second parameter indicates that auto-acknowledge should be used for the message.

```
QueueSession qSession=qConnection.createQueueSession(false, ➥
Session.AUTO_ACKNOWLEDGE);
```

To create a topic session, use this code:

```
TopicSession tSession=tConnection.createTopicSession(false,➥
Session.AUTO_ACKNOWLEDGE);
```

Create a JMS Destination

A JMS destination is either a queue or a topic. JMS destinations are deployed as managed objects in the server and need to use JNDI to look up their handle.

```
Object object = ic.lookup("queue/myQueue");
Queue queue=(Queue)PortableRemoteObject.narrow(object, Queue.class);
```

To look up a topic, use this code:

```
Object object = ic.lookup("topic/myTopic");
Topic topic=(Topic)PortableRemoteObject.narrow(object, Topic.class) ;
```

Create a JMS Producer or Consumer

To create a topic producer or subscriber, use this code:

```
TopicPublisher publisher=tSession.createPublisher(topic);
TopicSubscriber subscriber=tSession.createSubscriber(topic);
```

To create a queue sender or receiver, use this code:

```
QueueSender sender=qSession.createSender(queue);
QueueReceiver receiver=qSession.createReceiver(queue);
```

Send or Receive Messages

To publish a message to the topic, use this code:

```
TestMessage message=tSession.createTextMessage();
Message.setText("Test Message");
publisher.publish(message);
```

Use a topic subscriber to receive messages published to a topic:

```
Message message=subscriber.receive();
```

To send a message to a queue, use this code:

```
TextMessage message=qSession.createTextMessage();
Message.setText("Test Message");
sender.send(message);
```

Use a queue receiver to receive messages from the queue:

```
message message=receiver.receive();
```

Geronimo JMS Support

As noted, Geronimo uses ActiveMQ as its JMS server and supports the JMS 1.1 standard. J2EE application components can access the JMS server by using connection factories, queues, and topics. Application components can map JMS connection factories as environment resources, and queues and topics as administered objects, and access them from the code. Geronimo's JMS support is available as a prepackaged configuration: geronimo/activemq/1.0/car. The next sections describe how to utilize Geronimo to deploy and run JMS applications.

Start the JMS Server

To start the JMS server, start the configuration geronimo/activemq/1.0/car by using the following command:

```
java -jar deployer.jar geronimo/activemq/1.0/car
```

This command starts the configuration and thereby starts all its contained GBeans to bring up the ActiveMQ server listening on port 61616 for TCP transport (the URL is tcp://localhost:61616). You can change the port number in the var/config/config.xml file.

Note Clients running on the same JVM can access the server directly by using the URL vm://localhost.

You can deploy a new JMS server by creating a configuration with all the necessary GBeans and deploying it to the server. The JMS server can be deployed as a server-scoped service, an application-scoped service, or a module-scoped service, depending on whether you deploy the GBeans separately, as part of an application plan, or as part of a module plan. You can use the console application to configure the JMS server by selecting JMS Server on the Console Navigation menu.

Configure and Deploy JMS Resources

JMS resources include connection factories, queues, and topics. You deploy JMS resources as a connector module. (We will discuss connectors in detail in Chapter 8.) This process typically includes the following steps:

1. Create a deployment plan.

2. Deploy the connector.

The following code shows a sample deployment plan (the file name is dd/my-JMS-resources-plan.xml):

```
<connector xmlns="http://geronimo.apache.org/xml/ns/j2ee/connector" ➥
configId="SampleJMSResources" parentId="geronimo/activemq/1.0/car">
  <resourceadapter>
    <resourceadapter-instance>
      <resourceadapter-name>SampleJMSResources</resourceadapter-name>
      <config-property-setting name="ServerUrl">
          tcp://localhost:61616
      </config-property-setting>
      <!--
      <config-property-setting name="UserName">name</config-property-setting>
      <config-property-setting name="Password">passwd</config-property-setting>
      -->
      <workmanager>
        <gbean-link>DefaultWorkManager</gbean-link>
      </workmanager>
    </resourceadapter-instance>

    <!-- defines a ConnectionFactory -->
    <outbound-resourceadapter>
      <connection-definition>
        <connectionfactory-interface>javax.jms.ConnectionFactory
        </connectionfactory-interface>
        <connectiondefinition-instance>
          <name>SampleConnectionFactory</name>
          <implemented-interface>javax.jms.QueueConnectionFactory
          </implemented-interface>
          <implemented-interface>javax.jms.TopicConnectionFactory
          </implemented-interface>
          <connectionmanager>
            <xa-transaction> <transaction-caching /> </xa-transaction>
            <single-pool>
              <max-size>10</max-size>
              <min-size>0</min-size>
              <blocking-timeout-milliseconds>5000
              </blocking-timeout-milliseconds>
              <idle-timeout-minutes>0</idle-timeout-minutes>
              <match-one/>
            </single-pool>
          </connectionmanager>
```

```
                <global-jndi-name>jms/SampleConectionFactory</global-jndi-name>
              </connectiondefinition-instance>
            </connection-definition>
          </outbound-resourceadapter>
        </resourceadapter>

        <!-- defines a Topic -->
        <adminobject>
          <adminobject-interface>javax.jms.Topic</adminobject-interface>
          <adminobject-class>org.codehaus.activemq.message.ActiveMQTopic
          </adminobject-class>
          <adminobject-instance>
            <message-destination-name>SampleTopic</message-destination-name>
            <config-property-setting name="PhysicalName">SampleTopic
            </config-property-setting>
          </adminobject-instance>
        </adminobject>

        <!-- defines a Queue -->
        <adminobject>
          <adminobject-interface>javax.jms.Queue</adminobject-interface>
          <adminobject-class>org.codehaus.activemq.message.ActiveMQQueue
          </adminobject-class>
          <adminobject-instance>
            <message-destination-name>SampleQueue</message-destination-name>
            <config-property-setting name="PhysicalName">SampleQueue
            </config-property-setting>
          </adminobject-instance>
        </adminobject>

      </connector>
```

The preceding deployment plan contains the following sections:

Deployment plan header: This section defines a configId and a parentId for this configuration. The configId can be used to identify this configuration; for instance, when you use the deploy tool, you provide this value to start, stop, deploy, or undeploy this configuration. The default parentId should be `geronimo/activemq/1.0/car`.

JMS server connection details: The resourceadapter-instance element provides the details required for the resource adapter to connect to the JMS service broker. In our example, we specify that a JMS server is running and listening on port 61616. You also need to provide a work manager reference. A work manager is a component of the application server that the resource adapter can use to submit jobs for execution. This way, the resource adapter can utilize application server–managed thread pools to execute its work objects. The geronimo/j2ee-server/1.0/car configuration defines a work manager named DefaultWorkManager. You can use this work manager instance to configure your resource adapter.

Connection factory: A J2EE component uses a connection factory to create connection objects to interact with the resource adapter. This section defines the connection factory details that this resource adapter implements. Since we are deploying a resource adapter for JMS resources, the connection factory type should be `javax.jms.ConnectionFactory`. The connectiondefinition-instance element defines an instance of the connection definition. It includes a name that the connection factory is registered with, names of all interfaces that the connection factory implements, and a connection manager configuration. The connection manager is a component of the application server that interacts with the resource adapter to create managed connection objects. A connection manager can also provide a connection pool implementation. The global-jndi-name element specifies a name with which the connection factory should be registered with the JNDI service.

One or more admin objects: An admin object can be either a queue or a topic. You need to provide a message-destination-name and a physical name for every admin object that you define. The message-destination-name is the name with which the admin object will be registered, and the physical name is the actual name of the queue in ActiveMQ. You can have one or more logical queues configured for the same physical queue.

Once you have created the deployment plan for your JMS resources, you can deploy it in one of three ways: serverwide deployment, application-scoped deployment, or module-scoped deployment.

Serverwide Deployment

To deploy the JMS resources as a serverwide deployment, use the following command:

```
deploy.bat deploy dd/ my-JMS-resources-plan.xml ➡
 repository/activemq/rars/activemq.rar
```

Application-Scoped Deployment

To deploy the JMS resources as application-scoped resources, create an EAR file that contains the following files:

```
web-app.war
ejbs.jar
activemq.rar
sampleJMSResources-plan.xml
META-INF/application.xml
META-INF/geronimo-application.xml
```

The application.xml file should look like this:

```
<application …>
        <module><web>
                <web-uri>web-app.war</web-uri>
                <context-root>/webApp</context-root>
        </web></module>
        <module><ejb>ejbs.jar</ejb></module>
        <module><connector>activemq.rar</connector></module>
</application>
```

The geronimo-application.xml file should look like this:

```
<application …>
        <module>
                <connector>activemq.rar</connector>
                <alt-dd>sampleJMSResources-plan.xml </alt-dd>
        </module>
</application>
```

Here, the alt-dd element is used to specify the Geronimo-specific deployment plan that is packaged with the EAR. You can also choose to package the Geronimo-specific deployment plan inside the RAR, in which case you need to name this file geronimo-ra.xml.

Module-Scoped Deployment

To deploy JMS resources that are module scoped, include an additional resource element in the Geronimo deployment plan for that module, as shown here:

```
<web-app ...>
...
  <resource>
    <external-rar>
       activemq/rars/activemq-ra-3.1-M5.rar
    </external-rar>
    <connector xmlns="http://geronimo.apache.org/xml/ns/j2ee/connector" ➥
version="1.5" configId="SampleJMSResources" ➥
parentId=" geronimo/activemq/1.0/car">
...
    </connector>
  </resource>
</web-app>
```

The external RAR should refer to the path of the ActiveMQ RAR relative to the Geronimo repository (GERONIMO-HOME/repository).

Access the JMS Resources from a Stand-Alone Client

The following code shows how you can access the JMS connection factory from a stand-alone client and use it to communicate with the underlying JMS provider. This code listing shows how you can send a message to a queue. Later in this chapter, we will develop an MDB to receive the message sent by this client.

```
Properties props = new Properties();
props.setProperty("java.naming.factory.initial",
           "org.openejb.client.RemoteInitialContextFactory");
props.setProperty("java.naming.provider.url", "localhost:4201");
props.setProperty("java.naming.security.principal", "username");
props.setProperty("java.naming.security.credentials", "passwd");
```

```
InitialContext ic=new InitialContext(props);

Object obj=ic.lookup("jms/myJMSConnectionFactory");

QueueConnectionFactory qcf=( QueueConnectionFactory) ➡
PortableRemoteObject.narrow(obj, QueueConnectionFactory.class);

QueueConnection qConnection=qcf.createQueueConnection();

QueueSession qSession=qConnection.createQueueSession(false,  ➡
Session.AUTO_ACKNOWLEDGE);

Object object = ic.lookup("SampleQueue");
Queue queue=(Queue)PortableRemoteObject.narrow(object, Queue.class) ;

QueueSender sender=qSession.createSender(queue);

TextMessage message=qSession.createTextMessage();
message.setText("Sample Message");
sender.send(message);
```

The JNDI lookup name for the connection factory should be the value given for the element outbound-resourceadapter/connection-definition/connectiondefinition-instance/global-jndi-name in your deployment plan. The JNDI lookup name for a queue or a topic should match the value given in admin-object/adminobject-instance/message-destination-name in your deployment plan.

Access JMS Resources from Web Applications, EJBs, and Application Clients

You can access the deployed JMS resources from J2EE components, such as web applications, EJBs, and J2EE clients. The following code shows the same client logic discussed in the previous section implemented as a web application (a servlet):

```
InitialContext ic=new InitialContext();

Object obj=ic.lookup("java:comp/env/jms/myJMSConnectionFactory");
QueueConnectionFactory qcf=( QueueConnectionFactory) ➡
PortableRemoteObject.narrow(obj, QueueConnectionFactory.class);

QueueConnection qConnection=qcf.createQueueConnection();

QueueSession qSession=qConnection.createQueueSession(false,  ➡
Session.AUTO_ACKNOWLEDGE);

Object object = ic.lookup("java:comp/env/queue/myQueue");
Queue queue=(Queue)PortableRemoteObject.narrow(object, Queue.class) ;
```

```
QueueSender sender=qSession.createSender(queue);

TextMessage message=qSession.createTextMessage();
message.setText("Sample Message");
sender.send(message);
```

This code is the same as that shown in the previous section—the difference concerns the JNDI lookup. Since the servlet runs in the J2EE environment, you need not provide the connectivity details when you create the InitialContext reference. Also, in this case, you can use logical names (resource references) for JNDI lookup. You need to define these references in your web.xml file and resolve the references in your geronimo-web.xml file, as described here:

- Add a resource reference entry for the connection factory and a resource environment reference entry for each queue and topic reference in the web.xml deployment descriptor (or EJB standard deployment descriptor in the case of EJBs), as shown here:

```
<resource-ref>
  <res-ref-name>jms/myJMSConnectionFactory</res-ref-name>
  <res-type>javax.jms.ConnectionFactory</res-type>
  <res-auth>Container</res-auth>
  <res-sharing-scope>Shareable</res-sharing-scope>
</resource-ref>
<resource-env-ref>
  <resource-env-ref-name>queue/myQueue</resource-env-ref-name>
  <resource-env-ref-type>javax.jms.Queue</resource-env-ref-type>
</resource-env-ref>
```

- You need to resolve these references by linking them to the actual JMS resources in the Geronimo-specific deployment descriptor (geronimo-web.xml or openejb-jar.xml). For a web application, add the following entries in geronimo-web.xml:

```
<resource-ref>
  <ref-name>jms/myJMSConnectionFactory</ref-name>
  <resource-link>SampleConnectionFactory</resource-link>
</resource-ref>
<resource-env-ref>
  <ref-name>queue/myQueue</ref-name>
  <message-destination-link>SampleQueue</message-destination-link>
</resource-env-ref>
```

The resource-link element should match the value of the element connectiondefinition-instance/name in the JMS resources' deployment plan. Also, the message-destination-link element should match the value specified in the adminobject-instance/message-destination-name element in the JMS resources' deployment plan.

As of J2EE 1.4, you can configure a reference to a message destination (like a queue or a topic) by using a message-destination-ref element in the web.xml file. The advantage of using this approach over using a resource-env-ref element is that you do not need any corresponding entries in the Geronimo-specific deployment descriptor. A sample message-destination-ref element is shown here:

```
<message-destination-ref>
        <message-destination-ref-name>queue/myQueue</message-destination-ref-name>
        <message-destination-type>javax.jms.Queue</message-destination-type>
        <message-destination-usage>Consumes</message-destination-usage>
        <message-destination-link>SampleQueue</message-destination-link>
</message-destination-ref>

<message-destination>
        <message-destination-name>SampleQueue</message-destination-name>
</message-destination>
```

Here, the message-destination-name should match the value specified in the adminobject-instance/name element in the JMS resources' deployment plan.

From your web application (or from your EJB), you can access the JMS resources as shown here:

```
InitialContext ic=new InitialContext();
Object obj=Ic.lookup("jms/ myJMSConnectionFactory ");
Object object = ic.lookup("queue/myQueue ");
Queue queue=(Queue)PortableRemoteObject.narrow(object, Queue.class) ;
```

The JNDI name for the connection factory lookup should be the value of the element resource-ref/ref-name in the J2EE standard deployment descriptor for your component. Similarly, the JNDI name for the message destination lookup should be the value of the element resource-env-ref/ref-name or of the message-destination-ref/message-destination-ref-name element in the J2EE standard deployment descriptor of your component.

Message-Driven Beans

EJB 2.0 introduced a new type of EJB, message-driven beans. MDBs can receive JMS messages delivered to a queue or a topic from a JMS client. If you need to do things in parallel, using an MDB is the recommended way to achieve this. Consider this simple example—imagine you need to develop a search application that can search multiple data sources. For high-performance results, you need to search the different sources in parallel. If you put your search logic in your EJB, you cannot achieve parallel execution. The best approach is to have your EJB produce as many messages as there are data sources and have an MDB perform the actual search in a particular data source. The EJB can wait in a temporary response queue for a response. In this case, parallelism is achieved because the application server processes MDB execution in
a separate parallel thread.

The characteristics of an MDB are as follows:

- An MDB does not have a remote (or local) interface or a home interface.

- An MDB is stateless.

- An MDB has a single business method, onMessage(). This callback method is invoked when a message is delivered to the JMS destination that the MDB is configured with.

To create, deploy, and use an MDB, you must follow these steps:

1. Write the bean implementation class.

2. Write the bean standard deployment descriptor.

3. Write the Geronimo-specific deployment descriptor.

4. Package and deploy the MDB.

5. Write the MDB client.

Write the Bean Implementation Class

The first step is to write the bean implementation class. We will consider a sample MDB that can receive messages sent by the client JMS application that we developed earlier. The following code shows the bean implementation:

```
package samples.jms.client.mdb;

// imports

public class JMSClientMDB implements MessageDrivenBean,
MessageListener {
    private transient MessageDrivenContext mdc = null;

    public JMSClientMDB() {
    }

    public void setMessageDrivenContext(MessageDrivenContext mdc) {
        this.mdc = mdc;
    }

    public void ejbCreate(){ }

    public void onMessage(Message message) {
       try{
          if(message instanceof TextMessage){
               System.out.println("Message is :"+((TextMessage)message).getText());
          }
       }catch(Exception e){
          // handle exception
       }

    }

    public void ejbRemove(){ }

}
```

The container treats an MDB like it treats a stateless session bean. It creates and manages a pool of MDB instances. The container invokes the ejbCreate() method when an MDB instance is created, and when the container removes the instance, it invokes an ejbRemove() method. For every message that is delivered to the message destination, the container invokes the onMessage() method.

Write the Bean Standard Deployment Descriptor

The standard deployment descriptor for an MDB is the file ejb-jar.xml. You can use the same deployment descriptor for specifying your MDB that you use for your other EJB types. Figure 6-4 shows the elements of the deployment descriptor that are relevant to an MDB.

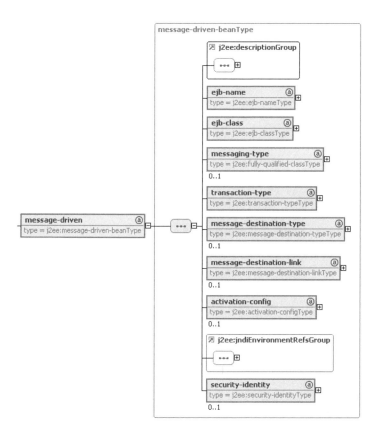

Figure 6-4. *Standard deployment descriptor elements for an MDB*

Table 6-1 describes these elements.

Table 6-1. *The ejb-jar.xml Elements Specific to MDBs*

Element	Description
ejb-name	This is a name for the MDB.
ejb-class	This is the fully qualified class name for the bean class.
messaging-type	This is the fully qualified class name for the messaging listener type. The default value is `javax.jms.MessageListener`.
transaction-type	This element specifies whether the transaction is container managed or bean managed. Its value should be either `Bean` or `Container`.
message-destination-type	This should be either `javax.jms.Queue` or `javax.jms.Topic`.
message-destination-link	This specifies a link to the actual message destination. This element should match the message-destination-name element of message-destination in the same deployment plan.
activation-config	This element specifies one or more name and value properties that are required by the JMS resource adapter providing the JMS connections to a message broker. The name and value properties are specific to the messaging type and the resource adapter. The following property names are recognized: destination, acknowledgeMode, messageSelector, destinationType, and subscriptionDurability.
jndiEnvironmentRefsGroup	This refers to a set of elements that includes resource references, EJB references, resource environment references, and message destination references.
security-identity	This element specifies the security identity with which the MDB should be invoked.

The deployment descriptor for the sample MDB is shown here:

```
<?xml version="1.0" encoding="UTF-8"?>

<ejb-jar version="2.1" xmlns="http://java.sun.com/xml/ns/j2ee" ➥
xmlns:xsi="http://www.w3.org/2001/XMLSchema-instance" ➥
xsi:schemaLocation="http://java.sun.com/xml/ns/j2ee ➥
http://java.sun.com/xml/ns/j2ee/ejb-jar_2_1.xsd">
  <display-name>JMS Client MDB</display-name>
  <enterprise-beans>
    <message-driven>
      <display-name>JMSClientMDB</display-name>
      <ejb-name>JMSClientMDB</ejb-name>
      <ejb-class>samples.jms.client.mdb.JMSClientMDB</ejb-class>
      <messaging-type>javax.jms.MessageListener</messaging-type>
      <transaction-type>Container</transaction-type>
      <activation-config>
        <activation-config-property>
          <activation-config-property-name>
              destination
          </activation-config-property-name>
```

```
            <activation-config-property-value>
                SampleQueue
            </activation-config-property-value>
        </activation-config-property>
        <activation-config-property>
            <activation-config-property-name>
                destinationType
             </activation-config-property-name>
            <activation-config-property-value>
                javax.jms.Queue
            </activation-config-property-value>
        </activation-config-property>
      </activation-config>
    </message-driven>
  </enterprise-beans>
</ejb-jar>
```

The activation-config-property elements named destination and destinationType are required, and they should be the physical queue name (as given in the resource deployment plan) and the admin object type (`javax.jms.Queue` or `javax.jms.Topic`).

Write the Geronimo-Specific Deployment Descriptor

A Geronimo-specific deployment descriptor is required to define various properties that are required for MDB deployment and execution. Figure 6-5 depicts the elements relevant to MDBs in the openejb-jar.xml Geronimo-specific deployment plan.

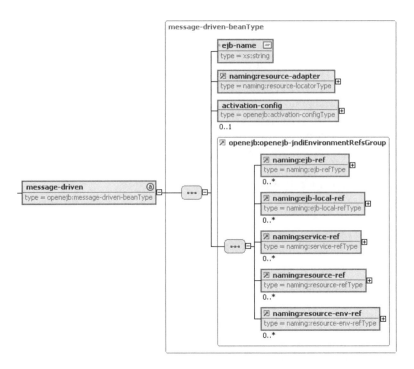

Figure 6-5. *Subelements of the message-driven element in the Geronimo-specific EJB deployment plan*

The following list describes these elements:

- *ejb-name*: This should match the ejb-name element in the standard deployment descriptor.

- *resource-adapter*: One or more message broker resource adapters can be installed with the Geronimo server. This element specifies which resource adapter this MDB should be associated with. You can either provide the JSR 77–style object name for the resource adapter or specify a resource adapter link, as shown here:

```
<resource-adapter>
        <resource-link>SampleJMSResources</resource-link>
</resource-adapter>
```

In this case, the resource-link value should match the resourceadapter-name value specified in the deployment plan for that resource adapter.

- *activation-config*: This specifies a set of activation-config properties (a pair of activation-config-property-name and activation-config-property-value elements) specific to ActiveMQ. There are two required properties: destinationType and destination. The destinationType property is similar to the message-destination-type element in the ejb-jar.xml file. The destination property should specify the physical name of a queue or a topic in ActiveMQ. Some of the other properties are username, password, and messageSelector.

- *openejb-jndiEnvironmentRefsGroup*: This defines elements for resolving references to EJBs, resources, message destinations, and administered objects.

The Geronimo-specific deployment plan for the sample application is given here:

```
<?xml version="1.0" encoding="UTF-8"?>
<openejb-jar
xmlns="http://www.openejb.org/xml/ns/openejb-jar" ➥
xmlns:naming="http://geronimo.apache.org/xml/ns/naming" ➥
xmlns:security="http://geronimo.apache.org/xml/ns/security" ➥
xmlns:sys="http://geronimo.apache.org/xml/ns/deployment" ➥
configId="JMSClientMDB"
parentId="geronimo/activemq/1.0/car">
  <enterprise-beans>
    <message-driven>
      <ejb-name>JMSClientMDB</ejb-name>
      <resource-adapter>
        <resource-link>SampleJMSResources</resource-link>
      </resource-adapter>
    </message-driven>
  </enterprise-beans>
</openejb-jar>
```

Here, notice the resource-adapter element that binds this MDB to the JMS resources' resource adapter SampleJMSResources.

Package and Deploy the MDB

You can package your MDB with other EJBs in a single EJB JAR file and then deploy the EJB JAR. In addition, you need to make sure that you have already set up the JMS message broker and the required message destinations (queues and topics).

Write the MDB Client

You can use the JMS client that we developed earlier in this chapter as the client for this MDB. First, deploy the MDB, and then run the JMS client. You will notice that the MDB's onMessage() method is invoked for every message that is put into the queue.

In general, an MDB client can be any J2EE component or a client program that uses JMS to send messages to the message destination that is set up for your MDB. From a J2EE component, you need to follow these steps to create and configure an MDB client:

1. Define a resource-ref element in the standard deployment descriptor file for obtaining a connection factory to the resource adapter.

2. Define a resource-ref element in the Geronimo-specific deployment plan to resolve the reference and map it to a deployed resource adapter instance.

3. For each queue or topic, define a resource-env-ref element in the standard deployment descriptor.

4. Define a corresponding resource-env-ref element in the Geronimo-specific deployment plan to resolve references to any admin object (queue or topic) defined in the resource adapter.

5. Look up the connection factory and the admin object by using their logical names specified in the standard deployment descriptor.

6. Use JMS API to send messages that need to be handled by the MDB.

Summary

In this chapter, you learned about JMS programming concepts and about how Geronimo supports JMS through the open source ActiveMQ message broker. You also learned about message-driven beans and how to develop, configure, and deploy them by using Geronimo. In the next chapter, we will explore enterprise applications.

CHAPTER 7

■■■

J2EE Enterprise Applications

Consider a typical three-tiered web application. It has a web presentation tier, a business tier, and a data access tier. You can package the presentation tier as a WAR, the business tier as an EJB JAR, and the data access tier as a utility JAR (or as a connector RAR). In this case, when you have dependent modules that need to be processed as a unit, you use an enterprise application.

In this chapter, you'll learn how to use Geronimo to deploy and run enterprise applications. You'll also familiarize yourself with the general characteristics of enterprise applications.

J2EE Application Overview

A J2EE application consists of one or more J2EE modules (which include EJB, web, application client, and J2EE connector modules) and an application deployment descriptor. It provides a convenient way of assembling, packaging, and deploying multiple dependent J2EE modules as a unit. A J2EE module is composed of one or more J2EE components (like servlets, JSPs, and EJBs) and represents the basic assembly unit that can be independently deployed into any J2EE-compliant container.

J2EE application development includes the following stages:

1. Application component creation

2. Application assembly

3. Application deployment

Figure 7-1 depicts the life cycle of a J2EE application.

Application component creation involves developing J2EE components and then packaging them as J2EE modules. As mentioned, a J2EE module can be one of the following types: web, EJB, application client, or resource adapter. A web module consists of one or more web components packaged as a WAR, an EJB module consists of one or more EJBs packaged as an EJB JAR file, an application client module consists of application client classes packaged as a JAR file, and a resource adapter module consists of J2EE connector components packaged as a RAR. (We will discuss J2EE connectors in detail in Chapter 8.) Packaged with a module is a module-specific deployment descriptor file that describes the module. If required, an individual module can be deployed without further development into a J2EE application server.

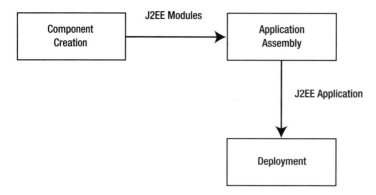

Figure 7-1. *J2EE application life cycle*

Application assembly involves assembling one or more J2EE modules to create a J2EE application. J2EE applications are packaged as EAR files. Basically, an EAR file is a JAR file with an .ear extension. The most significant difference between an EAR and a JAR is that the former contains enterprise application deployment descriptors, and hence the application server can identify and deploy all its application modules. Figure 7-2 depicts the composition of an EAR file.

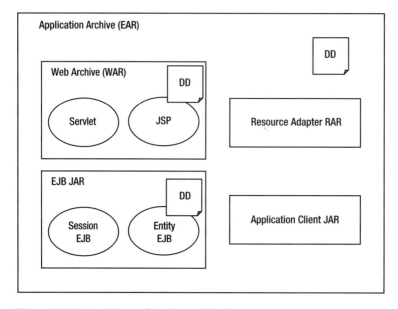

Figure 7-2. *Enterprise application packaging*

Besides containing module files, the application archive can contain utility JAR files that are referenced by its modules. Application module archives can specify dependencies by listing the dependent JARs as Class-Path entries in the JAR MANIFEST file.

In addition to packaging the application as an EAR file, the application assembler performs the following steps to assemble a J2EE application:

1. Links all internally satisfied dependencies of components in all modules in the application. Every ejb-link element in the module deployment descriptor needs to be properly linked with an EJB in the application.

2. If necessary, renames (or redefines) security role names defined in the modules. This is required when different modules in the same application define the same security role name to represent two different roles or when different modules define two different names to represent the same security role. Alternatively, the application deployment descriptor can define all the security roles that are common to the modules.

3. Assigns a unique context root for every web module in the application.

4. Resolves all dependencies that are specified in the MANIFEST file of every module. A module can use the JAR Class-Path mechanism to specify its dependencies with other JAR files. All JAR files that a module depends on need to be packaged with the EAR file. The assembler can put these files in any directory structure right under the root of the EAR file.

Figure 7-3 shows a typical EAR file.

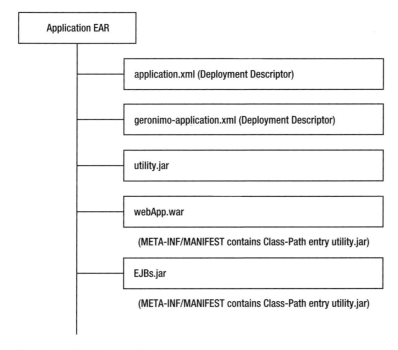

Figure 7-3. *Typical EAR file*

Here, the application.xml file is the deployment descriptor of the J2EE application. Often, additionally, an application assembler will create a new, module-specific deployment descriptor to override existing deployment descriptors that are packaged within a module. The assembler defines the alternate deployment descriptor by using the alt-dd element in the application.xml file. This way, the assembler can change deployment values without modifying the deployment descriptor packaged within a module.

The EAR file shown in Figure 7-3 contains a utility JAR, a web module (webApp.war file), and an EJB JAR (EJBs.jar file). The MANIFEST file of both the web module and the EJB JAR specifies a dependency on the utility JAR by using the Class-Path mechanism. All JAR files mentioned by using the MANIFEST Class-Path entry of a module are resolved relative to the module itself. Here is a simple MANIFEST file that shows how to use the Class-Path entry to specify dependencies:

```
Manifest-Version: 1.0
Class-Path: utility.jar
```

Now, let's turn to our enterprise application example, which will illustrate some of the steps we just discussed.

Sample Enterprise Application

In this section, we will create an enterprise application that contains a web application and an EJB application. Let's use the stateful session bean example we discussed in Chapter 4 and bundle the user management web client application and the corresponding user management stateful EJB as a user management EAR.

This sample EAR contains the following files:

```
META-INF/
META-INF/MANIFEST.MF
dd/
META-INF/application.xml
META-INF/geronimo-application.xml
dd/EJBs-geronimo-plan.xml
dd/webApp-geronimo-plan.xml
userMgmtStateful-1.0.jar
userMgmtStateful-1.0.war
```

The files userMgmtStateful-1.0.jar and userMgmtStateful-1.0.war are the EJB and web modules, respectively. The META-INF/MANIFEST.MF file is the JAR MANIFEST file, and you can use it to specify library dependencies, as discussed in the previous section. The file META-INF/application.xml is the enterprise application standard deployment descriptor, and the file geronimo-application.xml is the Geronimo-specific enterprise application deployment descriptor. In the next two sections, we will discuss these descriptors in detail. The file dd/EJBs-geronimo-plan.xml is the Geronimo-specific EJB deployment plan, and dd/webApp-geronimo-plan.xml is the Geronimo-specific web deployment plan. These two deployment plans override corresponding deployment plans packaged within the EJB and web modules, respectively. This way, the application assembler can override existing deployment-specific values at deployment time without making changes directly to the deployment plan supplied by the developer.

Creating the Standard Application Deployment Descriptor

The standard application deployment descriptor is a file named application.xml. The contents of this file specify all the modules the application contains. As noted, for each of these modules, you can also specify an alternate deployment descriptor (alt-dd), which enables the application assembler to override existing values in the standard deployment descriptor packaged within the module. The assembler can also use this alternate deployment descriptor file to specify new or modified security roles. Figure 7-4 depicts the elements of a J2EE application deployment descriptor.

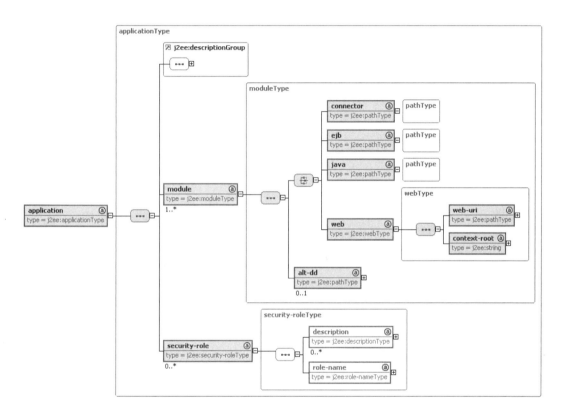

Figure 7-4. *J2EE application deployment descriptor elements*

A sample application deployment descriptor is shown here:

```
<application xmlns="http://java.sun.com/xml/ns/j2ee"
xmlns:xsi="http://www.w3.org/2001/XMLSchema-instance"
xsi:schemaLocation="http://java.sun.com/xml/ns/j2ee
http://java.sun.com/xml/ns/j2ee/application_1_4.xsd" version="1.4">

  <description>Sample application deployment descriptor</description>
  <display-name>Sample Application</display-name>
```

```
<module>
  <ejb>userMgmtStateful-1.0.jar</ejb>
</module>

<module>
  <web>
    <web-uri>userMgmtStateful-1.0.war</web-uri>
    <context-root>webapp</context-root>
  </web>
</module>

</application>
```

Creating the Geronimo-Specific Application Deployment Descriptor

In addition to providing the standard application deployment descriptor, you need to create a Geronimo-specific deployment descriptor. The Geronimo deployment descriptor is an XML file that is defined by the geronimo-application.xsd file. You can either package the Geronimo deployment plan within the application EAR or provide it as a separate file directly to the deploy tool (GERONIMO-HOME/bin/deploy.bat) when you deploy the application.

If you package the Geronimo deployment plan within the application EAR, the deployment plan needs to be a file named geronimo-application.xml. Figure 7-5 depicts the elements of the Geronimo-specific application deployment plan.

This file defines the application configId required to manage the application by using the deploy tool. The alt-dd element defines alternate Geronimo-specific deployment descriptors that need to be used for the modules. This is needed when the modules are not packaged with a Geronimo-specific deployment plan or when the application assembler decides to override the Geronimo-specific deployment plan with a new deployment plan.

A sample Geronimo deployment plan is shown here:

```
<application xmlns="http://geronimo.apache.org/xml/ns/j2ee/application"
configId="MyApp" parentId="geronimo/j2ee-server/1.0/car">

  <module>
    <ejb>userMgmtStateful-1.0.jar</ejb>
    <alt-dd>dd/EJBs-geronimo-plan.xml</alt-dd>
  </module>

  <module>
    <web>userMgmtStateful-1.0.war</web>
    <alt-dd>dd/webApp-geronimo-plan.xml</alt-dd>
  </module>

</application>
```

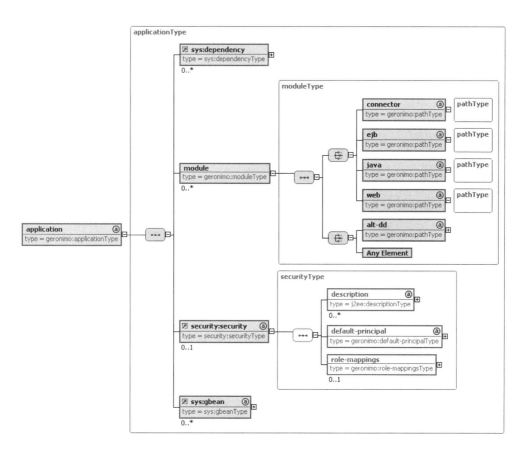

Figure 7-5. *Geronimo-specific application deployment plan*

While the application.xml file can define alt-dd elements for module-specific standard deployment descriptors, the Geronimo deployment plan can define alt-dd elements for module-specific Geronimo deployment plans. In the preceding example, note that we override the Geronimo deployment descriptors contained within the modules with the deployment descriptors given in the dd directory in the application EAR. The new EJB deployment descriptor is shown here:

```
<?xml version="1.0" encoding="UTF-8"?>
<openejb-jar
xmlns="http://www.openejb.org/xml/ns/openejb-jar"
xmlns:naming="http://geronimo.apache.org/xml/ns/naming"
xmlns:security="http://geronimo.apache.org/xml/ns/security"
xmlns:sys="http://geronimo.apache.org/xml/ns/deployment"
configId="MyApp/StatefulUserManagement"
parentId="geronimo/j2ee-server/1.0/car">
```

```
  <enterprise-beans>
    <session>
      <ejb-name>sfUserMgmt</ejb-name>
      <jndi-name>ejb/MyAppStatefulUserMgmt</jndi-name>
    </session>
  </enterprise-beans>
</openejb-jar>
```

The new web application deployment descriptor is shown here:

```
<?xml version="1.0" encoding="UTF-8"?>

<web-app xmlns="http://geronimo.apache.org/xml/ns/web"
 xmlns:naming="http://geronimo.apache.org/xml/ns/naming"
 xmlns:sec="http://geronimo.apache.org/xml/ns/security"
 configId="MyApp/StatefulUserMgmtClient" parentId="geronimo/j2ee-server/1.0/car">

<context-root>MyAppStatefulUserMgmtClient</context-root>
<context-priority-classloader>true</context-priority-classloader>

<ejb-ref>
  <ref-name>ejb/sfUserMgmt</ref-name>

  <target-name>geronimo.server:EJBModule=userMgmtStateful-1.0.jar,➥
J2EEApplication=MyApp,J2EEServer=geronimo,j2eeType=StatefulSessionBean,➥
name=sfUserMgmt</target-name>
</ejb-ref>

</web-app>
```

Notice that the configId values are overriden in the new deployment descriptors and that the web plan has totally redefined the EJB reference.

Deploying J2EE Applications in Geronimo

You can deploy and run a J2EE 1.4 (or earlier) application packaged as an EAR file in Geronimo. Deploy the EAR file as shown here:

```
java -jar deployer.jar userMgmtStateful-1.0.ear
```

Or, you can use this command:

```
deploy.bat deploy userMgmtStateful-1.0.ear
```

You can also deploy the application by providing the Geronimo deployment plan directly to the deploy tool, as shown here:

```
java -jar deployer.jar userMgmtStateful-1.0.ear my-application-deployment-plan.xml
```

Java Pet Store Demo

For more practice with enterprise applications, you can go to the Geronimo wiki for step-by-step instructions on running the Java Pet Store application on Geronimo (`http://wiki.apache.org/geronimo/PetStore`). The Geronimo source package ships with a diff file that has a record of all changes that should be made to the Pet Store application, which you can download from Sun's web site (`http://java.sun.com/j2ee//1.4/download.html#samples`), to run it on Geronimo. With the diff file, you can use the patch command on UNIX to make the necessary modifications automatically and then build it to create the deployable. Once you deploy the Pet Store application, you can access it at `http://localhost:8080/petstore`. The admin and supplier applications are available at `http://localhost:8080/admin` and `http://localhost:8080/supplier`, respectively.

Summary

Using enterprise applications enables you to process multiple dependent J2EE modules as a unit. In this chapter, you learned how to assemble, package, and deploy J2EE applications in Geronimo. In the next chapter, we will explore web services and J2EE connectors.

■ ■ ■

CHAPTER 8

Developing Web Services and J2EE Connectors

Web services define a standard way for interconnecting web applications. They expose service implementations to clients over the web infrastructure. In simple terms, a web service is a web application with no user interface. Client applications can build their own user interfaces around the exposed services. You can build your own search screens and still utilize your favorite search engine (exposing the search functionality as a web service) to perform the search. Geronimo implements JSR 109/921 (the enterprise web services specification) and allows you to create, deploy, and run web services. Internally, Geronimo uses Apache Axis to implement the SOAP transport and the required JAX-RPC support.

J2EE connectors are J2EE application components that provide connectivity to resource managers like databases, JMS providers, enterprise applications, and enterprise resource planning (ERP) systems. Geronimo uses connectors extensively; database connection pools and JMS provider connectivity are implemented and deployed as J2EE connectors. Thus, if you need to create a database connection pool or define a JMS connection factory and JMS administered objects (like a queue or a topic), you need to deploy a corresponding connector along with a plan to customize the definitions for this deployment instance.

The first section of this chapter discusses utilizing Geronimo server to create, deploy, and run web services. You will learn how to expose a J2EE component's functionality as web services and how to consume web services from J2EE components. In this chapter, you'll also explore the J2EE connector architecture by using Geronimo to create and deploy a simple connector.

Web Services

Figure 8-1 depicts the various possibilities of exposing and consuming web services in J2EE.

You can implement and expose a web service in J2EE in one of two ways: by using a JAX-RPC service endpoint or by using an EJB service endpoint. The choice of a particular endpoint type is primarily based on whether the business logic uses enterprise beans. If the business logic uses enterprise beans, it is often convenient to expose the EJB as the web service endpoint. If the application is primarily web tier based, you should use a JAX-RPC service endpoint.

You can consume a web service from your servlets, EJBs, JAX-RPC stand-alone clients, J2EE application clients, or SOAP clients. You do this by defining a web service reference in the J2EE component's standard deployment descriptor and resolving the reference in the Geronimo-specific deployment descriptor for that component by pointing to the target web service.

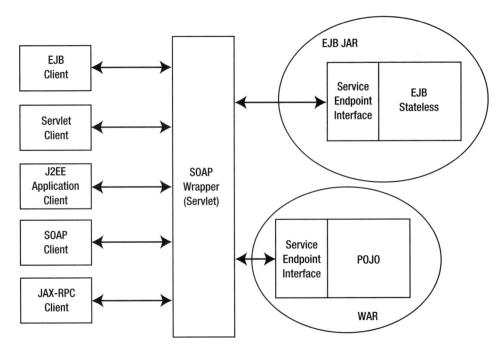

Figure 8-1. *Web services and clients*

Using Geronimo to Implement a Web Service

In this section, we'll discuss in more detail the two approaches to implementing web services.

JAX-RPC Service Endpoint Approach

With this approach, you use Geronimo to wrap your Java POJO-based service implementation as a servlet that delegates web service requests to your service implementation class. To implement your web service by using this approach, you need to follow these steps:

1. Write the service interface (service endpoint interface).

2. Write the service implementation.

3. Create the standard web deployment descriptor.

4. Create the Geronimo-specific web deployment descriptor.

5. Generate the Web Service Descriptor Language (WSDL) file and JAX-RPC mapping.

6. Create the web service deployment descriptor.

7. Package and deploy the web service.

Write the Service Interface

The service interface needs to be a valid RMI remote interface. Its methods should throw the RMI RemoteException in addition to any application-defined exceptions.

```
package samples.ws.web;

import java.rmi.Remote;
import java.rmi.RemoteException;

public interface Calculator extends Remote {

  public int add(int num1, int num2) throws RemoteException;
}
```

Write the Service Implementation

The service implementation is a plain Java class that implements the service interface methods.

```
package samples.ws.web;

import java.rmi.Remote;

public class CalculatorImpl implements Calculator {

  public int add(int num1, int num2){
    return num1+num2;
  }
}
```

The implementation class is not required to explicitly implement the service interface—it need only implement the methods defined in the interface. Also, please note that the implementation methods do not throw the RMI RemoteException.

Create the Standard Web Deployment Descriptor

The web service is deployed as a web application, and hence you need a web deployment descriptor (web.xml file).

```
<web-app>
  <display-name>WS Web App</display-name>
  <description>Web services Web Application</description>

  <servlet>
    <servlet-name>CalculatorServlet</servlet-name>
    <servlet-class>samples.ws.web.CalculatorImpl
    </servlet-class>
  </servlet>

  <servlet-mapping>
    <servlet-name>CalculatorServlet</servlet-name>
    <url-pattern>calculatorService</url-pattern>
  </servlet-mapping>
</web-app>
```

Here, you can see that the servlet-class element refers to the service implementation class even though it is not actually a servlet. JSR 109 requires the container to create a wrapper servlet and use it to dispatch web service requests to the service implementation. The servlet-mapping element defines a URL pattern (along with the context root for the web application) that can be used to access the web service. The web service will be available at `http://host:port/context-root/url-pattern`.

Create the Geronimo-Specific Web Deployment Descriptor

The Geronimo-specific deployment descriptor (geronimo-web.xml) is required to specify the web application context root and other details, like the Geronimo configuration ID for the application.

```
<?xml version="1.0" encoding="UTF-8"?>

<web-app xmlns="http://geronimo.apache.org/xml/ns/web" ➡
xmlns:naming="http://geronimo.apache.org/xml/ns/naming" ➡
xmlns:sec="http://geronimo.apache.org/xml/ns/security" ➡
configId="sample.sampleWS" parentId="geronimo/j2ee-server/1.0/car">

  <context-root>sampleWS</context-root>
  <context-priority-classloader>true
  </context-priority-classloader>
</web-app>
```

Generate the WSDL File and JAX-RPC Mapping

WSDL defines the web service in a language-neutral and standard way. A JAX-RPC mapping file maps standard web service types to Java as defined by the JAX-RPC specification. You can generate both the WSDL file and the JAX-RPC mapping from the Java service interface as implementation classes. Let's use Sun's Java Web Services Developer Pack (JWSDP) 1.4 to generate the WSDL file and the mapping file.

JWSDP requires you to create a file (let's call it config.xml) with the contents shown here:

```
<configuration xmlns="http://java.sun.com/xml/ns/jax-rpc/ri/config">
..<service name="CalculatorService" ➡
targetNamespace="http://samples.ws.web" ➡
typeNamespace="http://samples.ws.web" packageName="samples.ws.web">
    <interface name="samples.ws.web.Calculator" ➡
servantName="samples.ws.web.CalculatorImpl">
    </interface>
  </service>
</configuration>
```

Now let's run the wscompile tool, as shown here:

```
wscompile -cp %PATH-TO-SERVICE-CLASSES% -gen:server ➡
-mapping calSvc-mapping.xml config.xml
```

This will generate a WSDL file (named CalculatorService.wsdl), a mapping file named calSvc-mapping.xml, and the server-side classes. You don't need the server classes since the Geronimo runtime will provide them.

Create the Web Service Deployment Descriptor

Web services require a deployment descriptor to define the service endpoint interface, the service implementation, and how the service implementation should be linked to the J2EE components. This deployment descriptor is a file named webservices.xml and is packaged along with the web application.

```
<webservices xmlns="http://java.sun.com/xml/ns/j2ee" ➥
xmlns:xsi="http://www.w3.org/2001/XMLSchema-instance" ➥
xsi:schemaLocation="http://java.sun.com/xml/ns/j2ee ➥
http://www.ibm.com/webservices/xsd/j2ee_web_services_1_1.xsd" ➥
version="1.1">
  <webservice-description>
    <webservice-description-name>Calculator Web Service
    </webservice-description-name>
    <wsdl-file>WEB-INF/CalculatorService.wsdl</wsdl-file>
    <jaxrpc-mapping-file>
      WEB-INF/calSvc-mapping.xml
    </jaxrpc-mapping-file>
    <port-component>
      <port-component-name>
        Calculator
      </port-component-name>
      <wsdl-port>CalculatorPort</wsdl-port>
      <service-endpoint-interface>
        samples.ws.web.Calculator
      </service-endpoint-interface>
      <service-impl-bean>
        <servlet-link>
          CalculatorServlet
        </servlet-link>
      </service-impl-bean>
    </port-component>
  </webservice-description>
</webservices>
```

Here, the port-component element defines the mapping between the service endpoint and the J2EE component that provides the web service implementation. The element service-impl-bean/servlet-link specifies that the container should use the CalculatorServlet (see the definition in the web deployment descriptor) and should wrap the service endpoint implementation to expose it as a web service.

Package and Deploy the Web Service

This POJO-based web service is packaged as a WAR file. The contents and the structure of the WAR file are shown here:

```
jar -tvf calculatorWS.war
```

```
META-INF/MANIFEST.MF
WEB-INF/geronimo-web.xml (Geronimo web deployment descriptor)
WEB-INF/calSvc-mapping.xml (JAX-RPC mapping file)
WEB-INF/webservices.xml (web services deployment descriptor)
WEB-INF/CalculatorService.wsdl (WSDL file)
WEB-INF/classes/ (compiled classes, including service implementation)
WEB-INF/web.xml (web deployment descriptor)
```

You deploy the web service when you deploy this WAR file, as shown here:

```
java -jar deployer.jar calculatorWS.war
```

EJB Service Endpoint Approach

You can instead use a stateless session bean as the service implementation component. This way, the service can utilize the benefits of the EJB container. To use the EJB service endpoint approach, you need to follow these steps:

1. Write the service interface (service endpoint interface).

2. Write the service implementation.

3. Create the EJB standard deployment descriptor.

4. Create the Geronimo-specific EJB deployment descriptor.

5. Generate the WSDL file and JAX-RPC mapping.

6. Create the web service deployment descriptor.

7. Package and deploy the EJB JAR.

Write the Service Interface

As it was in the first approach, the service interface is a regular RMI interface.

```
package samples.usermgmt;

import java.rmi.Remote;
import java.rmi.RemoteException;

public interface Greeting extends Remote {

  public String sayGreeting(String to) throws RemoteException;
}
```

Write the Service Implementation

As noted, the service implementation is a stateless session bean.

```
package samples.usermgmt;

//imports

public class UserManagementBean implements SessionBean {

  private SessionContext context;
  public void ejbCreate() { }
  public void ejbRemove() { }
  public void ejbActivate() { }
  public void ejbPassivate() { }

  public void setSessionContext(SessionContext context)
  {this.context=context;}

  public String sayGreeting(String to){
    return "Greetings "+to;
  }
}
```

Here, the bean class does not implement the server endpoint interface (Greeting) directly but, rather, implements all the methods in that interface.

Create the EJB Standard Deployment Descriptor

You need to create the EJB JAR XML deployment descriptor with these contents:

```
<?xml version="1.0" encoding="UTF-8"?>

<ejb-jar xmlns="http://java.sun.com/xml/ns/j2ee" ➡
xmlns:xsi="http://www.w3.org/2001/XMLSchema-instance" ➡
xsi:schemaLocation="http://java.sun.com/xml/ns/j2ee ➡
http://java.sun.com/xml/ns/j2ee/ejb-jar_2_1.xsd" ➡
version="2.1">
  <enterprise-beans>
    <session>
      <ejb-name>UserMgmt</ejb-name>
      <home>
        samples.usermgmt.UserManagementHome
      </home>
      <remote>
        samples.usermgmt.UserManagement
      </remote>
      <service-endpoint>
        samples.usermgmt.Greeting
      </service-endpoint>
```

```
      <ejb-class>
        samples.usermgmt.UserManagementBean
      </ejb-class>
      <session-type>Stateless</session-type>
      <transaction-type>Container</transaction-type>
    </session>
  </enterprise-beans>
</ejb-jar>
```

The service-endpoint element defines the service endpoint interface. This also specifies home and remote interfaces for the EJB. If you do not need remote access for the EJB, these are not required.

Create the Geronimo-Specific EJB Deployment Descriptor

Create the openejb-jar.xml file with these contents:

```
<?xml version="1.0" encoding="UTF-8"?>
<openejb-jar xmlns="http://www.openejb.org/xml/ns/openejb-jar" ➥
xmlns:naming="http://geronimo.apache.org/xml/ns/naming" ➥
xmlns:security="http://geronimo.apache.org/xml/ns/security" ➥
xmlns:sys="http://geronimo.apache.org/xml/ns/deployment" ➥
configId="UserManagement" parentId="geronimo/j2ee-server/1.0/car">
  <enterprise-beans>
    <session>
      <ejb-name>UserMgmt</ejb-name>
      <jndi-name>ejb/UserMgmt</jndi-name>
    </session>
  </enterprise-beans>
</openejb-jar>
```

Generate the WSDL File and JAX-RPC Mapping

Run the JWSDP wscompile tool to generate the WSDL file and JAX-RPC mapping:

```
wscompile -cp %PATH-TO-SERVICE-CLASSES% -gen:server ➥
-mapping greetingSvc-mapping.xml config.xml
```

Here, the config.xml file has the following contents:

```
<configuration xmlns="http://java.sun.com/xml/ns/jax-rpc/ri/config">
  <service name="GreetingService" ➥
targetNamespace="http://samples.usermgmt" ➥
typeNamespace="http://samples.usermgmt" ➥
packageName="samples.usermgmt">
  ..<interface name="samples.usermgmt.Greeting" ➥
servantName="samples.usermgmt.UserManagementBean">
  ..</interface>
  </service>
</configuration>
```

The generated WSDL file is incomplete since it doesn't specify the service endpoint address. Geronimo needs this to make the service available. In the case of a servlet-based web service, this address is available from the web application context root and the URL pattern for the servlet. In the case of an EJB-based web service, you need to edit the WSDL file and provide this address. WSDL has a service/port/address element; you need to edit this element as shown here:

```
<soap:address ➥
location="http://localhost:8080/GreetingSvc/GreetingService"/>
```

Geronimo wraps the EJB service implementation with a servlet that delegates web service requests to the EJB.

Create the Web Service Deployment Descriptor

Name this file webservices.xml.

```
<webservices xmlns="http://java.sun.com/xml/ns/j2ee" ➥
xmlns:xsi="http://www.w3.org/2001/XMLSchema-instance" ➥
xsi:schemaLocation="http://java.sun.com/xml/ns/j2ee ➥
http://www.ibm.com/webservices/xsd/j2ee_web_services_1_1.xsd" ➥
version="1.1">
  <webservice-description>
    <webservice-description-name>Greeting Web Service
    </webservice-description-name>
    <wsdl-file>META-INF/GreetingService.wsdl</wsdl-file>
    <jaxrpc-mapping-file>
      META-INF/greetingSvc-mapping.xml</jaxrpc-mapping-file>
    <port-component>
      <port-component-name>
        Greeting
      </port-component-name>
      <wsdl-port>
        GreetingPort
      </wsdl-port>
      <service-endpoint-interface>
        samples.usermgmt.Greeting
      </service-endpoint-interface>
      <service-impl-bean>
        <ejb-link>UserMgmt</ejb-link>
      </service-impl-bean>
    </port-component>
  </webservice-description>
</webservices>
```

The service-impl-bean element specifies an ejb-link element, and its value needs to match the ejb-name element of an EJB in the same EJB JAR file. You can also give a fully qualified name (RELATIVE-JAR-PATH#ejb-name) of an EJB defined in a different EJB JAR file.

Package and Deploy the EJB JAR

You need to package the EJB and the deployment descriptors in a JAR file with the contents and the structure shown here:

```
jar -tvf userMgmt.jar
META-INF/MANIFEST.MF
META-INF/GreetingService.wsdl (WSDL file)
META-INF/ejb-jar.xml (EJB standard deployment descriptor)
META-INF/greetingSvc-mapping.xml (JAX-RPC mapping file)
META-INF/openejb-jar.xml (Geronimo EJB deployment descriptor)
META-INF/webservices.xml (web service deployment descriptor)
samples/usermgmt/Greeting.class (Service interface class)
samples/usermgmt/UserManagement.class (Remote interface class)
samples/usermgmt/UserManagementBean.class (Bean class)
samples/usermgmt/UserManagementHome.class (Home interface class)
```

Deploy the EJB JAR as shown here:

```
java -jar deployer.jar userMgmt.jar
```

Consuming Web Services

You can access a web service from a Java JAX-RPC client, a J2EE application client, any SOAP client, a servlet, or an EJB. In this section, we will discuss accessing web services from a JAX-RPC client, a servlet, and an EJB. We will discuss J2EE application clients in Chapter 9.

Stand-Alone JAX-RPC Client

JAX-RPC hides the complexity of web service messaging from developers, and it helps in mapping Java objects to and from SOAP messages. Developers use the JAX-RPC programming model to develop SOAP-based web service endpoints, along with their corresponding WSDL descriptors and clients. To use JAX-RPC, we need to have a JAX-RPC runtime. We can use either Sun's JWSDP or Apache Axis as the runtime. In our example, we will use Apache Axis.

A JAX-RPC client uses one of the following mechanisms to access a web service: static stubs, dynamic proxies, or dynamic invocation interface (DII). Many JAX-RPC implementations (like Apache Axis) provide tools that can generate static stubs from WSDL for accessing the web service. When you use dynamic proxies to access a web service, no pregeneration of code is necessary. Dynamic proxies are generated on the fly, and they can be used as a remote proxy to the web service. With the DII approach, no stubs or proxies need to be generated. Using DII is very similar to using Java reflection. You fill in generic objects representing a service call to the web service and use the generic DII objects to invoke the web service method. The following code shows a JAX-RPC client that uses DII to connect to the web service:

```
import org.apache.axis.client.Call;
import org.apache.axis.client.Service;
import org.apache.axis.encoding.XMLType;
import javax.xml.namespace.QName;
import javax.xml.rpc.ParameterMode;
```

```
// …
String endpoint ="http://localhost:8080/sampleWS/calculatorService";

Service  service = new Service();
Call call = (Call) service.createCall();
call.setTargetEndpointAddress( new java.net.URL(endpoint) );
call.setOperationName(new QName("http://samples.ws.web", "add"));
call.addParameter( "num1", XMLType.XSD_INT, ParameterMode.IN );
call.addParameter( "num2", XMLType.XSD_INT, ParameterMode.IN );
call.setReturnType( XMLType.XSD_INT );

Integer ret = (Integer) call.invoke( new Object [] { ➥
new Integer(5), new Integer(10) });

System.out.println("Got result : " + ret);
// …
```

This consumes the web service hosted at the address `http://localhost:8080/sampleWS/`
`calculatorService` and invokes its add() method.

Servlet Client

To access a web service from a servlet, you need to do the following:

1. Define a service reference in the web.xml deployment descriptor.

2. Resolve the service reference in the geronimo-web.xml deployment plan.

Define a Service Reference in the web.xml File

This step involves specifying a logical name for the service that you need to access from your
servlet code. Geronimo will create a javax.xml.rpc.Service instance to represent the web service and will then bind it with the given name (service reference name) in the JNDI
environment namespace. The following code shows a sample service reference configuration:

```
<service-ref>
  <service-ref-name>service/GreetingSvc</service-ref-name>
  <service-interface>javax.xml.rpc.Service</service-interface>
  <wsdl-file>WEB-INF/GreetingService.wsdl</wsdl-file>
  <jaxrpc-mapping-file>
    WEB-INF/greetingSvc-mapping.xml
  </jaxrpc-mapping-file>
  <service-qname xmlns:ns="http://samples.usermgmt">
    ns:GreetingService
  </service-qname>
</service-ref>
```

You can access the web service from your servlet as shown here:

```
InitialContext ic=new InitialContext();
Service svc =(Service)ic.lookup("java:comp/env/service/GreetingSvc");
QName svcQname=new QName("http://samples.ws.web","GreetingPort");
Greeting port=( Greeting)svc.getPort(svcQName, Greeting.class);
String greeting=port.sayGreeting("Tom"));
```

Resolve the Service Reference in the geronimo-web.xml File

To use the service, you need to resolve the service reference and point it to the target web service instance. You do this by including a corresponding service reference entry in the Geronimo web deployment descriptor of that web application, as shown here:

```
<web-app ...>
...
<service-ref xmlns="http://geronimo.apache.org/xml/ns/naming">
  <service-ref-name>service/GreetingSvc</service-ref-name>
  <port>
    <port-name>GreetingPort</port-name>
    <protocol>http</protocol>
    <host>localhost</host>
    <port>8080</port>
    <uri>/GreetingSvc/GreetingService</uri>
  </port>
</service-ref>
...
</web-app>
```

This specifies that the service is available at the location http://localhost:8080/GreetingSvc/GreetingService.

Figure 8-2 depicts the elements and the subelements of the service-ref element.

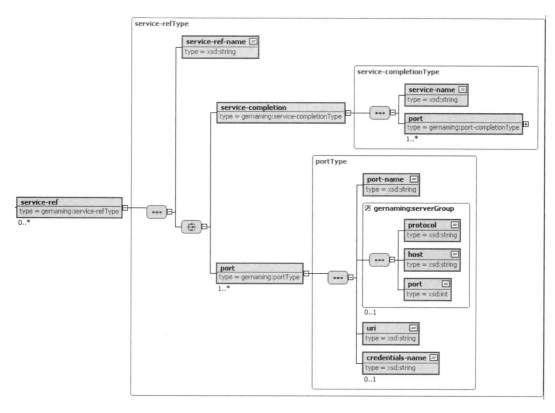

Figure 8-2. *The service-ref element in the Geronimo deployment descriptor*

Table 8-1 describes these elements.

Table 8-1. *The service-ref Element*

Element	Description
service-ref-name	This should match the service-ref-name in the standard deployment descriptor.
service-completion	This element can contain default values that Geronimo can use if the WSDL file given is incomplete. This element is not required if the WSDL file is complete.
service-name	This element specifies the name of the service if the given WSDL file does not contain a service element.
port	This element specifies one or more ports (corresponding to service endpoint interfaces). This value should match one of the ports defined in the WSDL file.
port-name	This is the port name as defined in the WSDL file.
host	This is the host where the service is available.
port	This is the network port value.

Table 8-1. *Continued*

Element	Description
uri	This is the path information required to access the web service.
credentials-name	This defines a credentials name that should be used to log in to a secure web service. This overrides any current security credentials that are available.
binding-name	This element should match a binding in the WSDL file.

EJB Client

You can also access a web service from an EJB. The mechanism is very similar to accessing a web service from a servlet. First, you need to add a service reference entry in the EJB standard deployment descriptor (ejb-jar.xml). Second, you need to resolve the service reference by providing a corresponding service reference entry in the Geronimo-specific EJB deployment descriptor (openejb-jar.xml).

J2EE Connectors

J2EE connector architecture defines a standard mechanism for J2EE application components to connect to EISs and use their resources. It requires the EIS vendor to provide a resource adapter that can plug in to any J2EE application server to provide connectivity to the EIS from any J2EE application component (like an EJB or a servlet). In this section, you'll review the J2EE connector architecture, and then you'll learn how to develop and deploy a J2EE connector.

Understanding J2EE Connector Components

Figure 8-3 depicts the various components involved in the J2EE connector architecture.

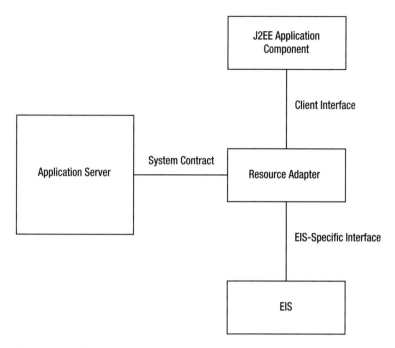

Figure 8-3. *J2EE connector components*

The following list gives a brief overview of these components:

EIS: An Enterprise Information System is any system that offers enterprise-level services to application clients. Examples include ERPs and legacy databases.

Resource: A resource in an EIS provides the EIS-specific functionality to clients. It is a record (or data) in a database system and a business object in an ERP.

Resource manager: A resource manager manages an EIS's shared resources. Often, the EIS is itself the resource manager. J2EE application components connect to the resource manager to access and use its resources. A transactional resource manager can participate in a local or a distributed transaction.

Connection: This identifies connectivity to the resource manager. The EIS client uses this to connect to the resource manager and perform transactions. A java.sql.Connection is a connection object that provides connectivity to a relational database.

Common Client Interface (CCI): This is a standard and common API clients use to access any EIS. The resource adapter is not required to support CCI. This is similar to how the JDBC Connection interface provides a vendor-independent API to perform database operations. Many connector vendors provide an EIS-specific connection interface rather than providing a CCI-compliant connection.

Resource adapter: A resource adapter is a J2EE application component, provided by the EIS vendor, that is designed to communicate with the EIS. In this sense, it is like a device driver, and it needs to support many system contracts (like life cycle management, security management, transaction management, connection management, and work management) with the application server to facilitate resource adapter pluggability with the application server. An outbound resource adapter supports synchronous requests by allowing client components to connect to the EIS by using a connection object and to perform EIS operations. An inbound resource adapter supports asynchronous processing by allowing messages to flow from the EIS into application components like message-driven beans (MDBs).

Developing, Packaging, and Deploying a J2EE Connector

In this section, we will create a simple resource adapter module that supports both outbound and inbound connectivity. This resource adapter will provide connectivity to a pseudo-EIS that produces sample text messages at preconfigured intervals. We will also discuss a web application that uses the outbound connection to communicate with the EIS through the connector, and then we'll examine an MDB that listens for messages flowing from the EIS through the connector's inbound resource adapter.

Outbound Connector

Our first example will be an outbound resource adapter. Before we delve into the code, let's look at how Geronimo and connector components interact when a connector is deployed and when the connector client uses the connector to perform operations.

Figure 8-4 shows the collaborations that take place between the application server and the connector during the deployment phase.

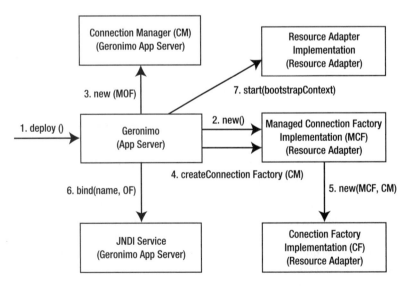

Figure 8-4. *Component interactions when a connector is deployed*

Geronimo examines the resource adapter deployment descriptor to get the class names of the resource adapter implementation class and the managed connection factory class. It uses the managed connection factory to create an instance of the connection factory implementation (SampleConnectionFactoryImpl in our example) and binds it with the JNDI service. It also invokes the start() method on the resource adapter implementation instance to allow the connector to perform any needed initialization.

Figure 8-5 depicts how a connector client uses the connector to perform operations on the EIS.

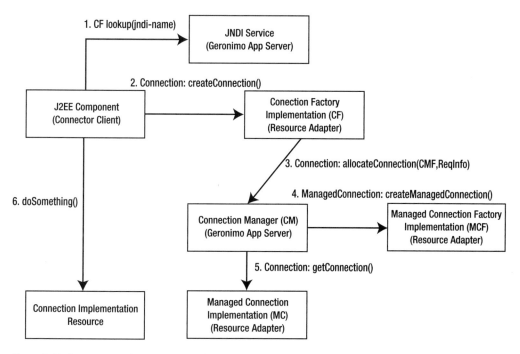

Figure 8-5. *Component interactions when a client uses the connector*

The connector client starts by performing a JNDI lookup to get the connection factory instance. It uses the connection factory to create a connection object that can be used to communicate with the underlying EIS. The connection factory, internally, invokes the connection manager to create a connection. The connection manager can implement connection pooling with the help of the managed connection factory, which the resource adapter provides. The connection manager invokes the matchManagedConnection() method or the createManagedConnection() method to get a managed connection and uses the managed connection to create the physical connection object. If the matchManagedConnection() method returns null, the application server (connection manager) creates a new managed connection instance instead of reusing any of the existing managed connections.

With this background, let us explore the various steps required to create an outbound resource adapter:

1. Create a connection manager implementation.

2. Create the connection factory interface.

3. Create the connection interface.

4. Create the connection implementation.

5. Create the connection factory implementation.

6. Create the managed connection factory implementation.

7. Create the managed connection implementation.

8. Create the resource adapter implementation.

9. Create the standard deployment descriptor.

10. Create the Geronimo-specific deployment descriptor.

11. Package and deploy the resource adapter.

Create a Connection Manager Implementation

A connection manager is a component of the application server. A connector can be used in a managed or a nonmanaged environment. In a managed environment, it runs in an application server environment, and the connection manager component of the application server is responsible for managing connection requests to the EIS. In a nonmanaged environment, the connector is used outside the environment of an application server, and it uses its own default connection manager implementation.

```
package samples.connectors.outbound;

import javax.resource.spi.*;
import javax.resource.*;
import java.io.Serializable;

public class ConnectionManagerImpl implements ConnectionManager, ➥
Serializable
{

  public ConnectionManagerImpl(){ }

  public Object allocateConnection(ManagedConnectionFactory mcf,➥
    ConnectionRequestInfo conReqInfo) throws ResourceException
  {
    ManagedConnection mc = mcf.createManagedConnection(null, ➥
conReqInfo);
    return mc.getConnection(null, conReqInfo);
  }
}
```

When the connector client uses a connection factory to create a connection, the connection factory invokes the connection manager's allocateConnection() method to allocate a connection.

Create the Connection Factory Interface

As noted, the connector client uses a connection factory to create a connection to the EIS. The DataSource class serves as a connection factory for JDBC clients, and JMSConnectionFactory is the connection factory for JMS clients. If the resource adapter supports CCI, it provides an implementation of <<TODO>> class. In our example, we will have a custom connection factory interface, as shown in the following code:

```
public interface SampleConnectionFactory
{

  public SampleConnection createConnection() throws ResourceException;

  // other create connection methods, if required
}
```

Create the Connection Interface

The connector client uses the connection object to invoke operations supported by the underlying EIS. With a JMS connection, JMS clients can send messages to and receive messages from a topic or a queue. We will define a custom connection interface with a very trivial method.

```
public interface SampleConnection
{

  public String doSomething(String text) throws ResourceException;

  public void close() throws ResourceException;
}
```

Create the Connection Implementation

Complete this step as shown here:

```
public class SampleConnectionImpl implements SampleConnection
{

  private ManagedConnectionImpl mc;
  public SampleConnectionImpl(ManagedConnectionImpl mc)
  {this.mc = mc;}

  public void close()throws ResourceException
  {
```

```
    if (mc == null) return;
    mc.setConnection(null);
    mc.sendEvent(ConnectionEvent.CONNECTION_CLOSED, null, this);
    mc = null;
  }


  public void associateConnection(ManagedConnectionImpl newMc)
  throws ResourceException
  {
    checkIfValid();
    // associate handle with new managed connection
    newMc.setConnection(this);
    mc = newMc;
  }


  public void checkIfValid() throws ResourceException
  {

    if (mc == null)
    {
      throw new ResourceException("INVALID_CONNECTION");
    }
  }


  public void invalidate()
  { mc = null; }

  public String doSomething(String text) throws ResourceException
  {
    checkIfValid();
    return "[From Sample Connection]"+text;
  }

}
```

A valid connection is one that is associated with a valid managed connection instance. The associateConnection() method associates this instance with a given managed connection.

Create the Connection Factory Implementation

In a managed environment, the application server registers an instance of the connection factory implementation with the JNDI service. The connector clients use a JNDI lookup to get a reference to the connection factory.

```
public class SampleConnectionFactoryImpl implements ➥
SampleConnectionFactory, Serializable, Referenceable
{

  private ManagedConnectionFactory mcf;
  private ConnectionManager cm;
  private Reference reference;

  public SampleConnectionFactoryImpl() { }


  public SampleConnectionFactoryImpl(➥
ManagedConnectionFactory mcf,ConnectionManager cm)
  {
    this.mcf = mcf;
    if (cm == null)
    {
      this.cm = new ConnectionManagerImpl();
    } else {this.cm = cm; }
  }


  public SampleConnection createConnection() throws ResourceException
  {
    SampleConnection con = null;
    con=(SampleConnection)cm.allocateConnection(mcf, null);
    return con;
  }

  public void setReference(Reference reference)
  {this.reference = reference;}

  public Reference getReference()
  {return reference;}
}
```

The client uses the connection factory instance to invoke the createConnection() method. The connection factory delegates this call to the connection manager to create a connection. The connection manager uses a managed connection factory to create the actual physical connection to the EIS.

Create the Managed Connection Factory Implementation

The managed connection factory serves as a factory for both the connection factory and the managed connection. When the resource adapter is deployed, the deployer creates an instance of the managed connection factory (the managed connection factory implementation class name is given in the deployment descriptor of the resource adapter), invokes its createConnectionFactory() method to create a connection factory, and makes it available to clients through JNDI.

```
public class ManagedConnectionFactoryImpl implements ➥
ManagedConnectionFactory, Serializable
{
  private transient PrintWriter out;

  public ManagedConnectionFactoryImpl() { }

  public Object createConnectionFactory(ConnectionManager ➥
conManager) throws ResourceException
  {
    SampleConnectionFactoryImpl cf = null;
    cf = new SampleConnectionFactoryImpl(this, conManager);
    return cf;
  }


  public Object createConnectionFactory() throws ResourceException
  {
    return new SampleConnectionFactoryImpl(this, null);
  }


  public ManagedConnection createManagedConnection(Subject ➥
subject, ConnectionRequestInfo cxRequestInfo) throws ResourceException
  {
    ManagedConnectionImpl mc = null;
    mc = new ManagedConnectionImpl(this, subject, cxRequestInfo);
    return mc;
  }


  public ManagedConnection matchManagedConnections(Set ➥
connectionSet, Subject subject, ConnectionRequestInfo cxRequestInfo)
throws ResourceException
  {return null;}

  public void setLogWriter(PrintWriter out) throws ResourceException
  {this.out = out;}

  public PrintWriter getLogWriter() throws ResourceException
  { return this.out; }


  public int hashCode() { // implement }

  public boolean equals(Object obj) // implement }


}
```

In a managed environment, the application server calls the createConnectionFactory() method by passing an application server–specific connection manager instance. In a nonmanaged environment, the client invokes a no-parameter version of the createConnectionFactory() method to create a connection factory. The application server's connection manager invokes the createManagedConnection() method for every new connection request. It also invokes the matchManagedConnection() method before creating a new managed connection in order to establish whether it can reuse any of the existing connections for the current request.

Create the Managed Connection Implementation

In a managed environment, the application server deals with managed connections. A managed connection serves as a wrapper to the actual physical connections to the EIS. The connector implementation can have one managed connection associate with one or more physical connections, or it can have simply a one-to-one relationship between the managed connection and the physical connection. For example, a JavaMail connector can have one managed connection for a store and a connection object for a folder within the store. A different folder in the same store will use a different connection but uses the same managed connection.

```java
public class ManagedConnectionImpl implements ManagedConnection
{
  private ManagedConnectionFactoryImpl    mcf;
  private SampleConnectionEventListener  eventListener;

  private SampleConnection connection;
  private PrintWriter logWriter;
  private boolean  destroyed;

  ManagedConnectionImpl(ManagedConnectionFactoryImpl mcf,➥
  Subject subject,ConnectionRequestInfo cxRequestInfo) ➥
  throws ResourceException
  {
    this.mcf = mcf;
    eventListener = new SampleConnectionEventListener(this);
  }

  public Object getConnection(Subject subject,➥
  ConnectionRequestInfo cxRequestInfo) throws ResourceException
  {
    checkIfDestroyed();
    if (null==connection)
    connection = new SampleConnectionImpl(this);
    return connection;
  }
}
```

```
  public void destroy() throws ResourceException
  {
    if (destroyed)  return;
    destroyed = true;
    ((SampleConnectionImpl)connection).invalidate();
    connection=null;


  }

  public void cleanup() throws ResourceException
  {
    checkIfDestroyed();
    ((SampleConnectionImpl)connection).invalidate();
    connection=null;
  }

  public void associateConnection(Object connection) ➥
  throws ResourceException
  {
    checkIfDestroyed();

    if (connection instanceof SampleConnection)
    {
      SampleConnectionImpl con =➥
      (SampleConnectionImpl) connection;
      con.associateConnection(this);
    } else {
      throw new IllegalStateException("INVALID_CONNECTION");
    }
  }

  public void setConnection(SampleConnection con){
    this.connection=con;
  }


  public void addConnectionEventListener( ➥
  ConnectionEventListener listener)
  {
    eventListener.addConnectorListener(listener);
  }
```

```java
  public void removeConnectionEventListener( ➥
    ConnectionEventListener listener)
  {
    eventListener.removeConnectorListener(listener);
  }

  public XAResource getXAResource() throws ResourceException
  {
    throw new NotSupportedException("NO_XATRANSACTION");
  }


  public LocalTransaction getLocalTransaction() throws ➥
ResourceException
  {
    throw new NotSupportedException("NO_TRANSACTION");
  }

  public ManagedConnectionMetaData getMetaData() ➥
  throws ResourceException
  {
    checkIfDestroyed();
    return new ManagedConnectionMetaDataImpl(this);
  }


  public void setLogWriter(PrintWriter out) ➥
  throws ResourceException
  {this.logWriter = out; }

  public PrintWriter getLogWriter() throws ResourceException
  {return logWriter; }

  private void checkIfDestroyed() throws ResourceException
  {
    if (destroyed) {
      throw new IllegalStateException("DESTROYED_CONNECTION");
    }
  }


  boolean isDestroyed()
  { return destroyed; }

  public ManagedConnectionFactoryImpl ➥
getManagedConnectionFactory()
  { return this.mcf;}
```

```
  public void sendEvent(int eventType, Exception ex)
  {
    eventListener.sendEvent(eventType, ex, null);
  }


  public void sendEvent(int eventType, Exception ex, Object ➥
connectionHandle)
  {
    eventListener.sendEvent(eventType, ex, ➥
connectionHandle);
  }

}
```

In our example, there is one physical connection (SampleConnection) per managed connection instance. Since the managed connection factory returns null for the matchManagedConnections() method, a new managed connection object is created for every request. The managed connection's getConnection() method is used to create a new physical connection.

Create the Resource Adapter Implementation

The resource adapter deployment descriptor specifies the name of a class that implements the ResourceAdapter interface. The application server creates a new instance of this class and calls its life cycle methods.

```
public class ResourceAdapterImpl implements ResourceAdapter, ➥
java.io.Serializable
{
  protected transient BootstrapContext  bootCtx;
  protected transient WorkManager    workManager;
  private  Work  worker;

  public ResourceAdapterImpl () { }

  public void start(BootstrapContext ctx) ➥
  throws ResourceAdapterInternalException
  {
    this.bootCtx = ctx;
    this.workManager = ctx.getWorkManager();
  }


  public void stop()
  {
    if(worker!=null){
      worker.release();
    }
  }
```

```
public void endpointActivation (MessageEndpointFactory ➡
endpointFactory, ActivationSpec spec) throws NotSupportedException
  {

    try {
      worker = new EndpointThread(endpointFactory,spec);
      workManager.scheduleWork(worker);
    }catch(Exception e){
      System.out.println("Error scheduling work"+e);
    }

  }


  public void endpointDeactivation (MessageEndpointFactory ➡
endpointFactory,  ActivationSpec spec)
  {
    worker.release();
    worker=null;
  }


  public XAResource[] getXAResources(ActivationSpec[] specs) ➡
  throws ResourceException
  {return null;}

}
```

The application server calls the start() method when it loads the resource adapter, and it calls the stop() method when it unloads the resource adapter. It passes a BootstrapContext object as a parameter to this method, and the resource adapter can use it to get a handle to workManager and XATerminator instances by calling the getWorkManager() and getXATerminator() methods. A work manager is a component of the application server that the resource adapter can use to submit work objects that need to be executed asynchronously. This way, the resource adapter can utilize the application server thread pool. We will discuss using the work manager and the methods endpointActivation() and endpointDeactivation() later in this chapter, when we discuss inbound connectivity.

Create the Standard Deployment Descriptor

The standard deployment descriptor of a resource adapter is a file named ra.xml.

```
<?xml version="1.0" encoding="UTF-8"?>


<connector xmlns="http://java.sun.com/xml/ns/j2ee" ➡
xmlns:xsi="http://www.w3.org/2001/XMLSchema-instance" ➡
xsi:schemaLocation="http://java.sun.com/xml/ns/j2ee ➡
http://java.sun.com/xml/ns/j2ee/connector_1_5.xsd" version="1.5">
```

```xml
<description>Sample adapter </description>
<display-name>SampleResourceAdapter</display-name>
<icon></icon>
<vendor-name>Sample</vendor-name>
<eis-type>SAMPLE</eis-type>
<resourceadapter-version>1.5</resourceadapter-version>

<resourceadapter>
  <resourceadapter-class>
    samples.connectors.ResourceAdapterImpl
  </resourceadapter-class>

  <outbound-resourceadapter>
    <connection-definition>
      <managedconnectionfactory-class>
        samples.connectors.outbound.ManagedConnectionFactoryImpl
      </managedconnectionfactory-class>
      <connectionfactory-interface>
        samples.connectors.outbound.SampleConnectionFactory
      </connectionfactory-interface>
      <connectionfactory-impl-class>
        samples.connectors.outbound.SampleConnectionFactoryImpl
      </connectionfactory-impl-class>
      <connection-interface>
        samples.connectors.outbound.SampleConnection
      </connection-interface>
      <connection-impl-class>
        samples.connectors.outbound.SampleConnectionImpl
      </connection-impl-class>
    </connection-definition>
    <transaction-support>NoTransaction</transaction-support>
    <reauthentication-support>false</reauthentication-support>
  </outbound-resourceadapter>

  <inbound-resourceadapter>
    <!--inbound definition -->
  </inbound-resourceadapter>
</resourceadapter>
</connector>
```

This defines the resource adapter implementation class name, the connection factory interface class name, the connection factory implementation class name, the managed connection factory implementation class name, the connection interface class name, and the connection implementation class name.

Create the Geronimo-Specific Deployment Descriptor

Geronimo supports J2EE Connector Architecture 1.5, with backward compatibility to version 1.0. The Geronimo-specific deployment descriptor is a file named geronimo-ra.xml (if you package it within the resource adapter module). You can instead provide the Geronimo deployment descriptor directly to the deploy tool, in which case the deployment descriptor's name can be anything.

```xml
<?xml version="1.0" encoding="UTF-8"?>
<connector xmlns="http://geronimo.apache.org/xml/ns/j2ee/connector" ➡
version="1.5" configId="SampleResourceAdapter" ➡
parentId="geronimo/j2ee-server/1.0/car">

<resourceadapter>

  <resourceadapter-instance>
    <resourceadapter-name>
      SampleResourceAdapterInstance
    </resourceadapter-name>
    <workmanager>
      <gbean-link>DefaultWorkManager</gbean-link>
    </workmanager>
  </resourceadapter-instance>

  <outbound-resourceadapter>
    <connection-definition>
      <connectionfactory-interface>
        samples.connectors.outbound.SampleConnectionFactory
      </connectionfactory-interface>
      <connectiondefinition-instance>
        <name>MySampleConnectionFactory</name>
        <connectionmanager>
          <no-transaction/>
          <single-pool>
            <max-size>10</max-size>
            <min-size>0</min-size>
            <blocking-timeout-milliseconds>
              5000
            </blocking-timeout-milliseconds>
            <idle-timeout-minutes>0</idle-timeout-minutes>
            <match-one/>
          </single-pool>
        </connectionmanager>
        <global-jndi-name>sra/scf</global-jndi-name>
      </connectiondefinition-instance>
    </connection-definition>
  </outbound-resourceadapter>
</resourceadapter>
</connector>
```

Figure 8-6 depicts an overview of the structure of the Geronimo deployment plan.

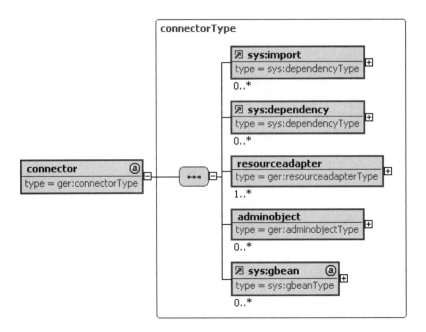

Figure 8-6. *Geronimo deployment plan*

The import and dependency elements in this plan are similar to those elements in every other Geronimo deployment plan. The resourceadapter element defines the resource adapter deployed with this plan, and the adminobject element defines all administered objects (like a queue or a topic in the case of a JMS connector) that are part of this resource adapter.

The resourceadapter element consists of two subelements—resourceadapter-instance and outbound-resourceadapter—which are shown in Figure 8-7.

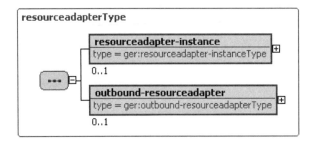

Figure 8-7. *The resourceadapter element in the Geronimo deployment plan*

The resourceadapter-instance defines the resource adapter, and the structure of its subelements is shown in Figure 8-8.

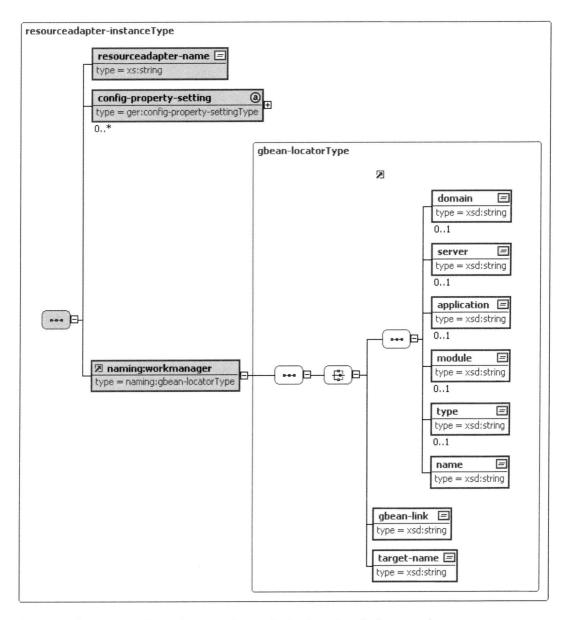

Figure 8-8. *The resourceadapter-instance element in the Geronimo deployment plan*

Table 8-2 describes these elements.

Table 8-2. *The resourceadapter-instance Deployment Elements*

Element	Description
resourceadapter-name	This element defines a name for the resource adapter. You use this name to refer to this resource adapter from other components (like from an MDB's Geronimo deployment plan).
config-property-setting	You can use this element to specify values for configuration properties defined for the resourceadapter element in the ra.xml deployment descriptor for the connector.
workmanager	A work manager is required for inbound connectors to use the application server's thread pool to submit work instances to be executed by the application server. Geronimo has a serverwide work manager already available, and if you need to use it, the gbean-link element should be the value DefaultWorkManager. This is the default implementation unless you want to define your own work manager implementation and refer it here to use it. If you use the target-name element to refer to the work manager, you need to provide the full object name of the work manager GBean.

The outbound-resourceadapter subelement of the resourceadapter element defines the outbound connection, as shown in Figure 8-9.

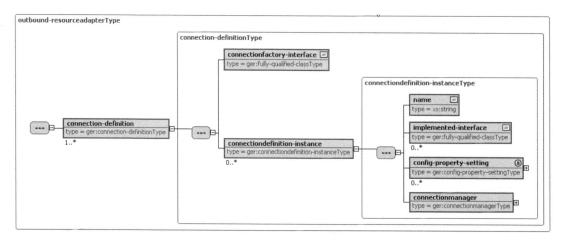

Figure 8-9. *The outbound-resourceadapter elements in the Geronimo deployment plan*

There needs to be a separate connection-definition element for every connectionfactory-interface that the resource adapter supports. The connectiondefinition-instance/name identifies the connection factory that is available to client components. You use this value to resolve connection factory resource references in the Geronimo deployment plan for these client components. The config-property-setting element specifies values for configuration properties defined for the outbound-resourceadapter element in the ra.xml deployment descriptor for the connector. You also need to define a connection manager to be used, as shown in Figure 8-10.

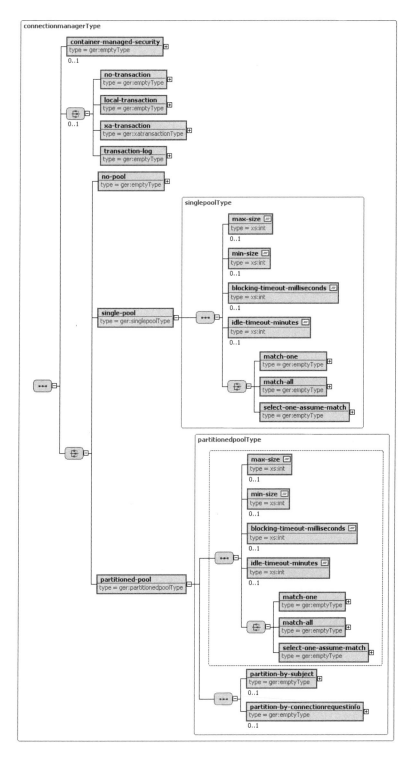

Figure 8-10. *The connectionmanager element in the Geronimo deployment plan*

Table 8-3 describes the connectionmanager element's subelements.

Table 8-3. The connectionmanager Deployment Elements

Element	Description
container-managed-security	This empty element specifies whether or not the container manages security.
no-transaction	If this element is present, the resource adapter does not participate in transactions.
local-transaction	If this element is present, the resource adapter participates in local transactions only.
xa-transaction	If this element is present, the resource adapter participates in distributed global transactions.
transaction-log	This setting is used for local-transaction JDBC resources only. When this setting is used, Geronimo makes them capable of participating in XA transactions.
connection pooling	You can use one of these settings for connection pooling: no-pool, single-pool, or partitioned-pool. With the no-pool option, connections are not shared, and every new request results in a new connection being created. The single-pool option uses a single connection pool, and a partitioned pool uses multiple connection pools partitioned by subject or by connection request information.
max-size	This specifies the maximum number of connections in the pool or for a partition, in the case of a partitioned pool.
min-size	This specifies the minimum number of connections in the pool or for a partition, in the case of a partitioned pool.
blocking-timeout-milliseconds	If all the connections in the pool are being used and the number of connections reaches the max-size setting, no more new connections are created. Every new request waits for this many milliseconds before it generates an error.
idle-timeout-minutes	Any connection idle longer than the time specified here qualifies for removal from the pool.
partition-by-subject	The pool is partitioned by subject type.
partition-by-connectionrequestinfo	The pool is partitioned by connection request information.
select-one-assume-match	With this setting, the connection pool takes one connection from the pool and assumes that it matches the current subject and connection request information. This setting is useful when the connection pool contains equivalent connections.
match-one	With this setting, the connection pool takes one connection from the pool and matches it with the current subject and connection request information before returning it to the requester. If the connection in the pool doesn't match, the connection pool throws an error. This setting can be used only with pools that contain equivalent connections.
match-all	With this setting, the connection pool matches all connection objects in the pool with the current subject and connection request information to find the matching connections, and returns them.

Package and Deploy the Resource Adapter

A resource adapter is packaged as a RAR file. A RAR file is a JAR file with a .rar file name extension and in our example has the following contents:

```
jar -tvf sampleRAR.rar
META-INF/
META-INF/MANIFEST.MF
META-INF/geronimo-ra.xml (Geronimo deployment plan)
META-INF/ra.xml  (deployment descriptor)
sampleConnector.jar (resource adapter classes JAR file)
```

To deploy the connector, use the following command:

```
java -jar deployer.jar deploy sampleRAR.rar
```

Connector Client

Now that we have finished deploying the sample outbound connector, we can try to invoke the connector from a web client. The first step is to define a resource reference in the web.xml deployment descriptor (or in the ejb-jar.xml file in the case of an EJB).

```
<resource-ref>
  <res-ref-name>mySampleConnectionFactory</res-ref-name>
  <res-type>
    samples.connectors.outbound.SampleConnectionFactory
  </res-type>
  <res-auth>Container</res-auth>
  <res-sharing-scope>Shareable</res-sharing-scope>
</resource-ref>
```

You need to resolve this reference in the geronimo-web.xml file (or in the openejb-jar.xml file in the case of an EJB) and point it to the connection definition of a resource adapter, as shown here:

```
<naming:resource-ref>
  <naming:ref-name>mySampleConnectionFactory</naming:ref-name>
  <naming:resource-link>
    MySampleConnectionFactory
  </naming:resource-link>
</naming:resource-ref>
```

The resource-link element should match the connection-definition/connectiondefinition-instance/name element in the geronimo-ra.xml deployment plan of the connector.

The connector client can get a reference to the connection factory, as shown here:

```
SampleConnectionFactory cf=(SampleConnectionFactory)ic.lookup(➥
"java:comp/env/mySampleConnectionFactory");
SampleConnection c=cf.createConnection();
String output=c.doSomething("Got Connected");
```

The res-ref-name element value should be used as the lookup name under the java:comp/env JNDI context.

Inbound Connector

An inbound connector allows messages to flow from the EIS to J2EE application components like MDBs. A JMS inbound connector can send messages posted to a queue or a topic to an MDB.

Before you learn how to create an inbound connector, let's explore what happens behind the scenes when an inbound connector is deployed, and let's examine how the connector manages message flow to application message endpoints.

Figure 8-11 depicts the deployer deploying an MDB (a message endpoint).

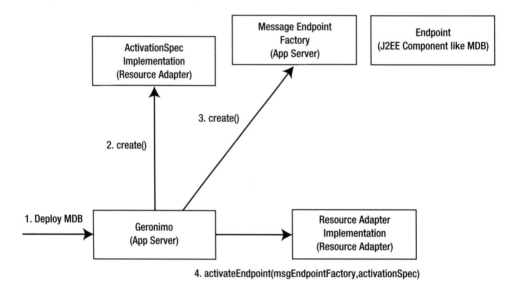

Figure 8-11. *Component interactions during MDB deployment*

When an MDB is deployed, the application server creates the required activationSpec object (the class name is obtained from the resource adapter deployment descriptor) and populates it with values given in the MDB deployment descriptor (the activation-config element). Geronimo invokes the resource adapter object's endpointActivation() method and provides the activation-Spec object and a message endpoint factory object. The resource adapter can use the message endpoint factory to get a reference to the endpoint (the MDB in this case) to send a message to it. The resource adapter might create more than one endpoint reference, depending on its logic for utilizing these endpoint references.

Next, let's consider what happens when the resource adapter delivers messages from the EIS to the MDB. Figure 8-12 depicts this process.

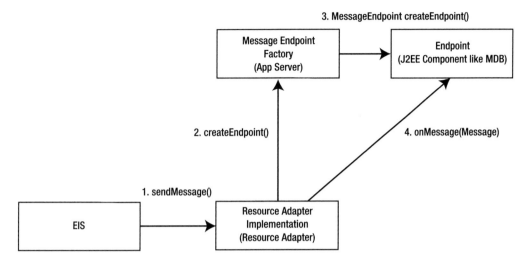

Figure 8-12. *Component interactions during the delivery of a message from the EIS to the MDB*

The resource adapter creates a reference to the endpoint by using the endpoint factory and calls its message listener interface methods to deliver messages from the underlying EIS.

Now, we'll turn to our inbound connector example. You must follow these steps to create an inbound connector:

1. Create a message class.

2. Create a message listener interface.

3. Create an ActivationSpec implementation.

4. Implement the resource adapter.

5. Create the standard deployment descriptor.

6. Create the Geronimo-specific deployment descriptor.

7. Package and deploy the inbound connector.

Create a Message Class

The connector delivers instances of this class to the MDB.

```
package samples.connectors.inbound;

public class SampleMessage
{
  private String msg;
  public SampleMessage(String msg)
  {this.msg=msg; }

  public String getMsg()
  {return msg;}
}
```

Create a Message Listener Interface

The MDB implements this listener interface to listen for messages from the connector.

```
public interface SampleMessageListener
{
  public void onMessage(SampleMessage message);
}
```

Create an ActivationSpec Implementation

A connector can specify the parameters required for activating an endpoint (a message consumer component or an MDB) by creating an implementation of the ActivationSpec interface. The ActivationSpec implementation is a JavaBean that has the configurable parameters as bean properties with setter and getter methods. When an MDB is defined, it can define values for these parameters in its deployment descriptor (by using the activation-spec element). When an MDB is deployed, the application server creates an instance of the connector-specific ActivationSpec implementation class, populates the bean properties, and passes the activationSpec object to the connector for endpoint activation. The ActivationSpec JavaBean should be configured according to details in the connector deployment descriptor, as well as to the message provider's specifics.

```
public class ActivationSpecImpl implements ➥
javax.resource.spi.ActivationSpec, java.io.Serializable
{
  private ResourceAdapter resourceAdapter = null;
  private String msg= new String("SAMPLE MESSAGE FROM CONNECTOR");
  private String interval=new String("500");

  public ActivationSpecImpl() { }

  public String getMsg()
  {return this.msg;}

  public void setMsg(String msg)
  {this.msg = msg;}

  public String getInterval()
  {return this.interval;}

  public void setInterval(String interval)
  {this.interval = interval;}

  public void validate() throws InvalidPropertyException
  { }

  public void setResourceAdapter(ResourceAdapter ra) ➥
  throws ResourceException
  {this.resourceAdapter = ra;}
```

```
public ResourceAdapter getResourceAdapter()
{return resourceAdapter;}

}
```

Implement the Resource Adapter

The application server invokes the endpointActivation() method when an MDB is deployed and invokes the endpointDeactivation() method when the MDB is removed. A resource adapter must implement the endpointActivation() and endpointDeactivation() methods in such a manner that the application server can make concurrent calls to them. An inbound resource adapter will enable message delivery to the endpoint when the endpoint is activated. We will use the same resource adapter class we used in the outbound connector scenario and implement the endpoint-related methods, as shown here:

```
public class ResourceAdapterImpl implements ResourceAdapter, ➥
java.io.Serializable
{
  // other methods

  public void endpointActivation (MessageEndpointFactory ➥
endpointFactory,ActivationSpec spec)throws NotSupportedException
  {

    try {
      worker = new EndpointThread(endpointFactory,spec);
      workManager.scheduleWork(worker);
    }catch(Exception e){
      log.error("Error scheduling work:"+e);
    }

  }

  public void endpointDeactivation (MessageEndpointFactory ➥
endpointFactory, ActivationSpec spec)
  {
    worker.release();
    worker=null;
  }

  // other methods
}
```

When an endpoint is activated, the connector starts a delivery thread to deliver messages to the endpoint. The connector uses the application server–provided work manager to start the delivery thread in order to utilize the application server–managed thread pool. When the application server invokes the endpointDeactivation() method, the connector stops the delivery thread. The delivery thread code is shown here:

```
public class EndpointThread  implements Work
{

  private boolean  active = false;
  private MessageEndpointFactory endpointFactory;
  private String msg;
  private static int  QUANTUM = 500;

  public EndpointThread(MessageEndpointFactory endpointFactory,➥
  ActivationSpec spec)
  {
    this.active  = true;
    this.endpointFactory=endpointFactory;
    ActivationSpecImpl specImpl=(ActivationSpecImpl)spec;
    this.msg=specImpl.getMsg();
    try{
        this.QUANTUM=Integer.getInteger(
        specImpl.getInterval()).intValue();
    }catch(Exception e){// handle}
  }

  public void release()
  {active = false;}

  public void run()
  {
    while (active)
    {
      try
      {
        Thread.sleep(QUANTUM);
        generateAndSendMessage();
      } catch(Exception e) {
        e.printStackTrace();
      }
    }
  }

  private void generateAndSendMessage(){
    try {
      SampleMessage sampleMessage=new SampleMessage(msg);
      MessageEndpoint endpoint=
      endpointFactory.createEndpoint(null);
      if(null!=endpoint){
        ((SampleMessageListener)endpoint).onMessage(sampleMessage);
      }
    } catch(Exception e){
```

```
    // handle exception
  }
 }

}
```

This is a very simple and trivial implementation in which the connector emulates an EIS message source just by creating a message at every preconfigured interval and then sending it to the endpoint. The connector creates the endpoint instance from the endpoint factory object the application server provided when the endpoint was activated. The endpoint will implement the message listener type in order to consume messages from the connector. Also, the endpoint can define the activation parameter values (msg and interval in our case) in its deployment descriptor. We will discuss an MDB endpoint in the "MDB Connector Client" section.

Create the Standard Deployment Descriptor

In this example, we can use the same deployment descriptor (ra.xml) that we used to define the outbound connector. The descriptor contents relevant for defining an inbound connector are shown here:

```xml
<?xml version="1.0" encoding="UTF-8"?>


<connector xmlns="http://java.sun.com/xml/ns/j2ee" ➥
xmlns:xsi="http://www.w3.org/2001/XMLSchema-instance" ➥
xsi:schemaLocation="http://java.sun.com/xml/ns/j2ee ➥
http://java.sun.com/xml/ns/j2ee/connector_1_5.xsd" version="1.5">

<!-- connector definition--same as for outbound connector-->

<resourceadapter>
  <resourceadapter-class>
    samples.connectors.ResourceAdapterImpl
  </resourceadapter-class>
  <outbound-resourceadapter>
    <!-- outbound definition -->
  </outbound-resourceadapter>

  <inbound-resourceadapter>
    <messageadapter>
      <messagelistener>
        <messagelistener-type>
          samples.connectors.inbound.SampleMessageListener
        </messagelistener-type>
        <activationspec>
          <activationspec-class>
            samples.connectors.inbound.ActivationSpecImpl
          </activationspec-class>
```

```
            <required-config-property>
              <config-property-name>
                msg
              </config-property-name>
            </required-config-property>
            <required-config-property>
              <config-property-name>
                interval
              </config-property-name>
            </required-config-property>
          </activationspec>
        </messagelistener>
      </messageadapter>
    </inbound-resourceadapter>

  </resourceadapter>
</connector>
```

Here, the message listener types specify the listener interface class that endpoints will have to implement to receive messages from this connector. If the endpoint is an MDB, the MDB should implement this listener interface. The connector also defines the required activation configuration parameters and the ActivationSpec implementation class name. When an endpoint is deployed, if you configure the endpoint to get messages from this resource adapter (by specifying the resource adapter name in the Geronimo-specific deployment descriptor for the endpoint), the application server creates an instance of the ActivationSpec class, populates it with values provided in the endpoint deployment descriptor, and passes it to the resource adapter for endpoint activation.

Create the Geronimo-Specific Deployment Plan

The Geronimo-specific deployment plan is the same as that of the outbound resource adapter that we created earlier in this chapter. The critical element here is the work manager. Its value needs to be a work manager implementation. To use the Geronimo default implementation, you should make its value `DefaultWorkManager`.

Package and Deploy the Inbound Connector

This step is the same as the step we used to package and deploy the outbound connector.

MDB Connector Client

Let's create a client (an MDB message endpoint) to connect to the inbound connector and receive messages from it. The first step is to create the MDB itself, as shown here:

```
public class SampleMDB implements MessageDrivenBean,➥
SampleMessageListener
{
  private transient MessageDrivenContext mdc = null;
  private static final Log log = LogFactory.getLog(SampleMDB.class);
```

```
public SampleMDB() { }

public void setMessageDrivenContext(MessageDrivenContext mdc)
{this.mdc = mdc; }

public void ejbCreate(){}

public void onMessage(SampleMessage message)
{
  log.info("RECEIVED MSG:"+message.getMsg());
}

public void ejbRemove(){ }

}
```

Here, the MDB implements the SampleMessageListener interface, which is the message listener type defined by the connector. In the listener method—onMessage()—the MDB just prints the message sent by the connector to the log.

The next step is to create the standard deployment descriptor (ejb-jar.xml) for the MDB, as shown here:

```
<?xml version="1.0" encoding="UTF-8"?>

<ejb-jar version="2.1" xmlns="http://java.sun.com/xml/ns/j2ee" ➥
xmlns:xsi="http://www.w3.org/2001/XMLSchema-instance" ➥
xsi:schemaLocation="http://java.sun.com/xml/ns/j2ee ➥
http://java.sun.com/xml/ns/j2ee/ejb-jar_2_1.xsd">
  <display-name>Sample Connector Client MDB</display-name>

  <enterprise-beans>
    <message-driven>
      <display-name>Sample MDB</display-name>
      <ejb-name>SampleMDB</ejb-name>
      <ejb-class>samples.connectors.client.mdb.SampleMDB</ejb-class>
      <messaging-type>
        samples.connectors.inbound.SampleMessageListener
      </messaging-type>
      <transaction-type>Container</transaction-type>
      <activation-config>

        <activation-config-property>
          <activation-config-property-name>
            Msg
          </activation-config-property-name>
          <activation-config-property-value>
            My Sample Message
          </activation-config-property-value>
        </activation-config-property>
```

```
        <activation-config-property>
          <activation-config-property-name>
            Interval
          </activation-config-property-name>
          <activation-config-property-value>
            200
          </activation-config-property-value>
        </activation-config-property>

      </activation-config>
    </message-driven>
  </enterprise-beans>
</ejb-jar>
```

Here, the key point to note is how the MDB defines values for the activation configuration properties. These should match the ActivationSpec elements of the resource adapter.

Finally, you need to create a Geronimo-specific deployment descriptor (openejb-jar.xml), as shown here:

```
<?xml version="1.0" encoding="UTF-8"?>
<openejb-jar ➥
xmlns="http://www.openejb.org/xml/ns/openejb-jar" ➥
xmlns:naming="http://geronimo.apache.org/xml/ns/naming" ➥
xmlns:security="http://geronimo.apache.org/xml/ns/security" ➥
xmlns:sys="http://geronimo.apache.org/xml/ns/deployment" ➥
configId="ConnectorMDBClient" ➥
parentId="SampleResourceAdapter">
  <enterprise-beans>
    <message-driven>
      <ejb-name>SampleMDB</ejb-name>
      <resource-adapter>
        <resource-link>
          SampleResourceAdapterInstance
        </resource-link>
      </resource-adapter>
    </message-driven>
  </enterprise-beans>
</openejb-jar>
```

The resource-link element links this MDB to the resource adapter from which it needs to consume messages. This value should match the value of the resourceadapter/resourceadapter-name element of the resource adapter's Geronimo-specific deployment plan (geronimo-ra.xml).

Summary

In this chapter, you learned about web services and J2EE connectors. You explored the details of creating, packaging, and deploying web services and J2EE connectors. You also saw how to consume web services from a web client and from an EJB. In the connectors section, you learned about invoking EIS-specific operations through the outbound connector interface and about consuming EIS messages by using an MDB. In the next chapter, you will learn about J2EE application clients.

CHAPTER 9

J2EE Application Clients

AJ2EE application deployed in Geronimo or in any J2EE 1.4–compliant application server can support the following application client types:

- A browser client or an HTTP client accessing J2EE web applications

- A stand-alone Java application accessing EJBs deployed in Geronimo

- A stand-alone non-Java application using CORBA to access EJBs deployed in Geronimo

- A web services client accessing web services deployed in Geronimo

- A J2EE application client accessing J2EE components deployed in Geronimo

In this chapter, you will learn how to create, configure, deploy, and run J2EE application clients.

Understanding J2EE Application Clients

A J2EE application client is a J2EE module that can run in a J2EE client container. This is the basic difference between a J2EE application client and a normal Java client (Java 2 Platform, Standard Edition [J2SE] client) application. This means that the J2EE application client module, much like other J2EE application modules (web, EJB, and connector modules), defines a standard that allows it to run inside a container. Another difference between a J2EE application client and a normal J2SE client concerns portability; J2EE application clients are more portable since they can utilize the container to resolve various references (like resource references) during runtime, whereas J2SE clients must implement an application server–dependent mechanism to achieve this.

A J2EE client is particularly useful when you need to utilize server resources, like a security realm or database connection pools. Let's say you need to invoke a protected EJB. Here, you need to provide a proper security context to access this EJB. You need a client that is portable across various application servers, and the only way to get this is to write a J2EE application client.

In this chapter, we will examine an application client that accesses the CMP entity bean we developed in Chapter 5. The following steps are required to create, deploy, and run a J2EE application client in Geronimo:

1. Create the client class.

2. Create the application client standard deployment descriptor.

3. Create the application client Geronimo deployment descriptor.

4. Create the client JAR.

5. Deploy and run the client JAR.

Create the Client Class

The code for the client class is shown here:

```
public class StudentClient{

public static void main(String[] args){
  try {

    System.out.println("Student EJB J2EE Client ...");

    InitialContext context=getInitialContext();
    StudentHome home=(StudentHome)PortableRemoteObject.narrow(
              context.lookup("java:comp/env/ejb/cmpStudent"),StudentHome.class);

    Random generator =new Random();
    Student student=null;
    // create students
    for (int i=1;i<=10;i++){
      student=(Student)PortableRemoteObject.narrow(home.create("f"+i,"l"+i),
              Student.class);
      int marks=generator.nextInt(101);
      student.setMarks(marks);
      System.out.println("Student [f"+i+"][l"+i+"]["+marks+"] created ... ");

    }

    System.out.println("Using findByPrimaryKey ...");

    Object obj = home.findByPrimaryKey("f1");
    student=(Student)PortableRemoteObject.narrow(obj,Student.class);
    System.out.println("Got Student ["+student.getFirstName()+
        "]["+student.getLastName()+"]["+student.getMarks()+"] ... ");
    System.out.println("Using Business Method ...");
    System.out.println("Student Passed:"+student.passed()+": ");

    System.out.println("Using Home Business Method...");
    int passPercentage=home.getPassPercentage();
    System.out.println("EJB Home Pass Percentage:"+passPercentage+":");
```

```
System.out.println("Using findAll ... ");
Collection list = home.findAll();
for (Iterator it=list.iterator();it.hasNext();){
  student=(Student)PortableRemoteObject.narrow(it.next(),Student.class);

  System.out.println("Got Student ["+student.getFirstName()+
    "]["+student.getLastName()+"]["+student.getMarks()+"][passed:"+
    student.passed()+"]...");

  student.remove();
  System.out.println("Student Removed... ");
}


}catch(Exception e){
....// handle exception
 }

}
```

The getInitialContext() method is listed here:

```
private static InitialContext getInitialContext()throws Exception{
  return new InitialContext();
}
```

This class is very similar to the stand-alone client we discussed in Chapter 5. The differences between the two clients involve the getInitialContext() method and the EJB lookup name. For a stand-alone client, you need to provide JNDI properties, such as the initial context factory and the URL, to the InitialContext class's constructor. By contrast, since the J2EE client runs on a client container, the container already knows the required JNDI configurations. For the EJB lookup, we can create an EJB reference (defined in the deployment descriptor, as shown in the next section) and utilize the Java component environment (java:comp/env) for looking up the reference name. For a stand-alone client, you need to use the JNDI name with which the EJB is registered in the server.

Create the Standard Deployment Descriptor

The standard deployment descriptor for an application client is an XML file named application-client.xml. The following code snippet shows the deployment descriptor for the sample client:

```
<?xml version="1.0" encoding="UTF-8"?>

<application-client xmlns="http://java.sun.com/xml/ns/j2ee"
    xmlns:xsi="http://www.w3.org/2001/XMLSchema-instance"
    xsi:schemaLocation="http://java.sun.com/xml/ns/j2ee
      http://java.sun.com/xml/ns/j2ee/application-client_1_4.xsd"
    version="1.4">
```

```
<ejb-ref>
   <ejb-ref-name>ejb/cmpStudent</ejb-ref-name>
   <ejb-ref-type>Entity</ejb-ref-type>
   <home>samples.cmp.student.StudentHome</home>
   <remote>samples.cmp.student.Student</remote>
</ejb-ref>

</application-client>
```

Here, an EJB reference is defined, and this reference name will be used in the client code to perform the JNDI lookup. Figure 9-1 shows the various elements of the standard deployment descriptor.

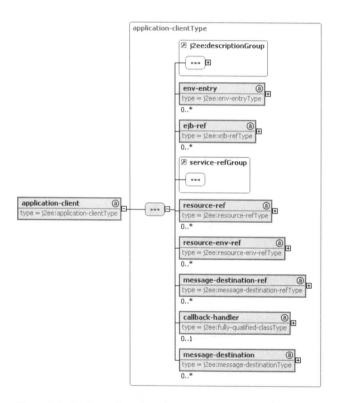

Figure 9-1. *J2EE application client standard deployment descriptor*

The following list describes these elements:

- *descriptionGroup.* The description group contains optional elements for specifying the description, the display-name, and the icon for the application client module.

- *env-entry.* This element defines environment entry values that the container will make available to the application at runtime through the JNDI component context (java:comp/env). A sample env-entry element is shown here:

```
<env-entry>
    <env-entry-name>logLevel</env-entry-name>
    <env-entry-type>java.lang.String</env-entry-type>
    <env-entry-value>DEBUG</env-entry-value>
</env-entry>
```

From your application component, you can now use JNDI to look up java:comp/env/logLevel to get the value provided in the deployment descriptor.

- *ejb-ref*: This element defines a reference to a target EJB by specifying a logical name that can be used in the code to refer to the EJB. A sample ejb-ref element is shown here:

```
<ejb-ref>
    <ejb-ref-name>ejb/userManagement</ejb-ref-name>
    <ejb-ref-type>Session</ejb-ref-type>
    <home>com.example.UserManagementHome</home>
    <remote>com.example.UserManagement</remote>
</ejb-ref>
```

You can now use the JNDI name java:comp/env/ejb/userManagement to get a reference to the EJB from your application code. To completely specify the EJB reference, you need to use the Geronimo deployment plan to resolve the reference and point it to the target EJB. You can also resolve the reference by providing an ejb-link element to the preceding ejb-ref element.

- *service-refGroup*: This defines the service-ref element that can be used to define a reference to a web service, as shown here:

```
<service-ref>
        <service-ref-name>service/GreetingSvc</service-ref-name>
        <service-interface>javax.xml.rpc.Service</service-interface>
        <wsdl-file>WEB-INF/GreetingService.wsdl</wsdl-file>
        <jaxrpc-mapping-file>
                WEB-INF/greetingSvc-mapping.xml
        </jaxrpc-mapping-file>
        <service-qname xmlns:ns="http://samples.usermgmt">
                ns:GreetingService
        </service-qname>
</service-ref>
```

You need to resolve the reference by defining a corresponding service-ref element in the Geronimo deployment plan for the component and pointing it to the target web service.

- *resource-ref*: You can use this element to define a reference to a resource like a database connection pool, as shown here:

```
<resource-ref>
    <res-ref-name>jdbc/sampleResource </res-ref-name>
    <res-type>javax.sql.DataSource</res-type>
```

```
        <res-auth>Container</res-auth>
        <res-sharing-scope>Shareable</res-sharing-scope>
    </resource-ref>
```

After you resolve the reference by defining a corresponding resource-ref element in the Geronimo-specific deployment plan for the application component, you can obtain a reference to the resource by using the name java:comp/env/jdbc/sampleResource to perform a JNDI lookup.

- *resource-env-ref*: This element allows you to define a reference to a connector-administered object, like a JMS queue or topic, as shown here:

```
<resource-env-ref>
    <resource-env-ref-name>queue/MyQueue</resource-env-ref-name>
    <resource-env-ref-type>javax.jms.Queue</resource-env-ref-type>
</resource-env-ref>
```

Here, also, you need to resolve the reference in the Geronimo deployment plan for that component.

- *message-destination-ref*: For JMS message destinations, you can also define a message destination reference (or define a resource-env-ref, which is a pre–J2EE 1.4 mechanism) to use an administered object like a queue or a topic, as shown here:

```
<message-destination-ref>
    <message-destination-ref-name>q/myQ</message-destination-ref-name>
    <message-destination-type>javax.jms.Queue
    </ message-destination-type>
    <message-destination-usage>Consumes</message-destination-usage>
    <message-destination-link>Queue1</message-destination-link>
</message-destination-ref>
```

The advantage of using a message-destination-ref element instead of a resource-env-ref element is that you can fully specify the message destination—you don't need to resolve the reference in the Geronimo deployment plan. The message-destination-link element should refer to a message-destination/message-destination-name element in the same deployment descriptor, as shown here:

```
<message-destination>
    < message-destination-name>Queue1</message-destination-name>
</message-destination>
```

- *callback-handler*: This element specifies a fully qualified class name of a callback handler (refer to http://java.sun.com/products/jaas/ for more details on callback handlers). The container uses an instance of this class to interact with the user to provide the required authentication information.

Create the Geronimo-Specific Deployment Descriptor

You need a Geronimo-specific deployment descriptor to resolve references defined in the standard deployment descriptor. You can provide this deployment plan in one of the following ways:

- Package it as an XML file within the application client JAR. In this case, its name should be geronimo-application-client.xml.

- Package it within the EAR file and refer to the deployment plan by using the alt-dd element of the Geronimo deployment plan for the EAR. In this case, you can use any name for the file.

- Provide the plan directly to the deploy tool. In this case, you can use any name for the file.

The deployment descriptor for the sample client application is shown here:

```
<application-client
xmlns="http://geronimo.apache.org/xml/ns/j2ee/application-client"
xmlns:naming="http://geronimo.apache.org/xml/ns/naming"
xmlns:security="http://geronimo.apache.org/xml/ns/security"
xmlns:sys="http://geronimo.apache.org/xml/ns/deployment"
configId="sample/myclient/serverConfigID"
clientConfigId="sample/myclient/clientConfigId"
parentId="geronimo/j2ee-server/1.0/car"
clientParentId="geronimo/client/1.0/car">

  <ejb-ref>
    <ref-name>ejb/cmpStudent</ref-name>

    <target-name>geronimo.server:EJBModule=StudentCMP,J2EEApplication=null, ➥
J2EEServer=geronimo,j2eeType=EntityBean,name=StudentCMPEJB</target-name>
  </ejb-ref>

</application-client>
```

The configId attribute specifies the configuration ID for this application on the server. This is useful when other configurations need to depend on this configuration (by referring to it as their parent configuration) to use the classes contained within the client JAR. The parentId attribute specifies the deployed configuration's parent configuration on the server. The clientConfigId attribute specifies a configuration ID that can be used to start and stop this configuration when it is run using a client container, and the clientParentId refers to the deployed configuration's parent configuration when it is run within the client container. The default value of clientParentId is org/apache/geronimo/Client.

Figure 9-2 depicts the subelements of the application-client element.

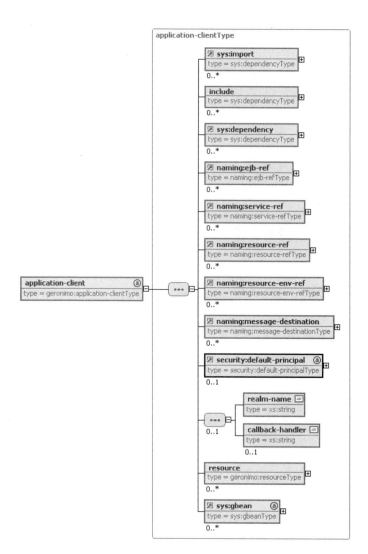

Figure 9-2. *Geronimo-specific deployment plan for a J2EE application client*

You learned about many of these elements in previous chapters, and we will not discuss them in detail here. Table 9-1 briefly describes these elements. It also describes the subelements shown in Figure 9-3.

Table 9-1. *Geronimo-Specific Deployment Plan Elements*

Element	Description
import, include, dependency	These elements are used to specify library dependencies for this configuration.
ejb-ref	This element is used to resolve an EJB reference and link it to a target EJB.
service-ref	This element is used to resolve a web service reference and link it to a target web service.
resource-ref	This element resolves resource references.
resource-env-ref	This element resolves references to administered objects, like a JMS queue or topic.
message-destination	This element can be used to resolve message destination references.
realm-name	Use this element to specify a security realm.
callback-handler	Use this element to specify a callback handler class for authentication.
resource	You can use this element to embed an inline definition of a resource adapter.
gbean	You can define GBeans that should be deployed along with this configuration.
default-principal	This element defines the default principal that should be used for unauthenticated requests.
default-principal: realm-name	This attribute specifies which realm the principal comes from.
principal	This element defines the default principal and has attributes for the name and class values for the principal.
named-username-password-credential	You can use this element to specify a default principal by providing its name, user name, and password.

Figure 9-3 depicts the subelements of the default-principal element.

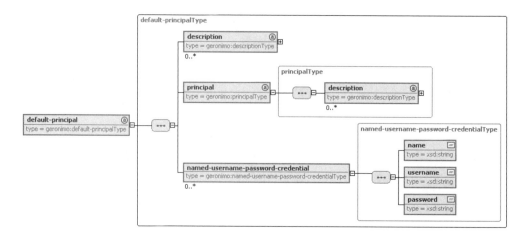

Figure 9-3. *The default-principal element*

Create the Client JAR

The client JAR should contain the client class files and resources. In addition, it should contain the following files: META-INF/application-client.xml, META-INF/geronimo-application-client.xml, and META-INF/MANIFEST.MF. The MANIFEST file should contain an entry for the Main-Class attribute pointing to a class that defines a method with the `public static void main(String[] args)` signature. The sample client JAR contains these directories and files:

```
META-INF/
META-INF/MANIFEST.MF
samples/
samples/client/
samples/client/student/
samples/cmp/
samples/cmp/student/
META-INF/application-client.xml
META-INF/geronimo-application-client.xml
samples/client/student/StudentClient.class
samples/cmp/student/Student.class
samples/cmp/student/StudentHome.class
samples/cmp/student/StudentPKey.class
```

Deploy and Run the Application Client

To deploy the client JAR, use the following command:

```
deploy.bat deploy studentJ2EEClient-1.0.jar
```

This command requires the Geronimo server to be running. To execute the client by using the client container, use the following command:

```
java -jar client.jar sample/myclient/clientConfigId
```

The general form of this command is `java -jar client.jar clientConfigId arg1 arg2…` argn.

Summary

In this chapter, you learned how to use Geronimo to create, package, deploy, and run J2EE application clients. In the next chapter, we will discuss some advanced Geronimo topics, in addition to miscellaneous topics we did not discuss in other chapters.

CHAPTER 10

Advanced Geronimo

This chapter focuses on some advanced features of Geronimo: security and JavaMail. It also covers miscellaneous topics, such as the Geronimo configuration deployment plan, that were not discussed in previous chapters.

You'll begin by looking at the Geronimo configuration plan and its various elements. You've used many of these elements in previous chapters, and here you'll examine each one in more detail.

Next, you'll cover Geronimo security. Geronimo uses Java Authentication and Authorization Service (JAAS) and Java Authorization Contract for Containers (JACC) to implement its security infrastructure. It provides a set of built-in security implementations (such as login modules for authentication) and allows you to customize the security system to your needs (e.g., by using custom login modules).

Finally, you'll learn about Geronimo's support for JavaMail, and you'll see how to use one or more GBeans to configure JavaMail and use it from your J2EE components.

Geronimo Configuration Deployment Plan

You use a configuration deployment plan to install Geronimo services and new configurations. As you learned in Chapter 2, at its core Geronimo is an IOC container. You introduce new functionality into the platform by deploying one or more GBeans. You do not deploy GBeans individually, however, but only as a group of GBeans known as a *configuration*. You deploy a configuration by creating a configuration deployment plan and deploying the plan into the Geronimo platform. When you download Geronimo, the Geronimo platform is set to run many configurations, such as the j2ee-server configuration. The j2ee-server configuration (geronimo/j2ee-server/1.0/car) defines GBeans that implement the J2EE server functionality, including the web container and EJB container. You may create your own configuration plan if you need to further extend the platform to support custom functionality.

This section describes the various elements of the deployment plan in detail. Most of the elements in a Geronimo configuration are also applicable to the Geronimo-specific deployment plans for other application components, such as an EJB or web component, whose deployment plans you saw in previous chapters. This is because you may also deploy custom services and GBeans along with your EJB or web components. However, if you need to deploy just the custom services, then you need to define these in a separate configuration plan.

Figure 10-1 depicts the structure of the Geronimo configuration deployment plan.

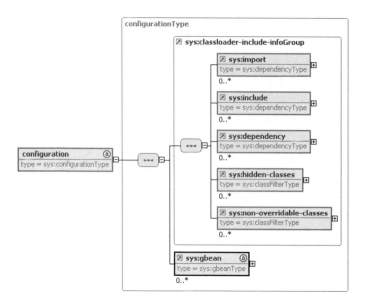

Figure 10-1. *Geronimo configuration deployment plan*

Chapter 2 demonstrated how to deploy a sample custom service. The configuration plan for that service is as follows:

```
<?xml version="1.0" encoding="UTF-8"?>
<configuration xmlns="http://geronimo.apache.org/xml/ns/deployment"
configId="sample/echoserver">
        <dependency>
                <uri>myservices/echoserver/1.0/jar</uri>
        </dependency>
        <gbean name="geronimo.apps:name=echoserver" class="EchoServer" >
                <attribute name="port" type="int">4545</attribute>
        </gbean>
</configuration>
```

As you can see, this deployment plan defines a GBean that implements an echo service. The service implementation is packaged as a JAR file and is available in the Geronimo repository. The dependency element specifies a dependency of this configuration to the JAR file. The elements of the deployment plan are as follows:

- configuration: This is the root element that defines a configuration with one or more services as GBeans. It has the following attributes:

  - configId: This required attribute defines an identifier for this configuration.

  - parentId: This optional attribute specifies a parent configuration. Please note that if this attribute is defined, the configuration can access the classes and libraries defined by the parent configuration.

- domain and server: If defined, these optional attributes specify the domain and J2EE server values for the configuration and its descendant configurations. A configuration is required to have either a parentId value or a domain and server value defined.

- inverseClassloading: This optional attribute is a Boolean value denoting whether inverse classloading should be enabled. Normally, classes to be loaded are searched for in the parent configuration's classloader first, and if they are not present, they are loaded from the current configuration's classloader. The inverseClassloading setting disables this behavior and allows the configuration to override the classes (such as the logging classes) present in its parent configurations.

- import: You may import one or more configurations and add them to the parent configurations list of the current configuration. You may specify the configuration to be imported as a URI, in which case you need to give the full configuration name as a string, or you can use a Maven style name. You specify a Maven style name as follows:

```
<import>
    <groupId>myapps</groupId>
    <artifactId>webapp</artifactId>
    <version>1.0</version>
    <type>war</type>
</import>
```

This import definition will be translated to the configuration name myapps/webapp/1.0/war (groupId/artifactId/version/type).

- include: Use this element to specify libraries available in the repository that should be linked with this configuration. Using the include element, the library will be physically copied from the repository and packaged along with the configuration during deployment time, so that the configuration can run whether or not the repository is available. The library needs to be specified either as a URI or as a Maven style name. The URI specified should be relative to the Geronimo repository. For example, you would use `<import> <uri>log4j/log4j/1.2.8/jar </uri></import>` (groupId/artifactId/version/type) to specify the library repository entry `'log4j/jars/log4j-1.2.8.jar'` (groupId/type/artifactId-version.type). If you use the Maven style name to specify the library, then you need to specify the groupId, artifactId, version, and type for the library as shown here:

```
<include>
    <groupId>log4j</groupId>
    <artifactId>log4j</artifactId>
    <version>1.0</version>
    <type>jar</type>
</include>
```

This include definition will be converted to the repository entry `log4j/jar/log4j-1.0.jar` (groupId/type/artifactId-version.type).

- dependency: This element refers a repository entry (library), which will be added to the classpath of the configuration. The dependency element is similar to the include element, except that it links to the actual library in the repository rather than copying and packaging it along with the configuration. You may use a URI or a Maven style name to specify the repository entry.

- hidden-classes: This element is a comma-separated list of fully qualified class names that should not be loaded from the parent configurations. This way, you can use your copy of the libraries and override what is provided along with Geronimo (or the parent configuration). The class names can also be partial names, such as java.util, in which case all classes starting with the given names will be hidden.

- non-overridable-classes: This element specifies a list of fully qualified class names (or partial names) that cannot be overridden by child configurations.

- gbean: This element defines a custom component or a new service. Figure 10-2 depicts its subelements.

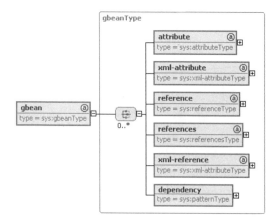

Figure 10-2. *GBean subelements*

- attributes: This element specifies the attribute's name, its type, and a value as shown here: `<attribute name="configFile">var/config/config.xml</attribute>`.

- xml-attributes: You can use this element to specify an attribute value using an XML string. Geronimo uses an XML Attribute Builder class to parse the XML and obtain the attribute's value. The following is a sample configuration:

```
<xml-attribute name="tssConfig">
  <tss:tss ...>
  ... TSS definition XML goes here
  </tss:tss>
</xml-attribute>
```

Here, Geronimo uses the name attribute to identify which XML Attribute Builder should be used to parse the XML contents.

- reference: This element specifies a reference name, a type, and a reference pattern as its value. This pattern identifies another GBean. The reference can also be used to communicate with this GBean. A reference is configured as shown here:

```
<reference name="Stores">
  <gbean-name>*:j2eeType=ConfigurationStore,*</gbean-name>
</reference>
<reference name="AttributeStore">
  <name>AttributeManager</name>
</reference>
```

- references: This element allows you to configure multipatterned references.

- xml-reference: You can use this element to specify XML reference values as an XML string. Geronimo uses an available XML Reference Builder class to parse the given XML and set the reference value.

- dependency: This element specifies a dependency of this GBean to other GBeans in the server.

Configuring Geronimo Security

J2EE defines a standard security model for J2EE application components such as web applications, EJB applications, connectors, and J2EE application clients. It includes authentication and authorization of application component clients. *Authentication* is the process by which the clients identify themselves (which may be through a login process) to the application component, and *authorization* is the process by which the application component enforces access privileges to the authenticated client.

Web applications support four authentication mechanisms: basic, form, digest, and certificate. Any J2EE-compliant web container is expected to support these mechanisms. Chapter 3 covered these mechanisms during the web applications discussion, and as you learned, you may restrict access to certain resources in a web application to a particular security role. You need to map these security roles to one or more principals that belong to a particular security realm using a Geronimo-specific deployment descriptor. Geronimo will not allow access to restricted resources until the user is authenticated using the configured mechanism and the authentication produces principals that are mapped to the corresponding security role.

J2EE defines both declarative and programmatic security for authorizing user access. You may create an EJB and use declarative security to enforce access to the EJB method to particular security roles. This way, only an authenticated user with the configured security role can invoke the EJB method. You may also implement programmatic security by using the methods isCallerInRole() and getCallerPrincipal() in your EJB code (or from a servlet or JSP) and restrict access accordingly.

In the sections that follow, you'll learn how to set up a security realm in Geronimo. You'll also walk through the steps required to create a new security realm and configure it to enable J2EE components to authenticate against.

Setting Up a Security Realm

J2EE defines a *security realm* as a collection of users and groups that are authenticated by the same authentication policy. A user authentication is performed against a security realm and, on successful authentication, this process produces one or more principals representing the identity of the user. A subject encapsulates these principals and represents an authenticated user with recognized identities (principals) to the application.

Geronimo uses Java Authentication and Authorization Service (JAAS) to implement security. JAAS provides a pluggable framework that allows integration of different authentication implementations. Table 10-1 shows the key concepts of JAAS.

Table 10-1. *Key Concepts of JAAS*

Concept	Description
Subject	A subject represents the client—either a user or an application—that needs to be authenticated.
Login module	A login module implements authentication logic. It may implement the necessary logic to authenticate a subject against an LDAP or a relational database. Geronimo provides many standard login modules; we will discuss these in detail later in this chapter.
Principal	A principal is like a token to identify the subject. A login module authenticates a subject and populates a subject instance with one or more matching principal instances. When a user logs in to the application by providing a user name and password, one or more configured login modules authenticate the user (subject), and the login module(s) may populate the subject with a principal object to denote the user name and one or more principal objects to denote the groups the user is a member of.
AppConfigurationEntry	This is a login configuration entry for an application (identified by an application name). The JAAS configuration may, at any time, store the login configuration of one or more applications. A configuration entry defines a login module and a control flag. The control flag, which can have the value REQUIRED, SUFFICIENT, REQUISITE, or OPTIONAL, controls how login modules are applied to an application. One application may be configured with more than one login module, and the security system authenticates the client using all the login modules one by one. If any login module has the control flag SUFFICIENT, a success on that login module will be considered as sufficient and the login process will end. For more information on the various control flags, refer to the JAAS documentation.
Configuration	The JAAS configuration encapsulates the configuration entries, and the security system uses the current configuration to authenticate a subject to an application.

The following sections describe two ways to configure and deploy a security realm: using the deploy tool and using the Geronimo console.

Configuring and Deploying a Security Realm Using the Deploy Tool

To configure a security realm in Geronimo, you need to create a deployment plan as follows:

```
<configuration xmlns="http://geronimo.apache.org/xml/ns/deployment"
configId="sampleSecurityRealm" parentId="geronimo/j2ee-server/1.0/caq">
<gbean name="samplePropertiesFileRealm"
class="org.apache.geronimo.security.realm.GenericSecurityRealm">
    <attribute name="realmName">
        samplePropertiesFileRealm
    </attribute>
    <reference name="ServerInfo">
        <name>ServerInfo</name>
    </reference>
    <xml-reference name="LoginModuleConfiguration">
        <login-config xmlns="http://geronimo.apache.org/xml/ns/loginconfig">
            <login-module control-flag="REQUIRED" server-side="true">
            <login-domain-name>
                some-properties-file-login
            </login-domain-name>
            <login-module-class>
                org.apache.geronimo.security.realm.providers.➥
PropertiesFileLoginModule
            </login-module-class>
            <option name="usersURI">
                var/security/some_users.properties
            </option>
            <option name="groupsURI">
                var/security/some_groups.properties
            </option>
            </login-module>
        </login-config>
    </xml-reference>
</gbean>
</configuration>
```

The GBean class should be org.apache.geronimo.security.realm.GenericSecurityRealm for a security realm, and the name should be the same as the realm name itself. The security realm defined here has one login module configured (using the xml-reference element), and it is the standard PropertiesFileLoginModule provided along with Geronimo. You may write your own login modules and use a configuration similar to the one shown here to create a realm that includes your new login module.

Table 10-2 lists the elements used within the xml-reference element of the security realm GBean to define a login module.

Table 10-2. *xml-reference Subelements to Configure a Login Module*

Element	Description
login-config	Use this element to configure a new login module (as shown in the previous code) or to reference (using JSR 77 object name syntax) an already configured login module.
login-module	Use this element to define a new login module.
control-flag	This element represents how a login-module is applied and denotes one of the following JAAS control flag values: REQUIRED, REQUISITE, SUFFICIENT, or OPTIONAL.
server-side	This element is set to true for most cases where the authentication is performed on the server side.
login-domain-name	Each login module is associated with a login domain, which enables a security realm to contain two instances of the same login module (e.g., an LDAP realm connecting to two different servers).
login-module-class	This element specifies the fully qualified name of the class implementing the login module.
option	A login module can take one or more options when it is initialized. Options are simply name/value pairs.

You may deploy a security realm with server-wide scope as follows (note that this example assumes the deployment file containing the security realm configuration is named securityRealmPlan.xml):

```
java -jar deployer.jar deploy securityRealmPlan.xml
```

You may also deploy a security realm as part of a J2EE application:

```
<application xmlns="http://geronimo.apache.org/xml/ns/j2ee/application" ➥
configId="SampleApplication" parentId="geronimo/j2ee-server/1.0/car">
<!-- other configurations -->
    <gbean name="SamplePropertiesFileSecurityRealm" ➥
    class="org.apache.geronimo.security.realm.GenericSecurityRealm">
    <!-- security realm configuration goes here -->
</gbean>
</application>
```

To deploy the security realm, deploy the application as usual.

Configuring and Deploying a Security Realm Using the Geronimo Console

You may also use the Geronimo console to configure and deploy a security realm. Select the Security/Security Realms link under the Console Navigation menu on the console application and you will see the screen shown in Figure 10-3.

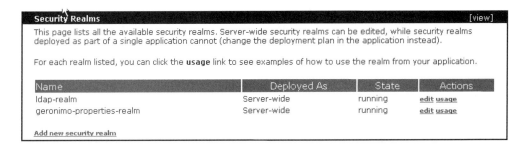

Figure 10-3. *Security Realms screen*

This screen displays all available security realms on the server. When you select the "Add new security realm" link, the screen in Figure 10-4 appears.

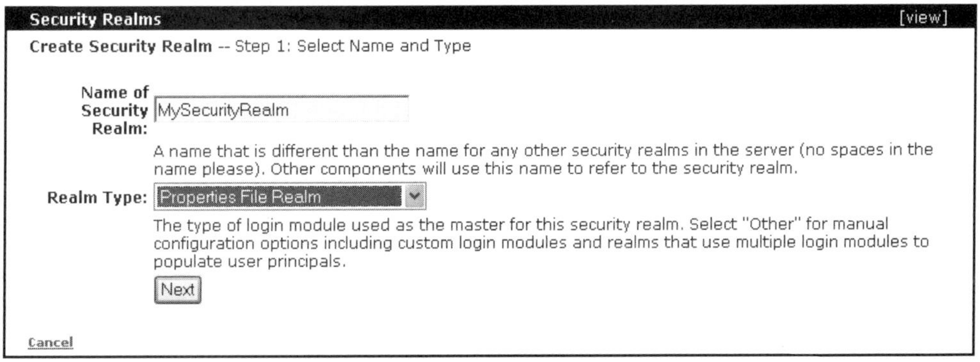

Figure 10-4. *Selecting the name and type of the security realm*

In this screen, you need to enter a name for your new security realm and choose a realm type (I selected the Properties File Realm type). Click the Next button to move on to the screen shown in Figure 10-5, where you enter the options for the selected realm type.

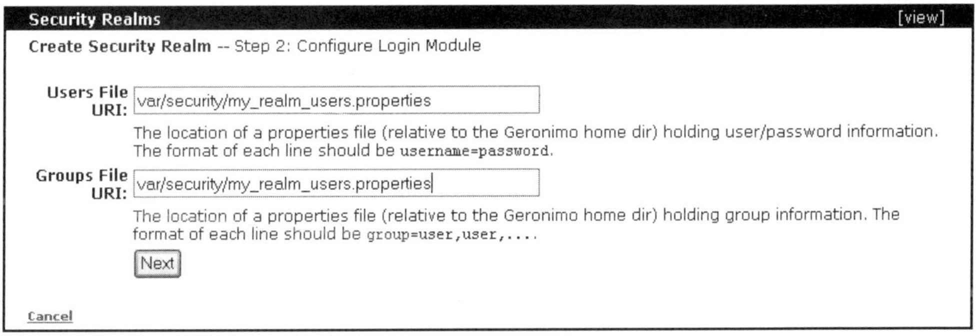

Figure 10-5. *Configuring the login module for the security realm*

For the properties security realm, you need to provide the user and group file names. The file names should be relative to the Geronimo root directory and the files should exist. When you've finished, click the Next button to display the screen in Figure 10-6.

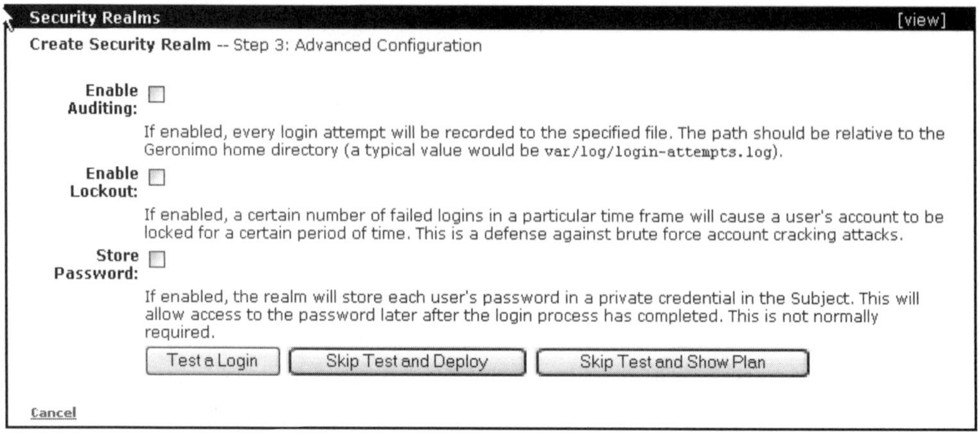

Figure 10-6. *The security realm deployment screen*

Click the Skip Test and Deploy button to deploy the security realm.

Implementing Standard Login Modules

As you have already seen, a login module implements the actual authentication logic. You can have a login module that authenticates using user information stored in a database or in LDAP. Geronimo ships with many commonly used login modules such as the following:

- Properties file login module

- SQL login module

- Certificate chain login module

- Geronimo password credential login module

- Certificate properties file login module

- Kerberos login module

Most application servers provide similar login modules for common situations. You may use these login modules to configure a security realm or you may even choose to create your own custom login module. (You'll learn how to write your own login module shortly.) A login module is configured for a realm by using the login-module element as explained in the previous section and specifying the login module implementation class along with a set of options (properties) that it expects.

In the following sections, you'll see how to configure and use some of the standard login modules provided with Geronimo: the properties file login module, SQL login module, and Kerberos login module.

Properties File Login Module

The properties file login module uses one property file to store user names and another property file to store user group information. You configure a properties file login module as follows:

```
<gbean name="samplePropertiesFileRealm"
class="org.apache.geronimo.security.realm.GenericSecurityRealm">
<!-- security realm configuration -->
<xml-reference name="LoginModuleConfiguration">
    <login-config xmlns="http://geronimo.apache.org/xml/ns/loginconfig">
        <login-module control-flag="REQUIRED" server-side="true">
            <login-domain-name>
            some-properties-file-login
            </login-domain-name>
            <login-module-class>
            org.apache.geronimo.security.realm.providers. ➥
PropertiesFileLoginModule
            </login-module-class>
            <option name="usersURI">
            var/security/some_users.properties
            </option>
            <option name="groupsURI">
            var/security/some_groups.properties
            </option>
        </login-module>
    </login-config>
</xml-reference>
</gbean>
</configuration>
```

The usersURI property should point to a property file (relative to the Geronimo root) with content similar to the following:

```
UserName1 = password1
UserName2 = password2
UserName3 = password3
```

The groupsURI should point to another properties file that stores user group information:

```
Group1 = UserName1, UserName2
Group2 = UserName3
Group3 = UserName2, UserName3
```

SQL Login Module

You may use a SQL login module if the user and group information is stored in a database. This is implemented using the class org.apache.geronimo.security.realm.providers. SQLLoginModule. The options in Table 10-3 are required to configure a SQL login module.

Table 10-3. *SQL Login Module Configuration Options*

Option	Description
jdbcURL	The JDBC URL that should be used to connect to the database.
jdbcUser	The user name.
jdbcPassword	The password.
jdbcDriver	The JDBC driver class name.
userSelect	The SQL query that when executed returns a list of user name and password combinations. This query should return a resultset similar to the following: `select username, password from userTable`
groupSelect	The SQL query that when executed returns a list of group name and user name combinations. This query should return a resultset similar to the following: `select groupname, username from userGroupsTable`

Kerberos Login Module

Geronimo uses the Kerberos login module provided with Sun's JDK; hence, you may use all its options to configure this module. For details, please refer to the Sun documentation for this login module.

Configuring Security for Web Applications

You learned how to secure your web application in Chapter 3, where you used the built-in geronimo-properties-realm to authenticate the application. This section summarizes the steps required to enable security for web applications.

To configure security in a web application, perform the following steps:

1. Define a security role in web.xml:

```
<web-app ...>

<security-role>
<role-name>adminUser</role-name>
</security-role>
...
</web-app>
```

2. Specify a protected resource list in web.xml:

```
<web-app ...>
...
<security-constraint>
  <web-resource-collection>
    <web-resource-name>My Protected Resources</web-resource-name>
    <url-pattern>/admin/*</url-pattern>
  </web-resource-collection>

  <auth-constraint>
    <role-name>adminUser</role-name>
```

```
    </auth-constraint>
  </security-constraint>
  ...
</web-app>
```

3. Specify a login configuration in web.xml:

```
<web-app ...>
...
<login-config>
  <auth-method>BASIC</auth-method>
  <realm-name>MySecurityRealm</realm-name>
</login-config>
...
</web-app>
```

4. Map security roles to one or more principals in the target security realm using the Geronimo deployment descriptor:

```
<sec:security>
  <sec:default-principal realm-name="MySecurityRealm">
    <sec:principal class="org.apache.geronimo.security.realm.➥
providers.GeronimoUserPrincipal"  name="default"/>
  </sec:default-principal>

  <sec:role-mappings>
    <sec:role role-name="adminUser">
      <sec:realm realm-name="MySecurityRealm">
        <sec:principal class="org.apache.geronimo.security.realm.➥
providers.GeronimoGroupPrincipal" name="admins" ➥
designated-run-as="true"/>
        <sec:principal class="org.apache.geronimo.security.realm.➥
providers.GeronimoGroupPrincipal" name="seniors"/>
      </sec:realm>
    </sec:role>
  </sec:role-mappings>
</sec:security>
```

Here, the logical role adminUser is mapped to two group principals, one named admins and the other named seniors, from the MysecurityRealm. You may use the logic role name adminUser from your code to denote a user that belongs to the physical group admins or the group seniors.

Implementing a Custom Login Module

As mentioned in a previous section, you may need to develop a custom login module when none of the Geronimo-provided login modules satisfies your authentication requirements. The following code listing shows how to create a simple custom login module:

```
public class MyLoginModule implements LoginModule {
  private Subject subject;
  private CallbackHandler handler;
  private String user;
  private String userPropertyFile;
  public void initialize(Subject subject,
  CallbackHandler handler,Map sharedState, Map options) {
    this.subject = subject;
    this.handler = handler;
    userPropertyFile=options.get("usersFile");
    // read property file and load user information to a map
  }
  public boolean login() throws LoginException {
    NameCallback nc = new NameCallback("Enter User name");
    PasswordCallback pwc = new PasswordCallback("Enter Password",
    false);
    handler.handle(new Callback[]{nc, pwc});
    user = nc.getName();
    String pw = new String(pwc.getPassword());
    // validate the account by checking user name and password
    // if found valid, return true; otherwise, return false
    return credentialsValid;
  }
  public boolean commit() throws LoginException {
    subject.add(new MyUserPrincipal(user));
    return true;
  }
...
}
```

MyUserPrincipal is a sample principal class, as shown here:

```
public class MyUserPrincipal implements Principal, Serializable {
  private String name;
  public MyUserPrincipal(String name) {
    this.name = name;
  }
  public String getName() {return name;}
  public String toString() {return name;}
  public boolean equals(Object o) {
    return o instanceof UserPrincipal &&
    ((UserPrincipal)o).name.equals(name);
  }
  public boolean hashCode() {return name.hashCode();}
}
```

To deploy this login module, compile and package the login module classes as a JAR file and include this as a dependency in the deployment plan for a new security realm that specifies this new login module as one of its login modules.

Configuring Geronimo for HTTPS

To configure Geronimo for HTTPS connectivity, perform the following steps:

1. Create a private key and signed certificate.

2. Configure an HTTPS connector.

3. Deploy and start the HTTPS connector.

First, you can use the JDK keytool utility to generate a private key and a self-signed certificate and store them in a key store file. You may also use a signed certificate from a certificate authority (CA) instead of a self-signed certificate. The example in this section uses a self-signed certificate, but be aware that using a CA signed certificate is very similar except for the process of obtaining a certificate and importing it to the key store using the keytool.

To create a private key and a self-signed certificate, use the following command:

```
keytool -genkey -alias myprivatekey -keyalg RSA -validity 365 ➥
-keystore mykeystore
```

You need to enter a password for the key store, a password for the private key, the first name and last name (enter the hostname of the server for these), and several other details. Refer to the JDK keytool documentation for more information. The end result is a private key with the name myprivatekey stored in the key store with the file name mykeystore. The keytool also creates a self-signed certificate.

Next, you need to configure an HTTPS connector. An HTTPS connector can be configured as a GBean in a deployment plan as follows:

```
<gbean name="MyHTTPSConnector"➥
class="org.apache.geronimo.jetty.connector.HTTPSConnector">
  <attribute name="port">9009</attribute>
  <attribute name="keystoreFileName">
  var/security/mykeystore
  </attribute>
  <attribute name="keystoreType">JKS</attribute>
  <attribute name="keystorePassword">password</attribute>
  <attribute name="keyPassword">password</attribute>
  <attribute name="clientAuthRequired">false</attribute>
  <attribute name="secureProtocol">TLS</attribute>
  <attribute name="maxThreads">100</attribute>
  <attribute name="minThreads">5</attribute>
  <reference name="JettyContainer">
    <module>geronimo/j2ee-server/1.0/car</module>
    <name>WebContainer</name>
  </reference>
  <reference name="ServerInfo">
    <module>geronimo/j2ee-server/1.0/car</module>
    <name>ServerInfo</name>
  </reference>
</gbean>
```

The keystoreType should be JKS and the secureProtocol value should be TLS or SSL (for IBM JDK). The clientAuthRequired attribute specifies whether the client should have a certificate in addition to the server.

Finally, to deploy this HTTPS connector configuration, simply deploy the deployment plan file containing this GBean configuration.

Configuring JavaMail

To use JavaMail from a J2EE component (such as a servlet or an EJB), perform the following steps:

1. Download Sun JavaMail and Java Activation Framework (JAF), and include these as dependencies to your configuration's deployment plan. To do so, add the following JAR to the Geronimo repository either by using the Geronimo console or by manually adding the JAR to the Geronimo repository directory:

```
<dependency>
  <uri>javamail/activation/1.0/jar</uri>
</dependency>
<dependency>
  <uri>javamail/mail/1.0/jar</uri>
</dependency>
```

2. In your deployment plan, add these GBean definitions:

```
<dependency>
  <uri>geronimo/geronimo-mail/1.0/jar</uri>
</dependency>
<gbean name="SMTPJavaMailProtocol"
class="org.apache.geronimo.mail.SMTPTransportGBean">
  <attribute name="host">myhostname</attribute>
  <attribute name="port">25</attribute>
  <attribute name="from">myemailid@hostname.com</attribute>
</gbean>
<gbean name="MyMailSession"
class="org.apache.geronimo.mail.MailGBean">
  <attribute name="transportProtocol">smtp</attribute>
  <attribute name="useDefault">false</attribute>
  <attribute name="properties">
    mail.debug=true
  </attribute>
  <reference name="Protocols">
    <name> SMTPJavaMailProtocol</name>
  </reference>
</gbean>
```

3. Finally, define a resource reference for the J2EE component. You define a resource reference in the standard J2EE deployment descriptors for the component (web.xml or ejb-jar.xml):

```
<resource-ref>
  <res-ref-name>mail/SampleMailSession</res-ref-name>
  <res-type>javax.mail.Session</res-type>
  <res-auth>Container</res-auth>
  <res-sharing-scope>Shareable</res-sharing-scope>
</resource-ref>
```

4. Resolve the resource reference in the Geronimo-specific deployment descriptor:

```
<resource-ref>
  < ref-name>mail/SampleMailSession</naming:ref-name>
  <resource-link>MyMailSession</resource-link>
</resource-ref>
```

The resource-ref/ref-name element should match the resource-ref/res-ref-name element value in the standard deployment descriptor and the resource-link should match a GBean name of type org.apache.geronimo.mail.MailGBean.

You may use the mail session from your J2EE component as follows:

```
InitialContext context = new InitialContext();
javax.mail.Session session =
(Session)ctx.lookup("java:comp/env/mail/SampleMailSession");
```

By using the JavaMail GBeans provided with Geronimo, you can simplify your application code and use the standard mechanism to access the JavaMail resources.

Summary

You can extend and customize the Geronimo platform by adding your own services, and in this chapter you learned how to create a deployment plan for those new services as well as how to deploy them into Geronimo. You also examined Geronimo's security implementation and how to configure and deploy built-in and custom security realms. Finally, you learned how to configure JavaMail resources in Geronimo and use them from your J2EE applications.

Throughout this book, you explored many Java enterprise programming concepts and how to apply them using the Geronimo application server. You've covered web applications, EJB applications, message-driven beans, J2EE connectors, enterprise applications, and J2EE client applications. You've also examined the Geronimo architecture in great detail. I hope this book has provided you with an excellent introduction to the Geronimo application server.

Index

You Need the Companion eBook

Your purchase of this book entitles you to its companion eBook for only $10.

We believe this Apress title will prove so indispensable that you'll want to carry it with you everywhere, which is why we are offering the companion eBook for $10 to customers who purchase this book now. Convenient and fully searchable, the eBook version of any content-rich, page-heavy Apress book makes a valuable addition to your programming library. You can easily find, copy, and apply code—and then perform examples by quickly toggling between instructions and the application. Even simultaneously tackling a donut, diet soda, and complex code becomes simplified with hands-free eBooks!

Once you purchase this book, getting the $10 companion eBook is simple:

❶ Visit **www.apress.com/promo/tendollars/**.

❷ Complete a basic registration form to receive a randomly generated question about this title.

❸ Answer the question correctly in 60 seconds and you will receive a promotional code to redeem for the $10 eBook.

2560 Ninth Street • Suite 219 • Berkeley, CA 94710

eBookshop

Offer valid through 10/06.